SUFFERING

SUFFERING

A SOCIOLOGICAL INTRODUCTION

Iain Wilkinson

polity

First published in 2005 by Polity Press

Polity Press
65 Bridge Street
Cambridge CB2 1UR, UK

Polity Press
350 Main Street
Malden, MA 02148, USA

ISBN: 0-7456-3196-7
ISBN: 0-7456-3197-5 (paperback)

A catalogue record for this book is available from the British Library and has been applied for from the Library of Congress.

Typeset in 10.5pt on 12pt Palatino
by BookEns Ltd., Royston, Herts.
Printed and bound in Great Britain by MPG Books,
Bodmin, Cornwall.

For further information on Polity, visit our website: www.polity.co.uk

CONTENTS

PREFACE AND ACKNOWLEDGEMENTS

I first began to prepare notes for a sociological study of 'the problem of suffering' while reflecting upon the interrelationship between 'risk consciousness' and the social experience of anxiety. I was particularly struck by the extent to which media representations of 'risk' are concerned not so much with the ways we calculate the likely occurrence of adverse events, as with the suffering caused when taking risks leads to disastrous consequences for human life. More often than not, 'risk' is communicated for public attention in graphic portrayals of bodies in pain and harrowing images of people in mourning and distress. To my mind, it seemed that sociologists were not giving sufficient attention to these matters. While alert to the power of the mass media to intensify public disputes over the reality of dangers presented as possible 'risks' to our health and safety, they displayed no interest in dwelling directly on the ways in which the social meaning of these phenomena are related to 'the problem of suffering'. I was troubled by the possibility that this amounted to a failure to attend to the *human significance* of risk.

My writing began as a series of reflections upon the extent to which public expressions of anxiety about risk involve people's fears about being made vulnerable to suffering. I considered the possibility that individuals may experience their knowledge of risk as a type of 'pain' that has the potential to become a 'problem of suffering'. However, I soon discovered that this involved far more than a debate regarding the ways in which sociologists approach the study of risk. It seemed that by inquiring into the cultural dynamics of pain and suffering, I was increasingly being made to take issue with the general character of sociological thinking and styles of writing.

I was disturbed to note that, while sociologists have an elaborate range of languages at their disposal for conceptualizing the misery of our human condition, generally speaking, they do not address their inquiries to the experience of suffering. The concept of suffering rarely, if at all, features as a category of sociological analysis, and, most certainly, is unlikely to be identified as part of the lexicon of sociological theory. For the most part, sociologists have not concerned themselves with 'the problem of suffering' *per se*.

I could not ignore the nagging suspicion that there was something in this that left sociology with a diminished account of the social reality of human experience. This was further fuelled by noting the extent to which 'human suffering' is explicitly addressed as a pressing matter of concern by philosophy, theology, the arts and medical science. In other disciplines there are well-established traditions of inquiry into the 'origins', 'nature' and 'meaning' of this experience. Outside sociology, scholars have worked hard to develop styles of writing that aim to involve readers in a fuller sense of what happens to people in situations of great personal distress. While it is readily acknowledged that concepts of 'pain' and 'suffering' have contested meanings, in other areas of study researchers do not shy away from treating these as important for exploring the quality of people's experiences of self and society.

However, it was only when I discovered a new cross-disciplinary literature addressed to the topic of 'social suffering' that I began to organize my thoughts into a more systematic programme of study. The writings of Arthur Kleinman, Veena Das, Nancy Scheper-Hughes, and Pierre Bourdieu on the ways in which people *experience* their pains, hardships and oppression helped me to clarify my concerns and develop them to the point where I could reflect critically upon their sociological meaning and value. These writers inspired me to begin 'serious' work on a 'sociology of suffering' that aims not only to develop new conceptions of the social constitution of pain and suffering in human experience, but also, new agendas for sociological research and thinking.

This book is part of a 'work in progress'. It details my attempts to understand the concept of 'social suffering' and its relevance for sociology. It offers a sociological conception of 'the problem of suffering' as well as some reflections upon what 'the problem of suffering' implies for the task of sociology. At the same time as I am concerned to explore the social constitution of human suffering, I am also interested in exploring the potential for the social representation of this experience to influence people's moral attitudes and behaviours. While large parts of my discussion are devoted to investigating the impact of human suffering on the dynamics of social change, I give particular attention to the ways in which this might be related to developments within the cultural politics of compassion.

Each chapter is written as an invitation to dialogue and debate. By no means do I consider my work to represent an exhaustive account of all that might be involved in a 'sociology of suffering'. I certainly do not claim to have charted all the ways in which sociology might inform our understanding of what suffering does to people. Moreover, I expect readers to both approach and respond to my writing with a sense of *dissatisfaction*. Not only do I accept that there are aspects to 'human suffering' that defy meaning and understanding, but I also venture to place this at the heart of my sociological account of this phenomenon. I argue that in so far as we may be prepared to 'think with suffering', then we should be prepared to confront the failures of our scholarship and the limitations of our creative thinking. However, I am also intrigued by the extent to which such failing might lead us to better understanding the nature of human suffering.

I would like to thank Gerard Delanty for giving me the initial encouragement to write this book. I am grateful to Jonathan Clark, Keith Hayward, Steve Miles, David Morgan, Alan Petersen and Paul White for taking the time to read and comment on some draft chapters, although in no way should they be held responsible for what I have written here. Conversations with Joan Chandler, Matthew David, Gill Dunne, Elizabeth Ettorre, Moira Maconachie and Kevin Meethan helped shape my thoughts and keep me writing. Without the love, patience and support of my wife, Anna Taylor, I doubt whether I would have been able to see this project through to completion. Her life and work constantly inspire me. I dedicate this book to the memory of David Morgan, who taught me to appreciate the wonder of humanity and the value of a sociological imagination.

I

INTRODUCTION: SUFFERING, SOCIAL SCIENCE AND THE CHALLENGE TO SOCIOLOGY

Wherever humanity records its voice, then it always speaks of suffering. It appears that we cannot keep silent or remain unmoved before its presence. While suffering has always comprised the experience of humanity, we cannot impassively accept this as a normal and inevitable part of our human condition. This is because suffering hurts too much. The problem with suffering is that it involves us in far *too much* pain. The pain of suffering so dominates the senses that it cannot be simply ignored or blithely returned to its proper place. It is all at once excruciating and overwhelming, and as such it is entirely unacceptable. It must be fought against.

Suffering leaves us in no doubt that it is decisively against us. Its purpose, if it can be said to have a purpose, appears to be fundamentally opposed to our humanity. It works to obliterate all the pleasure and hope we have in life. Suffering destroys our bodies, ruins our minds, and smashes our 'spirit'. Indeed, to her great horror, Hannah Arendt observed that in the most extreme forms of suffering we may even be deprived of the category of 'being human' as a way of relating to ourselves and others, so that the very concept of humanity is made utterly 'superfluous' (Arendt 1973: 454–5). Simone Weil declares that the affliction of suffering is 'an uprooting of life, a more or less attenuated equivalent of death' (Weil 1950: 77). Its effect is to reduce us to nothing.

Yet in suffering we come across one of the greatest enigmas in human existence. This wholly violating and destructive experience has repeatedly been looked upon as that which may reveal the most basic truths about our humanity (Bowker 1970). The phenomenon which seems most fundamentally opposed to us is also conceived to disclose an essential part of the truth about what we are fundamentally for. Whilst with one voice we emphatically denounce this experience as a desecration of our humanity, with another we declare it to have the potential to reveal us in our most sanctified form. It seems that we cannot resist questioning the meaning of suffering, and under this compulsion we are inclined to recognize the meaning of our humanity to be at stake.

In this regard, Max Weber would have us identify the problem of suffering as 'the driving force of all religious evolution' (Weber 1948b: 122–3). Indeed, in this process he conceives the cultural aporia experienced in face of 'the brute fact that suffering exists' to be a constant factor within the development of the forms of rationality with which we venture to interpret the meaning of our world (Parsons 1966: p. xlvii; Morgan and Wilkinson 2001; Tenbruck 1989; Weber 1948c, 1948d). Similarly, Karl Marx recognizes the sensuous knowledge of suffering to be a vital force within the dialectics of social change. Where he first explains religion as an 'illusory sun' that shines in 'protest against real suffering' (Marx 1977: 64), he later goes on to prophesy that it is as a result of the suffering caused by the immiseration of the proletariat that they shall ultimately dispense with this illusion, and, as a class for themselves, act to abolish the material conditions which are responsible for their misery (Marx 1959a: 134). Furthermore, both Emile Durkheim and Sigmund Freud appear convinced that by dwelling upon the social psychology of human suffering, they are advancing towards a clearer account of the progress of our 'civilisation' (Durkheim 1964: 233–55; Freud 1985).

Nevertheless, it is perhaps surprising to note that, whereas such figures consider the phenomenon of suffering to disclose some basic truth about the definitive character of society, the actual quality of the *lived experience* of suffering rarely appears as the direct focus of sociological study. Of course, it is possible to suggest that a problem of suffering is almost always implicit within the topics of sociological research; indeed, one might go so far as to declare that sociology is always concerned with the causes and consequences of human suffering in one form or another. In modern times, sociologists have worked as hard as any group to expose the character of modernity as an age of great social injustice, cultural poverty and moral anxiety. In secular society it is the social sciences which now provide the majority of people with a 'common-sense' glossary of terms for representing the misery of our human condition. In the final analysis, it may well be entirely appropriate to label all sociological discourse as discourse on suffering.

However, in recent years, and from a number of different directions, commentators have been inclined to represent the social sciences in general, and sociology in particular, as failing to give due consideration to what the *experience* of suffering actually *does* to people (Kleinman 1995, 1996; Kleinman et al. 1997; Das 1997a; Bourdieu et al. 1999; Frank 2001; Morgan and Wilkinson 2001). While a great many publications are devoted to detailing the dramatic and tragic events of modern history, and although commentaries on risk, crisis and insecurity feature heavily within the literature of social science, and despite the fact that news media present us with a daily catalogue of disasters from around the globe, it is argued that something most vital is always being left 'outside' of our accounts of the *human significance* of these events and experiences. Where more information is available to us than ever before on the extent of poverty, the incidence of war and the dimensions of catastrophe, it is claimed that our knowledge of what it means for people to suffer these in *experience* remains woefully deficient.

This new 'awakening' to the need for the social sciences to inquire more substantially into the existential components of the phenomenon of suffering is not easy to explain. There is no single event that stands out as having had the obvious effect of making 'the problem of suffering' a matter for sociological debate. It is not at all clear why only now, in this most violent period of human history (Bennett 2001: 54–102; Glover 1999; Hobsbawm 1994; Mann 1999), researchers should become especially preoccupied with making sense of human experiences of suffering. Moreover, when one considers the interdisciplinary nature of this inquiry (Graubard 1996), it seems strange that sociology, which unlike theology or philosophy, has no long-standing tradition of debate on the subject, should be identified as the discipline with a particular responsibility to create a new framework for under-standing what suffering actually is and, further, for advising us on what we might do to combat its deleterious effects upon peoples' lives (Kleinman 1996; Das 1997a).

It is possible to identify at least four groups of writers who, while working on separate problems and with different audiences in mind, have arrived at a shared understanding that something most vital remains to be 'said' about the phenomenon of suffering and, further, that sociologists ought to be providing us with the language to 'say' what this is. Moreover, almost without exception, researchers appear convinced that in so far as it may be possible to create more 'authentic' representations or 'essential' accounts of the ways in which people live in and through their suffering, then politicians, experts and publics might not only be moved to acknowledge the hurts we inflict upon one another, but also our collective responsibility 'to do something about' this tragic state of affairs.

First, in medical anthropology, 'social suffering' features as a new topic of research for those working to account for the socio-cultural components of the pain experience. Generally speaking, such inquiries take the form of a critical dialogue with established biomedical accounts of pain, so as to expose the limitations of a Cartesian conception of bodily sensation (Bendelow and Williams 1995a, 1995b, 1998). In this context, biomedicine is criticized not only for neglecting to give proper attention to the socio-cultural dynamics of pain care (Frank 2001; Illich 1976: 140–60), but also, for failing to address the extent to which the pain sensation takes place as a product of the interaction between neurophysiological processes, social contexts and cultural meaning (Kotarba 1983; Kleinman 1988; Morris 1991; Kleinman and Kleinman 1991; Horn and Munafò 1997: 68–88). Attempts are made to make the form and significance of the lived experience of human suffering a part of the diagnostic language of medicine and, thereby, an object of clinical and caring concern. By developing new ways of 'thinking with suffering' it is maintained that it may be possible to revolutionize medical understanding of bodily pain as well as the ways in which people acquire the emotional/cognitive resources to cope with this experience (Morris 1998: 107–34).

In second place, a struggle to give formal expression to the phenomenon of human suffering features prominently in the works of ethnographers who seek to have their writing 'bear witness' to the experience of people living under the impact of extreme social hardships and events of political atrocity (Bourdieu et al. 1999; Das 1995, 1997a, 1997b; Das et al. 2000, 2001; Scheper-Hughes 1992, 1998; Skultans 1998). In this context, the use of academic texts to portray what suffering actually *does* to people is identified as a vital part of the political process of making the human experience of adversity a matter of public concern. Moreover, some go so far to express the hope that, where it is possible to have a broader public acknowledgement of what it means for people to live in suffering, then those that suffer may know some manner of healing for the hurts they experience. For example, in labouring to devise 'languages of pain through which social science [can] gaze at, touch or become textual bodies in which this pain is written' (Das 1997a: 67), Veena Das not only seeks to perform a public 'work of mourning' for the violence, abduction and rape experienced by women in India's internecine ethnic wars, but also to equip them with a portion of the cultural resources they require to experience some emotional healing for their trauma (Das 1997b: 570–2). For Das, it is in the struggle to express what seems inexpressible in devastating experiences of violence and loss, that social science addresses the moral and political challenge to amplify the human suffering that 'society' would rather leave in silence. In seeking to articulate the existential reality of what happens to people in suffering, she aims to make her work 'speak' on behalf of people in pain, and thereby draw society into public debate on the experience of suffering it imposes on people 'as a price of belonging' (Das 1997b).

Thirdly, it is with the same intention of arousing a fuller acknowledgement of the human suffering caused by social injustice and political repression that a growing number of researchers have sought to acquire a better understanding of the role of mass media in the formation of moral consciousness and humanitarian concern (Boltanski 1999; S. Cohen 2001; Ignatieff 1998; Kleinman 1995; Kleinman and Kleinman 1997; Moeller 1999; Shaw 1996; Tester 1994, 1999, 2001). However, in almost every instance, researchers are convinced not only that the content of media messages falls short of providing a proper account of the real substance and meaning of human suffering, but also that publics are all too easily left in the position of being able to ignore or deny their moral responsibility to address the plight of victims. A number hold to the view that the appropriation of images of suffering as commercial news 'infotainment' gives rise to a culture of 'promiscuous voyeurism' that erodes the possibility of audiences responding to the suffering of distant 'others' with compassion and moral outrage (Ignatieff 1998; Kleinman and Kleinman 1997). Yet there is no overall agreement as to how we should conceptualize the socio-political or psychological dynamics of this problem. It has become popular to suggest that audiences are liable to be wearied by the experience of repeatedly being brought face to face with mediated spectacles of human misery, and that we should expect them to display signs of 'compassion fatigue' (Kinnick et al. 1996). Others seek to identify this more as 'states of denial' and argue that our natural psychological response is to turn a blind eye and enter into a conspiracy of silence when faced with media representations of human agony and utter despair (S. Cohen 2001; Cohen and Seu 2002). Moreover, some would rather have us attend to the ways in which audiences are likely to feel morally and politically detached from mediated spectacles of human suffering as a consequence of habitually adopting the role of 'spectator' in relation to the worlds presented to them by mass media (Boltanski 1999). Nevertheless, while there is no agreement as to the bearing of mass media upon social conscience and moral behaviour, the majority of these writers hold to the view that a cultural politics of compassion is sustained by the quality of people's mediated experiences of human suffering.

Fourthly, at some point in these efforts, all the above writers are liable to make reference to, or certainly repeat, a central preoccupation of recent sociological studies of the Holocaust: that is, 'to grasp the event itself' so as to 'generate the shocking immediacy worthy of the subject' (Fine and Turner 2000: 1). It is perhaps surprising to note that in the twenty years following the Second World War, with the notable exception of Hannah Arendt (Arendt 1963a, 1968, 1973, 1994a; Arendt and Jaspers 1992), there have been remarkably few serious attempts to devise new languages for expressing precisely what happens to people's humanity when this is subjected to the violence and violation of industrial genocide (Aschheim 1997; Morgan and Wilkinson 2001). It is only in recent years that growing numbers of social scientists have sought to align themselves with her historical and political project to understand 'the difficulties of understanding' these events (Bauman 1989; Fine 2000, 2001; Mann 1999; G. Rose 1996; Wilkinson 2001b). In this context, once again attention is focused on the effort to construct modes of representation which bear authentic testimony to the experience of the victims of atrocity, with the understanding that, where it may be possible to make more 'visible' what happens to people in suffering, we might then arrive at a better position from which to address the apparent insufficiency of our categories of thought for making proper sense of the 'truths' which the Holocaust reveals about the moral condition of our humanity.

What are we to make of this increasing preoccupation with 'social suffering'? While conditions of modernity have always been identified as a potential source of anguish, distress and human misery, why is it only now that concerted efforts are being made to bring the *lived experience* of suffering within the domain of sociological analysis? Moreover, what kinds of hopes and expectations should we attach to these developments? Might 'thinking with suffering' provide us with opportunities to reappraise the value of sociology for contemporary society? Might it be on these grounds that social science is best placed to articulate the fundamental concerns of humanity? Indeed, are these the most forceful terms by which we can invigorate public debate about the moral meaning of our times?

With regard to the 'unimaginable' horrors of events such as 'Auschwitz', 'Hiroshima' and 'the Gulag', perhaps we should always expect there to be a considerable interval of time before people arrive at a position from which to explore their historical significance for the meaning of 'civilization'. In his final work, *The Drowned and the Saved*, Primo Levi suggests that it is perfectly normal for there to be a 'decanting' of experience whereby 'events acquire their chiaroscuro and perspective only some decades after their conclusion' (Levi 1989: 8). It may still be the case that we have barely begun to equip ourselves with cultural resources adequate to grasp the measure and meaning of the atrocities that brought Isaiah Berlin to regard the twentieth century as 'the most terrible century in human history' (cited in Hobsbawm 1994). Accordingly, the literature on 'social suffering' can be addressed in part as a further development within the ongoing struggle to interpret the history of our times in due recognition of the unprecedented extremes of violence and torture that have destroyed the lives of millions of people around the globe (Graubard 1996: p. viii).

Indeed, in so far as the last 30 years may be distinguished as a time in which organizations such as Amnesty International and Human Rights Watch have accumulated and disseminated an unprecedented amount of documentary evidence which exposes the increasing incidence of human rights atrocities (Amnesty International 1973, 1984, 1996, 2000, 2002), perhaps we should anticipate that this will have an increasing impact upon the cultural discourses through which we look back upon our past and negotiate the possible futures that await us (Bennett 2001: 54–78). Further, where it is estimated that during the course of the twentieth century as many as 170 million people were murdered by governments (Rummel 1996) and as many as 190 million people still live in conditions that run a high risk of degenerating into genocide or politicide (Harff and Gurr 1996), then we might expect social scientists to preoccupy themselves with the task of understanding the social conditions under which people are liable to indulge themselves in extremes of violence.

There is no doubt that the upsurge of academic debate on 'social suffering' is inspired to a considerable extent by efforts made by non-governmental organizations (NGOs) to draw public attention to the plight of populations suffering under the impact of war, political oppression and conditions of material scarcity. Certainly, much of this writing is explicit in identifying itself with campaigns to advance the cause of humanitarianism. Researchers tend to give open expression to the political motives that lead them to work at bringing the brute facts of suffering to the fore of academic debate. Moreover, where so much of this commentary aims to have us dwell upon the *lived experience* of individual sufferers, then researchers are more than willing to admit the extent to which their professional activities are driven by the force of moral sentiment (S. Cohen 1996, 2001; Das 1994, 1997a, 1997b; Kleinman and Kleinman 1997; Scheper-Hughes 1992, 1998).

Such open expressions of moral feeling suggest an elective affinity between the literature on social suffering and the increasing attention that Western social science now devotes to the place of emotional experience within the dynamics of social life. Where over the last thirty years sociologists have been more interested in exploring the social construction of emotion, as well as the role of emotional states within the dynamics of social change (Williams 2001), then this may well be looked upon as a development that was always likely to have the effect of making human suffering a disciplinary concern. On these grounds it is possible to recognize the efforts made by writers such as Veena Das (1997a, 1997b) to make the existential components of suffering a matter of public debate, to both reflect and consolidate an emphasis within our culture upon the significance of embodied states of feeling for revealing the essential character of the interrelationship between self and society (Bennett 2001: 178–97; Wilkinson 2001a). Indeed, in this context Bryan Turner identifies not only a possibility for sociology to free itself from the cognitivist bias of its classical inheritance (Barbalet 2001: 16–20), but also opportunities for it to gather the moral and intellectual resources to engage anew in debates on human rights (Turner 1993). With Chris Rojek he argues that it is particularly with reference to the universal experience of embodied states of suffering that sociology might be equipped to promote a universal concept of human rights; for whatever our cultural or political differences, it is with reference to the vulnerability of lived experience that we uncover the grounds upon which to assert our common humanity (Turner and Rojek 2001: 108–29).

In this regard, it is possible to gather evidence in support of the contention that debates on 'social suffering' are partly inspired by the frustrations of social scientists who consider their creativity to be constrained by the conventions of disciplinary boundaries. Certainly, this literature contains some of the strongest overtures to the value of cross-disciplinary study (Graubard 1996). Generally speaking, when researchers turn to address the nature of human suffering, they tend to express a great deal of frustration in face of the perceived inability of their professional terms of analysis to provide them with a sufficient account of their object of study (Wilkinson 2001b). In this context, efforts are made to break down the barriers that drive academics into narrow fields of expertise so as to bring them to a position where they can formulate a clearer representation of the diverse realities of human experience. More specifically, it is not only with a concern for the progressive development of new areas of research, but also, in a movement to combat a technocratic ideology that recognizes the authenticity of human misery only in its reduction to 'objective' terms of measurement, that commentators such as Arthur Kleinman are opposed to having the debate on suffering restricted to any single discipline of study (Kleinman 1988; Kleinman and Kleinman 1997). Accordingly, there appears to be a clear association between these developments and the appearance within the humanities and social sciences of a more pronounced scepticism towards the institutional cultures and intellectual biases of Western academe.

In an age of intensifying forces of globalization, 'social suffering' is presented as a field of research that has the potential to make a profound and lasting contribution to the reformulation of our intellectual and ethical concerns (Graubard 1996). The effort to provide a better account of what actually happens to people in suffering is understood to reflect not only a moral demand to reinterpret the meaning of modern history for our multicultural age, but also, a concern to 'humanize' the ways we relate to one another as global citizens. We are hereby challenged to incorporate within our accounts of modernity, a fuller acknowledgement of what occurs to the humanity of those who suffer under the extremes of economic hardship, social injustice and political oppression. In dwelling on what suffering *does* to people, and by developing new ways of *thinking with* the pain and distress of embodied experience, it is suggested that we might arrive at a position from which to radically reappraise the moral and political value of contemporary social science (Wilkinson 2001b). Moreover, it is claimed that in so far as it may be possible to expose a greater part of the social meaning of human suffering within the texture of our writing, and make this central to the ways we account for the value and justice of our times, then we might be best equipped to provoke politicians and publics into taking action against the conditions that cause too many people to live in far too much pain (Kleinman 1995; Das 1994, 1997a, 1997b).

Aims and objectives

At one level, this book is written as a ground-clearing exercise. It provides a summary overview of the analytical concerns that characterize contemporary efforts to make the *lived experience* of suffering a focal point of sociological and political concern. Accordingly, an emphasis is placed upon the extent to which, while working on a diverse range of projects, commentators identify similar kinds of ethical questions, epistemological issues and political dilemmas as defining the agenda for research into human suffering. It gives more attention to the conceptual problems and moral dilemmas that highlight commonalities of interest than to those matters which expose positions of mutual hostility or disciplinary bias. It offers a sociological conception of 'the problem of suffering' and details some of the possible ways in which this might impact upon the trajectories of political and moral debate on our times.

   At another level, it is also written to involve readers in a series of analytical perplexities and conceptual difficulties that appear to seriously disrupt the possibility of us ever acquiring an *adequate* account of what suffering actually does to people. In this regard, I am particularly interested to explore the capacity for some terrible part of suffering to always retain the appearance of being beyond all we can understand and say. While I attend to the ways in which the experience of suffering might be moderated and transformed at the level of cultural meaning, I am particularly concerned to have us dwell upon the capacity for components of this complex to remain wholly 'unspeakable' and radically opposed to reason. Indeed, I argue that if we are to better grasp some measure of the pain of suffering and its power to ruin human life, then we need to work at recognizing the ways in which the negative force of this experience is comprised by an overwhelming and deeply antagonistic sense of senselessness. I contend that a vital part of 'the problem of suffering' *consists* in a compulsive struggle to reconstitute a positive meaning for self and society against the brute force of events whereby all matters of human value and dignity are made to appear violated and betrayed.

In this regard, I am particularly interested to develop a sociological understanding of the ways in which experiences of suffering involve us in fundamental questions of origins, significance and purpose. I am concerned to have us consider the potential for the intellectual and moral tensions borne in the face of what suffering does to people, to serve as a force of cultural innovation with far-reaching political and practical ramifications. I aim to focus attention upon the ways in which processes of social and political change are initiated and influenced by people's involvement in the apparent senselessness of violence, injustice and oppression. I seek to explore the means by which 'the problem of suffering' is made to comprise social consciousness and thus impassion us with political concern for the most searching questions of humanity.

With this emphasis, I argue that research on 'social suffering' amounts to a case of social science becoming a form of critical praxis. I suggest that it is in the context of an open struggle against the limits of language, sense and meaning that writing on this subject acquires the potential to involve readers in some part of the moral confusion and intellectual torment of suffering in lived experience. I am concerned to highlight strategies of writing on this topic that, in the words of Hannah Arendt, are designed to 'solve no problems' and 'assuage no suffering', so as to make known 'a seemingly unendurable reality' (1968: 27–9). I explore the possibility that it is through a manner of writing that openly confronts our *failure* to make proper sense of suffering that we are drawn to debate the primal meaning and value of our cultural reality. I maintain that writing so as to involve readers in the great difficulty of understanding what suffering does to a person's humanity is an appropriate sociological response to this phenomenon (Morgan and Wilkinson 2001).

The early chapters of the book offer a series of critical reflections on the cultural formations and social processes that appear to constitute the lived experience of suffering. In later chapters I am more interested in charting some of the ways in which cultural representations of 'the problem of suffering' acquire the power to shape moral sentiment and direct social behaviour. Accordingly, I move from an investigation of the social constitution of human suffering to an exploration of the possible social consequences of the ways this is communicated for public attention. In this context, I am particularly keen to have us dwell upon the social conditions under which individuals acquire both a heightened sensitivity towards the experience of pain as well as a greater imagination for the suffering of others. As my discussion develops, I aim to involve readers in debates on the potential for our social consciousness of 'the problem of suffering' to spur political debate on the terms of human rights and to inspire us to take moral actions on behalf of the suffering of strangers in distant lands.

This project involves a critical appraisal of recent attempts to bring experiences of embodiment and emotion within the domain of sociological analysis. I suggest that a critical sociology of suffering requires us to engage with the development of new understandings of the ways in which matters of bodily feeling are constituted as products of social meaning. It seeks to have us dwell upon the ways in which people acquire sensuous knowledge of the moral character of society. It aims to uncover the cultural dynamics of social sentiment. In what follows, I am concerned not only to have us dwell upon the potential for new sociologies of the body and emotion to inform our understanding of human suffering, but also to investigate the extent to which research into this phenomenon might advance our knowledge of what is *vitally* at stake for people in the ways they embody conditions of modernity.

However, I do not treat this so much as a reason to distance ourselves from 'old-fashioned' sociological conceptions of self and society, but rather as an opportunity to appraise the continuing relevance and value of 'classical' traditions of inquiry. To this end, I draw attention to some of the neglected passages of writing in the works of Marx, Durkheim and Weber where the social character of human suffering is identified as a pressing concern. I argue that all these founding figures identify 'the problem of suffering' as a force of cultural innovation and social change and, further, that they all recognize this as a phenomenon that requires sociological analysis in its own terms. I maintain that in so far as there is no long-standing tradition of sociological research into suffering *per se*, then this is a topic which our discipline has failed to acknowledge and develop as an important part of its heritage. I contend that each of these writers still has something original and important to contribute to our understanding of the ways in which 'the problem of suffering' is made to comprise social consciousness. Moreover, I suggest that it is in the context of a critical dialogue with these theorists that writers on 'social suffering' might find some of the intellectual resources they need to bring analytical depth and historical insight to their inquiries.

In writing this book I have frequently been made to confront the limits of sociological methods of inquiry. I have continually been brought to the understanding that sociological terms of analysis fall short of providing us with an *adequate* account of what suffering does to people. At no point have I been satisfied with the meanings that sociology assigns to the suffering of humanity. But rather than see such difficulties as reason to abandon this project, I have ventured to approach them as an opportunity for learning. I have decided that facing up to the inadequacies of our scholarship may be a necessary part of the task of *thinking with* suffering. Accordingly, at the same time as I present readers with the beginnings of a critical 'sociology of suffering', I seek to involve them in a 'sociology of sociology'. As a means to investigate the social significance of human suffering, I encourage readers to grapple with some of the popular ways in which social scientists represent the cultural history of modern societies. In order for us to apprehend some part of what suffering does to a person's humanity, I wish to have us dwell upon the limitations of sociological conceptions of thought, feeling and action. When addressing the task of writing on 'the problem of suffering', I ask us to reflect upon the political value of the ways sociologists approach the study of human society and the possibilities for this to change. This is an invitation to share in the perplexities of my thinking about both 'the problem of suffering' and the character of sociology.

In chapter 2 I begin to explore the social constitution of human suffering and dwell upon some of the ways in which this may be approached as an object of sociological investigation. This chapter takes the form of a critical dialogue with contemporary research into the social dynamics of pain, and the possibility for this to be moderated at the level of cultural meaning. At the same time as I explore the socio-cultural dimensions of pain and suffering, I am particularly attentive to the ways in which people struggle to make sense of these experiences. I reflect upon the capacity of human suffering to appear 'senseless', 'meaningless' and 'for no purpose'. Moreover, I investigate the possibility that by failing to arrive at an adequate account of what suffering 'is' in human experience, scholars may better understand some part of its power to torment our humanity. In this context, I aim to introduce readers to the possibility of understanding 'the problem of suffering' as a dynamic force within the development of our culture and society.

In chapter 3, I attempt to recover the contrasting ways in which Marx, Durkheim and Weber conceive of the social character of human suffering. I argue that each of these writers provide us with valuable insights into ways in which our encounters with 'the problem of suffering' are liable to intensify under conditions of modernity. I underline the ways in which their theories contribute to a groundwork from which to develop distinctively sociological approaches to the study of 'human suffering' and its impacts upon the dynamics of social change. In this context, I also venture to identify the potential for questions relating to the social character of human suffering to provide us with new interpretations of the relevance of classical sociological theory to today's world.

In chapter 4 I offer an analysis of contemporary literature on 'social suffering' in the context of a critical dialogue with Hannah Arendt's writing on the 'evil' of totalitarianism. While Marx, Durkheim and Weber each provide us with unique insights into the potential for 'the problem of suffering' to have dynamic impacts upon the development of society, they never consider the possibility that by writing about the quality of this experience they might also add force to this process. I argue that, in the context of social science, Hannah Arendt and writers on 'social suffering' are pioneers of new approaches to writing about the condition of our humanity. I maintain that the novelty of this lies in the effort to generate styles of writing that involve readers as much as possible in *experiencing* the moral confusion and intellectual frustration of attempting to make sense of suffering, on the understanding that, within this struggle we are made to address fundamental questions of human value, origins and purpose. By comparing some of the strategies employed by Arendt and writers on 'social suffering' as they set about their task, I also highlight some of the political risks and ethical dilemmas that are associated with this manner of writing.

Chapter 5 develops some reflections upon Durkheim's contention that the same social processes that give rise to self-centred egoism and the torment of anomie, may also involve us in 'a broader pity for all sufferings' and 'sympathy for all that is human' (Durkheim 1973b: 48–9). I attend to the possibility that social conditions that increase our sensitivity to pain, might also involve us in a greater imagination for the suffering of others. Moreover, I venture to suggest that the increasing amount of attention that social science pays to the topic of 'social suffering' can be interpreted as a sign of the intensifying force of 'moral individualism' within society. This involves me in a series of controversial debates over the interrelationship between the social representation of suffering and the cultural politics of compassion. It leads me to examine the role of sociology within efforts to advance the concerns of 'humanity'.

Chapter 6 builds on matters raised in the previous chapter with a critical exploration of the social significance of 'mediatized' experiences of human suffering. Here I am not so much concerned to explore the potential for mass media to exhaust our capacity to feel compassion for others, as I am in the extent to which they might cultivate this to the point where we readily accept that we have a moral duty to care for the needs of strangers in distant lands. I treat seriously the possibility that, where we are regularly positioned by the mass media as moral spectators at the spectacle of human misery, we might also acquire a greater imagination for the suffering of humanity. I outline an agenda for research that concentrates more upon the task of tracing how people are moved to acknowledge and respond to 'distant suffering', than upon the extent to which they are inclined to deny the moral demands this places upon them.

In chapter 7 I relate these discussions to debates on the current 'crisis' of Western sociology. I summarize the main arguments of the previous chapters so as to outline the possible agendas of research that these set in place. I argue that in this work we may find the inspiration for a sociology that 'speaks' with compassion to the problems of humanity in a global society. I suggest that a 'critical sociology of suffering' may be a necessary part of our future attempts to engage sociology in the struggle to tell the truth about our world, so as to imagine how it can be made to change.

These chapters are designed to court controversy and provoke debate. In many ways they are more involved with highlighting *the difficulty of understanding* the problem of suffering than with the possibility of making this abundantly clear to the 'light' of sociology. I have no interest in 'winning arguments'; rather, my concern is for the potential for such terms of discussion and analysis to serve as a means to revitalize critical sociological thinking on the problems of modernity and the project of building humane forms of society. My hope is that through their critical response to my work, readers may be brought not only to question their involvement and place within the suffering of humanity, but also to more sociological thinking.

2

WHAT IS SUFFERING?

Suffering is common to us all, yet can only be known uniquely as our own. While being able to recognize and respond to the outward signs of a person's distress, we can never actually enter into the realms of their personal experience of suffering. The very fact that suffering is such a deeply personal experience may well be part of the explanation for why it remains so difficult for commentators to agree on a definition of what 'it' is (Illich 1976: 146–8). While the attention of a person 'in' suffering is captivated by pain, the felt reality of this experience cannot be openly shared with other people. The 'unsharability' of suffering appears to be such that there is always something 'in' this that confounds representation and defies our capacity to provide an outward formal expression of the contents of our experience (Scarry 1985: 4–5). Indeed, the 'unsharability' of suffering may well be one of its most essential attributes; it may be precisely as a result of suffering being locked in the realms of personal experience that it succeeds in causing us so much distress and harm.

A further part of the problem of arriving at an adequate definition of suffering may be connected with the fact that suffering appears to occur in such a wide variety of forms. While always personal, it seems that suffering has the potential to damage and disrupt every aspect of our personhood (Cassell 1982). It may well be the case that suffering always involves an element of physical pain (Weil 1950: 77–8; May 1969: 150); yet the majority of commentators emphasize that it is always much more than this. We identify suffering as taking place in experiences of bereavement and loss, social isolation and personal estrangement. Suffering is said to comprise feelings of depression, anxiety, guilt, humiliation, boredom and distress. People are held to suffer under the yoke of material deprivation, with the perpetuation of social injustice, and from the denial of their civil liberties. Suffering has the potential to take place in every part of our lives. It may all at once be physical, psychological, social, economic, political and cultural. Accordingly, those who venture to fashion symbolic forms of culture to reveal the character of suffering may always have their work exposed as woefully inadequate by efforts to account for the multidimensionality of this experience. In the final analysis, there may be no symbolic forms of culture that are adequate to represent *all* the ways in which suffering may afflict our humanity. Perhaps we ask too much of our capacity for language when we seek to represent a phenomenon which appears to be so dynamically adapted to the purpose of negating every aspect of our being?

Moreover, in recognizing that, whatever else it might be, suffering is always most definitely *against* us, perhaps we come as close as possible to understanding why the precise 'meaning' of the content of this experience remains so painfully obscure. For part of the negativity of suffering appears to consist in its capacity to oppose and destroy the 'meaning' of language. Indeed, in this regard, the apparent insufficiency in our accounts of suffering may be judged to be not so much related to the problem of addressing the multidimensionality of this experience, but rather, a particular result of the extent to which the 'sheer aversiveness' (Scarry 1985: 53) of suffering defies representation. Accordingly, Arthur Frank argues that the most significant part of suffering concerns what we cannot say about the pains of our adversity (Frank 2001: 354). He writes:

> Suffering involves experiencing yourself on the other side of life as it should be, and no thing, no material resource, can bridge that separation. Suffering is what lies beyond such help. Suffering is the unspeakable, as opposed to what can be spoken; it is what remains concealed, impossible to reveal; it remains in darkness, eluding illumination; and it is dread, beyond what is tangible even if hurtful. Suffering is loss, present or anticipated, and loss is another instance of no thing, an absence of what was missed and now is no longer recoverable and the absence of what we fear will never be. At the core of suffering is the sense that something is irreparably wrong with our lives, and wrong is the negation of what could not have been right. Suffering resists definition because it is the reality of what is not. Anyone who suffers knows the reality of suffering, but this reality is what you cannot 'come to grips with'. (Frank 2001: 355)

This chapter presents a critical review of the problem of conceptualizing human suffering as an object of sociological investigation. Of course, following Simmel (1971), one might well argue that every experience of life must in some part remain 'unformulable', and thus that the experience of suffering is by no means remarkable in this regard. Nevertheless, I take seriously the view that there is something particularly significant and awful in the capacity of suffering to defy representation that demands attention. Almost without exception, when writers venture to address this topic they appear to labour under the analytical burden of never being able to provide an *adequate* account of their main object of study (Kleinman et al. 1997; Wilkinson 2001b). The capacity of suffering to resist conceptualization is deemed to be a particular cause for concern, for the majority of researchers are left with no doubt that it is through this that suffering attains a substantial portion of its power to violate and destroy our lives. Accordingly, the struggle to create symbolic forms of culture to bestow a proper 'meaning' upon suffering is generally approached not only as intellectual endeavour, but also as part of an urgent work of social reconstruction and psychic healing (Das 1997a; Kleinman 1988; Morris 1991).

From the outset of my discussion I would have us reflect upon the extent to which writing on this topic is liable to court ethical controversy. A number of writers maintain that the very attempt to conceptualize human suffering may itself have the unintended consequence of intensifying experiences of pain and misery. For example, Arthur Frank contends that what became most distressing in his experience of being a cancer patient was not so much the embodied pain of his affliction, but rather the very suggestion that he could, and should, find a way to talk about his suffering. For, as the above quotation affirms, what he held to be most significant about his experience of pain was the sense in which it consisted in being 'unspeakable'. Indeed, that suffering is a reality 'you cannot "come to grips with"' is precisely what he most desperately wanted people to recognize about his experience as he searched for a way to live with and beyond what was happening to him. Accordingly, following writers such as George Steiner (1967), one might argue that we should keep silent before extremes of human suffering, on the understanding that words are always bound to trivialize this to a point that is morally objectionable.

However, there is a paradox here, for the ethical standpoint of silence in the face of suffering needs to be defended with comment and analysis. It is with a sense of urgency that these writers are at pains to explain precisely when there is a need for silence. It is in bearing narrative witness to the embodied experience of suffering that Frank labours to have us recognize silence as the most humane and productive response to his condition (Frank 1995, 1996). His narrative has to work at silencing forms of biomedical discourse that he understands to have the effect of increasing his suffering. Indeed, one might go so far as to suggest that in this context the standpoint of silence is argued for as loudly as possible!

Moreover, in raising the question of precisely when it may be best to keep silent in the face of suffering, one is liable to encounter a further, and perhaps even more disturbing, ethical quandary; for, particularly in the context of reports of 'human atrocity', the majority of writers appear to be far more concerned to expose the extent to which an attitude of silence is all too easily adopted by those with the power and responsibility to address the gross violation of people's human rights (S. Cohen 2001). For example, Veena Das works to alert social science to the danger of 'mimicking society's silence' towards the victims of suffering; for where we neglect to make the attempt to give formal expression to what suffering *does* to people, she contends, we are liable to compound the misery of those with no voice to register the trauma of their experiences of physical violence and social injustice (Das 1995, 1997a, 1997b). Furthermore, Gillian Rose raises the disquieting suggestion that a retreat into silence in face of events such as the Holocaust may be to 'mystify something we dare not understand, because we fear that it may be too understandable, all too continuous with what we are' (G. Rose 1996: 43). Accordingly, writers may be far more inclined to share in Hannah Arendt's horror at the capacity of expert 'double-talk' to work at silencing the harsh reality of lived experiences of disorder, hunger, massacre and slaughter (Arendt 1968: 7–9). Here, the greater danger is identified as the extent to which an attitude of silence does not so much disclose more of the truth about human suffering as contrive to 'degrade' it all to no more than a 'meaningless triviality'.

In what follows, I take seriously the possibility that there may be no means of arriving at a satisfactory resolution of these dilemmas. I focus upon the ways in which 'the problem of suffering' amounts to a 'terminal aporia' for human thought and moral behaviour (Ricoeur 1995). My discussion is designed to expose a series of analytical impasses that highlight some part of the intellectual and moral frustrations in which human suffering takes place. Accordingly, the title of this chapter is intended to bring critical questions to the minds of my readers. I work under the conviction that it is by involving ourselves in the difficulty of understanding what suffering is in human experience that we may arrive at a better position from which to appreciate something of what suffering *does* to people.

By no means am I seeking to deny the potential for elements within our culture and society to have a significant bearing upon the ways we feel and respond to suffering. Indeed, in this chapter, and throughout the rest of this book, I am concerned to analyse the cultural and social determination of this experience; I aim to explore how human suffering results from the ways in which individuals embody social conditions of modernity. However, *at the same time*, I would have us consider the possibility that there is *always* some part of 'the problem of suffering' that (so it seems) defies cultural meaning and moral purpose. While I aim to be alert to the ways in which human suffering is a product of particular forms of culture and society, I also attend to the ways in which the apparent 'senselessness' of this experience impacts upon the quality of our relationships with self and others. Thus I aim to trace the dialectics of the interrelationship between 'the problem of suffering' and society. Indeed, I am particularly interested in exploring the ways in which our struggles to relate to the meaning, or rather meaninglessness, of suffering serve as a force of cultural innovation and social change.

I begin with a critical review of the modern tradition of defining suffering in contradistinction to pain. In this context, I note some of the ways in which the sociological critique of Cartesianism in biomedicine is working to bring this tradition to an end. I aim to illustrate how the conceptual distinction between pain and suffering is obscured by evidence suggesting that a significant portion of the bodily experience of pain is constituted at the level of culture and society. For the purposes of this chapter, I concentrate not so much upon what this reveals about the substance of pain as upon the difficulty that this adds to the task of conceptualizing the nature of human suffering. As my discussion develops, I pay increasing attention to the ways in which our failure to arrive at an adequate conception of human suffering may serve as an opportunity for understanding what suffering *does* to people. I want us to reflect upon the potential of the failures of our scholarship to provide us with insight into the existential torment of suffering and their capacity to determine the ways we work to create cultural meaning and social purpose.

Suffering as embodied experience

In modern times there is a well-established tradition of defining suffering in contradistinction to pain (Amato 1990; Bowker 1970; Cassell 1982; R. B. Edwards 1984; Finn 1986; Hick 1966; Robinson 1978; Shaffer 1978). Where it is generally understood that there is a close association between pain and suffering, it is also assumed that 'pain is more objective than suffering' (Finn 1986: 4), and it is by distinguishing between pain as a form of physiological sensation and suffering as a subjective psychological response to pain that one might begin to piece together a fuller understanding of the distinctive attributes of these phenomena. Phenomenologically speaking, pain is conceived to have 'a specific bodily place' (R. B. Edwards 1984: 515), whereas the locus of suffering is held to be far more extensive than this. In contrast to pain, the domain of suffering is held to extend beyond the bounds of mere bodily sensation so as to encompass our entire experience of personhood in body, mind and 'spirit' (Amato 1990: 15; Cassell 1982). Moreover, at this level of analysis it is also observed that, while an element of physical pain always appears to comprise part of the experience of suffering (R. B. Edwards 1984: 515), it is possible to have pain with no suffering. For example, there are cases where patients who have had leucotomies and women undergoing childbirth report themselves to be feeling intense sensations of pain, but not minding this (Shaffer 1978: 1182). In some exceptional circumstances it seems possible to have an intense physiological pain experience without the distress of *suffering* pain. Indeed, it appears that certain types of pain may even be construed as a positive pleasure to a point where pain is 'enjoyed' with none of the negative connotations of suffering (P. L. Berger 1969: 55; Shaffer 1978: 1182).

Most commentators share in the understanding that such conceptual distinctions in large part derive from the influence of the Cartesian split between mind and body on Western thought. René Descartes's theory of a physical pain mechanism, as outlined in *The Treatise of Man* ([1664] 1972), is conceived to be largely responsible for instigating an approach towards the study and treatment of pain as a purely physiological entity (Bendelow and Williams 1995a, 1995b). Up until the mid-1960s Western conceptions of pain, particularly in the context of biomedicine, were dominated by the understanding that this bodily sensation results from a noxious physical stimulus transmitting pain

information along a specific pathway to receptors in the brain
(Horn and Munafò 1997: 4). On this view, 'the conquest of pain'
(Fairley 1978) takes place when it is possible either to block the
transmission of pain information along the pain pathway or dull
the sensitivity of the pain receptors; pain is hereby understood to
be a purely anatomical phenomenon which is most appropriately
addressed as a medical problem. By contrast, suffering is held to be
more a state of mind or a mode of consciousness which is bound to
the dynamics of social perception and cultural awareness (Hick
1966: 354–8). In this model it is commonly agreed that there is no
simple way of bringing suffering under the technical control of
medicine, for its 'treatment' is held to be highly dependent upon
the vagaries of an individual's sense of self-dignity and social value
(Finn 1986). Under the influence of Cartesianism, the problem of
pain is approached as a technological quest to master and control
an 'objective' bodily sensation, while the problem of suffering
tends to be represented as a 'subjective' matter of moral
conscience, cultural outlook and personal psychology (Amato
1990: 1–20; Illich 1976: 140–60).

However, over the last 30 years, researchers have become
increasingly alert to the extent to which the sensation of pain
cannot be explained in exclusively physiological terms, to a point
where the conceptual dichotomy between pain and suffering is
obscured. Where studies now place an emphasis upon the extent to
which sensory experience appears to be comprised of a dynamic
interaction between physiology, psychology and culture, it has
become much harder to maintain a clear conceptual distinction
between the constituents of pain, on the one hand, and the
condition of suffering, on the other (DelVecchio Good et al. 1992;
Kleinman 1988; Kleinman et al. 1997). Here commentators argue
that we are witness to a revolutionary transformation in Western
conceptions of somatic experience, for the emergent paradigm in
pain research is understood to require that we abandon
Cartesianism in favour of a conception of bodily sensation that
gives due recognition to the ways in which our physiological
experience of the world is moderated not only by psychological
disposition, but also by the social dynamics of cultural reproduction and exchange (Leder 1990; Morris 1998: 107–34). Accordingly, it is not just the case that suffering appears as a possible
result of an intense and prolonged experience of pain but, further,
that the actual feeling of pain appears to be inextricably bound to
the extent to which we are caught up in a state of suffering
(Kleinman and Kleinman 1991).

Within the domain of medical research, Roland Melzack and Patrick Wall's Gate Control Theory, which aims to highlight the extent to which psychological and cognitive variables modulate the physical sensation of pain, has advanced this paradigm shift in the conceptualization of pain and suffering by lending the authority of 'hard science' to the understanding that socio-cultural factors comprise an important part of the pain experience (Melzack and Wall 1965, 1988; Wall 1999). Maryann Bates argues that this theory has had the effect of adding renewed legitimacy to the insights of earlier studies of the impact of cultural variables on pain, perception, tolerance and behaviour (Bates 1987; Beecher 1956; Zborowksi 1952; Zola 1966). Among experts in the field of pain research, it is now generally accepted that socio-cultural factors not only influence the ways in which people respond to pain, but also *constitute* a significant portion of the bodily sensations which are labelled in these terms (Horn and Munafò 1997; V. N. Thomas 1997).

However, it is particularly as part of the effort to explain the dramatic increase in reports of chronic pain syndrome that researchers have been alerted to the sociocultural conditioning and composition of somatic experience (Morris 1991: 65–78; DelVecchio Good et al. 1992). Chronic pain, which in the terms of medical discourse is usually defined as 'pain which has persisted beyond the normal tissue healing time' (3–6 months), is estimated to afflict as many as 46.5 per cent of the general British population (Elliott et al. 1999). Nevertheless, it should be noted that estimates vary considerably, depending upon the design of epidemiological surveys and the particular characteristics of the samples of population in question (ibid.). In the most comprehensive cross-national study of this phenomenon to date, it was found that between 5 per cent (Nigeria) and 33 per cent (Chile) of populations experienced chronic pain (Gureje et al. 1998). However, despite such wide variations, expert opinion generally holds to the view that this amounts to a problem of epidemic proportions with huge social and economic costs (Margoles and Weiner 1999: pp. xi–xiv; B. H. Smith 2001).

While back problems and arthritis are the most commonly reported causes of chronic pain (Elliott et al. 1999: 1251), in the case of afflictions such as fibromyalgia, respondents may report feeling pains all over their body which cannot be linked to any discernible physiological cause (Romano 1999). Even when chronic pain can be linked to some degenerative physical condition, it is becoming increasingly apparent that there are major socio-economic and cultural components to this experience which have a moderating effect on the intensity of painful feelings. Indeed, in a recent editorial in *The British Journal of General Practice*, Blair Smith goes so far as to advise his colleagues that, on the basis of the accumulated findings of epidemiological surveys that repeatedly document the association between chronic pain and experiences of emotional distress, work problems and family breakdown, then they should understand this problem to be 'multidimensional both in its aetiology and in its impact' (B. H. Smith 2001: 525). Accordingly, if medical practitioners are to become more effective in pain care, they should be prepared not just to dispense analgesic drugs but also to make socio-economic factors and psychosomatic experiences a part of their clinical concern (ibid.).

The medical practitioner and anthropologist Arthur Kleinman has gone further than most to bring such knowledge to bear upon the practice of medicine, and over the last twenty years has documented a series of powerful cases of the aetiological significance of social and cultural conditions in the embodied experience of pain and disease (Kleinman 1986, 1988, 1992, 1996; Kleinman and Kleinman 1991). His research has repeatedly sought to highlight the extent to which the onset and response to chronic forms of mental and physical illness are mediated by the cultural meanings through which people relate to their personal social worlds. Moreover, he claims that by conducting 'mini ethnographies' of his patients he has often arrived at a position to provide more effective and humane care through 'the empathic witnessing of [their] existential experiences of suffering and practical coping with the major psychosocial crises that constitute the menacing chronicity of that experience' (Kleinman 1988: 10).

However, the significance of this work goes beyond its call for a radical reappraisal of the practice and goals of Western medicine; for Kleinman would have us dwell not only upon the ways in which his 'illness narratives' expose the 'cultural elaboration' of somatic experience, but also upon the extent to which this highlights the moral and political values that impinge upon the social reproduction and exchange of the forms of culture in which pain is *suffered*. Indeed, writing with colleagues at the Harvard Medical School's Department of Social Medicine, he explicitly identifies his work as an attempt to make questions about the nature of human suffering central to the study of painful bodily sensations and the effort to improve the techniques and practices of pain relief (DelVecchio Good et al. 1992). Accordingly, the intimacy of the association between pain and suffering is thought to be such that there are circumstances where the effective relief of pain may not require us to concentrate so much upon what is physically or mentally 'wrong' with a person, but more upon the socio-cultural processes in which their bodily feelings are constituted as an experience of suffering.

Such an emphasis encourages us to consider the extent to which there are occasions when bodily feelings of pain, and particularly those of chronic pain, are an idiom of personal distress which arises more as a consequence of the social frustrations and cultural contradictions in which people are made to live than as a result of psychological pathology, physical injury or disease. In his cross-cultural comparisons of chronic illness experiences in China and North America, Kleinman repeatedly highlights the intimacy of the association between somatic experience and the social and political frustrations which appear to have a structuring effect upon the personal meanings that individuals acquire and create for their lives (Kleinman 1986, 1988, 1992). Moreover, he understands the differences in the ways in which Chinese and North Americans appear to experience their symptoms and respond to various kinds of treatment as an indication of the extent to which embodied experience is embedded in culture. His case studies repeatedly document the extent to which physiological health and healing are contingent upon the character of the social relationships and symbolic forms of culture which provide people with their sense of self and social purpose. In this context, every experience of pain is conceived to take place within and, further, be derived to some extent from a particular culture of suffering. The conceptual distinction between pain and suffering is thus obscured to the point where it can no longer be sustained. Indeed, where biomedicine may still persist in maintaining a clear distinction between these two phenomena, this is deemed to obstruct the advancement of our understanding of the complexity of pain in its variety of manifestations within the density of lived experience (Kleinman and Kleinman 1991).

At this point in its development, pain research is confronted with a range of analytical conundrums which call for a radical reappraisal of the intellectual traditions that have shaped Western conceptions of embodied experience. Moreover, for the most part, those working to develop our understanding of the nature of human suffering in this context are inclined to the view that, where medical anthropology exposes the intimacy of the association between negative states of bodily feeling and the social dynamics of cultural reproduction and exchange, then this may have a revolutionary impact not only upon biomedical science, but also upon the science of society (Bendelow and Williams 1995a, 1995b; Graubard 1996; Kleinman et al. 1992, 1997; Morris 1991). However, I would add that, more often than not, it appears that where this research becomes most controversially engaging is where these 'new' understandings of human suffering are exposed as still inadequate to account for the 'reality' of this phenomenon. More often than not, it seems that the radical impulse of this work thrives more on the frustrations derived from its continued failure to provide a sufficient account of its main object of study than on the advances it makes towards the establishment of a comprehensive socio-cultural theory of embodied suffering.

'New' problems of suffering

When it comes to identifying the new fields of investigation that emerge in the wake of these developments, commentators, whatever their differences of opinion, are generally emphatic in declaring Cartesianism redundant. For example, Simon Williams and Gillian Bendelow affirm that 'at an analytical level the study of pain and human suffering demands the dissolution of former dualistic modes of thinking' (Williams and Bendelow 1998: 160). Likewise, Arthur Kleinman and colleagues maintain that in this context 'the dichotomy between mind and body upheld by both medical and psychological research is invalid and unavailing' (Kleinman et al. 1992: 11). However, if we are now to work at 'transcending' these 'false dualisms' (Bendelow and Williams 1995a, 1995b) so as to arrive at a more adequate conception of the lived 'reality' of human suffering, how might we proceed? What kinds of questions should we be asking ourselves, and are we yet in a position to answer them?

As a basic point of emphasis researchers tend to agree that the development of a more analytically sophisticated account of pain and suffering must strive to give due recognition to the ways in which the embodied experience of these phenomena is both shaped by culture and moderated by the quality of our social relationships. On this view, we must now embark upon an attempt 'to ground sociosomatic processes ... in a developed theory of the interconnection between the social body and the physical body' (Kleinman 1996: 204). For what is required here is no less than 'an embodied approach to pain that combines the physical, affective and cultural dimensions of human suffering in a seamless web of lived experience' (Williams and Bendelow 1998: 168). But there is certainly no consensus as to how this might be achieved. Indeed, at present this project appears to have not so much cleared the way for a more holistic account of our social embodiment as to have alerted researchers to the magnitude of the analytical problems which remain to impede a unified account of the integration of bodily feelings within the dynamics of culture and society.

Perhaps above all else, it has served to make commentators sensitive to the apparent inadequacy of the language of social science for expressing the content of embodied experience. While seeking to present this as 'the outcome of cultural categories and social structures interacting with psychophysiological processes' (Kleinman and Kleinman 1991: 277), writers continue to struggle to give adequate formal expression to what our social embodiment actually amounts to in lived experience. Accordingly, having criticized biomedicine for its reductionist accounts of bodily feeling, social scientists are inclined to turn this critique back upon themselves. For example, Mary-Jo DelVecchio Good and colleagues maintain that where researchers work to highlight the ways in which the human experience of suffering 'is resistant to incorporation into biomedical and psychological theorising', they should likewise concern themselves with the extent to which this 'eludes' the analytical grasp of social science (DelVecchio Good et al. 1992: 199). On this view, the sociological repre-sentation of suffering can only amount at best to a fragmentary account of the ways in which suffering takes place within the flow of lived experience, and thereby is deemed to always fall short of providing us with sufficient knowledge of what suffering does to people. The attempt to classify the content of embodied suffering is held to be a necessarily exclusionary practice; and the terminology of social science, in common with every technical language of expertise, is understood to be too orderly to disclose the dynamics of the social and cultural processes in which this disorderly experience is constituted.

Moreover, where ethnography is most often presented as the method best suited to diminish 'the gap between experience and objectification' (DelVecchio Good et al. 1992: 200), it is still perceived to run the risk of committing acts of 'symbolic violence' upon the qualitative experience of personal suffering (Bourdieu 1999: 607–26; Frank 2001). For example, while, on the one hand, Arthur Frank celebrates the power of 'illness narratives' to express bodily feelings in words that have the potential to become a powerful force in social life, on the other, he emphasizes the inadequacy of such texts to express the corporeal reality of those 'in' suffering (Frank 1995, 1996, 2001). He maintains that where researchers are necessarily committed to 'the stylistics of universality', they will never be able to provide an authentic representation of the personal sense of violation that comprises the trauma of suffering in lived experience. For Frank there is no method or style of writing which is sufficient to capture the standpoint of the individual within the 'mute embodied sense of absence' that, on this understanding, makes the essential part of their suffering 'unspeakable' (Frank 2001).

In this context, Frank suggests that 'the more we seek to understand the body ... the more we unsettle attempts to explain it' (Frank 1996: 103). In a similar vein, Arthur and Joan Kleinman report that their efforts to create 'experience near categories' for representing what is 'vitally at stake' for individuals within 'the immediacy of [the] felt quality' of suffering are always being exposed as insufficient to interpret the existential reality of this phenomenon. Accordingly, it seems that the narrative attempt to expose a greater part of the embodied experience of suffering does more to frustrate our terms of analysis than it achieves in 'objectifying' a person's bodily feelings of distress. Here suffering consistently appears to be 'more than we can say or understand' (Kleinman and Kleinman 1991: 278).

However, for the Kleinmans, this apparent failure of social science to provide a sufficient account of human suffering may not so much expose an inevitable discrepancy between symbolic forms of representation and sensory experience as serve to highlight a cultural poverty which is specific to the rational-technical frameworks with which we are disposed to construct knowledge of self and society. Where these researchers work to alert us to the cultural conditioning of pain in human experience, they would also have us question the extent to which our capacity to represent what happens to people 'in' suffering is contingent upon the cultural reality in which we are made to live. Accordingly, they maintain that it may yet be possible for us to transcend 'the dichotomy between thought and sensation which is inscribed in [our] language', for it may be more a matter of language than we are able to imagine at present (Kleinman et al. 1992: 12).

In his efforts to promote a 'biocultural' model of pain, David Morris has gone further than most to argue that our experience and knowledge of suffering are always relative to 'the specific cultural narratives' through which we relate to the exigencies of self and others. He maintains that in so far as we may be empowered to work creatively to transcend the textual constraints which define the dominant 'plot of suffering' in modern society, then there is no reason why we should not devise languages which allow for a more authentically meaningful account of this experience than has hitherto seemed possible. In this context, he celebrates the 'postmodern' turn within the cultural discourse of modernity for the extent to which this allows for the possibility of 'a richer narrative of recovered voices' to break through the silence imposed on individuals by 'the modernist myth that suffering is a quintessentially private act' (Morris 1998: 192–201). For Morris, the conceptual and analytical frustrations that characterize the attempt to represent human suffering are essentially a consequence of our cultural history, and in no way should be taken to betray the existence of some core element in suffering which is irreducible to language. On this view, there is no raw datum in suffering that exists somehow beyond the bounds of articulation; rather, this is entirely a matter of cultural perception, which is always open to textual modification (Morris 1998: 216).

However, such an argument can be sustained only as a matter of speculation. While there is a wealth of documentary evidence to highlight the cultural contingency of the ways in which we relate to suffering, it is quite another thing to suggest that what we know as suffering is entirely a matter of culture. For the most part suffering is written about in terms of a challenge to our culture: that is, as a phenomenon which has the appearance of being 'against' and 'outside' what we are culturally disposed to see as a 'normal' and 'necessary' part of our moral universe. At the most basic level, the task of theodicy (or secular anthropodicy/ sociodicy) is always conceived as the effort to reconcile our normative ideals with a lived experience of reality which appears to breach the bounds of moral acceptability to a point that defies reason (Morgan and Wilkinson 2001). In human history, the *sufficiency* of the cultural meanings we assign to suffering is constantly brought into question and this intrigue could as well speak of a component of experience that somehow defies cultural sensibility (Kung 1977: 428). Accordingly, we may here be faced with the paradox that while suffering is an inevitable part of our experience of culture, there is always something 'in' suffering that resists cultural articulation; a part of suffering appears to exceed the creative bounds of cultural expression, and yet we still know that 'it' is there.

On my understanding, this is what Emmanuel Levinas refers to as 'useless suffering' when he attempts to give voice to a component of the experience of suffering that, while imposing itself *on* consciousness, in some part remains 'unassumable' *in* consciousness (Levinas 1988). He suggests that:

> Taken as an experienced content, the denial and refusal of meaning which is imposed as a sensible quality is the way in which the unbearable is precisely borne by consciousness, the way this not-being-borne is, paradoxically, a sensation or a given. This is a quasi-contradictory structure, but a contradiction which is not formal like that of the dialectical tension between the affirmative and the negative which arises for the intellect; it is a contradiction by way of sensation: the plaintiveness of pain, hurt [*mal*] ... the least one can say about suffering is that in its own phenomenality, intrinsically, it is useless, 'for nothing'. (Levinas 1988: 156–8)

Accordingly, there is clearly no agreement among commentators as to how we should interpret the cultural significance of the analytical frustrations that arise within the attempt to make the lived *experience* of human suffering a topic of debate in social science. In the above examples we encounter a clear conflict of interpretations with regard to what this reveals about the cultural dynamics of human suffering. On the one hand, following Levinas and Frank, we may take the view that there is something 'in' suffering itself that in all times and places imposes a limit upon our cultural capacity for self-expression; while under the guidance of Kleinman and Morris, we may understand this aporia as perhaps no more than a contingent product of culture which in time may be consigned to history. Moreover, in looking to the documentary evidence of our cultural history, I would suggest that there is no way of privileging one position over the other as any more plausible; rather, it appears that each may have its moment of 'truth'. While it is possible to find plenty of good examples of the apparent cultural contingency of suffering, likewise it is possible to put forward a strong case in support of the view that there is a permanent insufficiency in our cultural capacity to account for the human significance of this phenomenon.

Recovered voices

In seeking to highlight the apparent cultural contingency of suffering, researchers, for the most part, have looked to the writings of Ancient Greece and the Christian Middle Ages for documentary evidence of contrasting conceptions and, by implication, alternative experiences of human suffering (Amato 1990: 43–73; R. B. Edwards 1979, 1984; Fairley 1978; Illich 1976; Morris 1991: 244–66; Perkins 1995; Rey 1993; Williams and Bendelow 1998). Moreover, in the attempt to recover the 'voices' of our forebears, some would even raise the disquieting suggestion that we were once far better culturally equipped to recognize the socio-cultural constitution of pain, and thereby more concerned to address the social causes and meaning of human suffering. On this view, where sociology works to expose the conceptual weaknesses and ideological hazards of Cartesian dualism, it might also lead us to better appreciate the greater human sensibility and meaningfulness of pre-modern accounts of pain and suffering.

It is commonly accepted that the 'social character' (Fromm 1942: 239–53) of Ancient Greece was quite different from that of the modern age; for, whereas we are culturally disposed to classify our experience of the world into analytically distinct categories, it appears that the Greeks were much more inclined 'to see things as an organic whole' (Kitto 1957: 169). This mind-set is understood to be in evidence in the ways in which the ancient Greeks appear to have drawn no firm categorical distinctions between bodily pain and so-called pains of the soul (R. B. Edwards 1984: 515). While they possessed a wide range of words to refer to different sensations of pain (Rey 1993: 10–40), all unpleasant qualities of feeling, generically speaking, be they physical, emotional, mental or social, were deemed to belong to the same order of experience. On this basis, Rem Edwards suggests that if we are now to work at creating modes of language which are more suited to represent the socio-cultural constitution of pain today, then we might do no better than 'return' to adopt some of these classical frames of reference in order to promote a more holistic account of human experience (R. B. Edwards 1984: 518–22).

In developing this line of argument, David Morris maintains that we would do well to work at recovering the wisdom of Greek tragedy. He celebrates the ways in which this genre of literature locates pain and suffering as an inevitable and socially meaningful aspect of human existence; for he claims that, while on the one hand tragedy seeks to make explicit some part of the wasteful senselessness of these phenomena in lived experience, on the other, there is a constant emphasis upon our human potential to 'rise to moments of awesome fortitude, grandeur, and almost inconceivable endurance' (Morris 1991: 262). On this basis, Morris argues that our classical ancestors appear to have been culturally endowed not only to be able to acknowledge what happens to individuals 'in' the midst of their personal experiences of suffering but, further, to face the task of enduring hardship with the possibility of 'transcending pain in the pursuit of a choice or goal' (Morris 1991: 266).

Similarly, Ivan Illich celebrates the human value of a pre-modern approach to suffering which conceives of pain not so much as a physiological sensation to be controlled and conquered by means of analgesic drugs, but more as a personal experience to be endured. However, he develops a more controversial line of argument in claiming that, where it was once the case that 'pain was recognized as an inevitable part of the subjective reality of one's own body in which everyone constantly finds himself [sic], and which is constantly being shaped by his [sic] conscious reactions to it' (Illich 1976: 141), this not only inspired people to work at making a *virtue* of their suffering, but also served to have 'a limiting effect on the abuses of man by man [sic]'. On this reading, the 'traditional' concern to address the social and metaphysical meaning of personal suffering has the effect of nurturing a greater human capacity for self-reliance as well as the virtue of compassion in the face of the suffering of other people. By contrast, our 'medical civilization' with its pain-killing technologies is held to have a corrosive effect upon our humanity, in so far as it deprives us of the social opportunities to bestow a proper cultural meaning upon suffering, and so 'anaesthetizes' our capacity to feel for the misery of others. Indeed, in an attempt to press home the full provocation of his argument, he even declares:

> What the bomb did in Hiroshima might guide us to an understanding of the cumulative effect on a society in which pain has been medically 'expropriated'. Pain loses its referential character if it is dulled, and generates a meaningless, questionless residual horror. The suffering for which traditional cultures have evolved endurance sometimes generated unbearable anguish, tortured imprecations, and maddening blasphemies; they were also self-limiting. The new experience that has replaced dignified suffering is artificially prolonged, opaque, depersonalised maintenance. Increasingly, pain-killing turns people into unfeeling spectators of their own decaying selves. (Illich 1976: 159–60)

However, the views of writers such as Edwards, Morris and Illich rest heavily upon one-sided and, perhaps, excessively simplistic readings of our cultural history. It is possible to find more nuanced, and certainly less positive, interpretations of the ways in which 'traditional' societies conceived of their pains and coped with suffering. For example, with reference to the Greco-Roman world-view, Judith Perkins maintains that it is not so much in the tradition of tragedy, but more in the classical romance literature and in the writings of Stoic philosophers, that one encounters this period's most popular attitudes towards bodily feelings of pain and suffering. She argues that these narratives 'functioned as part of a cultural script that represented poverty, pain and suffering as unauthentic human conditions ... [which had the effect of] estranging those experiencing them from legitimate society' (Perkins 1995: 204). On this reading, the Stoic virtues of forbearance and emotional restraint betray a society that has little regard or sympathy for what happens in the lived experience of those 'in' suffering.

As far as Perkins is concerned, it is only from the time of the Roman Christian Empire that 'those belonging to the category of sufferers', such as the sick, the elderly, the handicapped and the poor, acquire 'cultural visibility' (Perkins 1995: 7). She maintains that, in Western history, it is only under the influence of Christianity that we witness the development of a cultural discourse which portrays the self as 'a body liable to pain and suffering' (Perkins 1995: 3). In this regard, Perkins would persuade us that it is largely as a consequence of the ways in which Christian discourse on suffering proved more adequate to represent the experience and interests of the majority of people that the cultural appeal of the Greco-Roman world-view began to wane. She contends that the popularity of the Christian world-view and support for the Church grew as people came to identify narratives on 'the suffering self' as a more authentic representation of their personal and social concerns.

Yet, when it comes to assessing the contribution of Christianity to our cultural self-understanding, there are widely contrasting accounts of the adequacy of this world-view for addressing the problem of human suffering. Once again, we are presented with a clear conflict of interpretations. Whereas, on the one hand, it is suggested that the sacred meanings which Christianity bestows upon suffering have the effect of equipping people with the cultural resources to live through and beyond this experience, on the other, it is conceived to leave them vulnerable to experience more intensive forms of psychological and social distress.

On the positive side, in so far as the Christian religion disposes people to read moral and providential meaning into their pain and suffering, a number of writers maintain that 'traditional' societies were less vulnerable to experience the existential anxieties that seemingly comprise a large part of suffering in the modern age (Giddens 1994: 65–6; Illich 1976: 140–60). Moreover, where it is assumed that believers draw a direct connection between the experience of suffering and the ethics of personal conduct, then this is conceived not only to make them more alert to the social aetiology of personal distress, it also makes them more concerned to address the moral condition of their society (Bowker 1997; Hewitt 1983). Accordingly, there is a tendency here to understand the failure of modern society to pay attention to the socio-cultural constitution of suffering as the residuum of a process of intellectual secularization.

By contrast, it is possible to develop a far more negative reading of the impact of Christianity upon the ways in which people relate to the suffering of self and society. In the first instance, there is evidence to suggest that Christian narratives on the value of suffering for the saintly life may serve to promote an attitude of 'stoic indifference' towards the plight of others. For example, Roseleyne Rey holds to the view that during the Christian Middle Ages, the masochistic self-denial of monastic society worked to divert concern away from the attempt to alleviate bodily feelings of pain (Rey 1993: 48–9). In a similar vein, Peter Fairley argues that at this time, little thought was given to the task of relieving the distress of physical pain, for in following the example of Christ's crucifixion, it was popularly assumed that it was right and proper for all to display the marks of suffering (Fairley 1978: 23).

However, in emphasizing the negative influence of Christianity upon the ways in which people experience and respond to suffering, most critical attention is given to the theological teaching that suffering takes place as an act of divine retribution. It appears that, more often than not, the denizens of 'traditional' society interpreted human suffering not so much as a sign of godliness, but rather as punishment sent by God for wrongdoing. Indeed, Marc Bloch maintains that in feudal society this teaching served to make the majority of people morbidly preoccupied with the imminent threat of hell and damnation. He argues that the popular understanding that 'everyday' events of famine and disease were signs of God's judgement upon the sin of society cultivated a social mentality which was disposed to collective outbursts of anxiety that bordered on the brink of mass hysteria (Bloch 1961: 72–87).

Some of the most extreme examples of the psychologically and socially debilitating effects of this doctrine can be found in histories of the impact of plague upon Western European societies where repeatedly, it appears that the suffering of disease and death was compounded by the widespread conviction that this should be taken as a sign of God's judgement upon humanity (Deaux 1969; Gottfried 1983; Ziegler 1969). Moreover, in Paul Slack's account of *The Impact of Plague in Tudor and Stuart England* (1985) plague is conceived not only as a source of great anxiety, but also as the ideological justification for the brutal enforcement by public authorities of strict measures of quarantine upon the poorest sections of society. Accordingly, it seems that this theology worked as a cultural spur to the institutionalization of bureaucratic structures that functioned to advance the social stigmatization of those least equipped to defend their own interests. In its origins, quarantine was designed to separate 'righteous' society from sinners marked out by suffering; those on the wrong side of the *cordon sanitaire* were forced to endure not only the distress of their affliction as social outcasts, but also, the conviction that in this they were experiencing the very wrath of God.

On this account, one of the unintended consequences of these 'public health' measures was to establish a secular space in society for combating epidemic disease, which over the long term served to make people increasingly sceptical towards the doctrines that, in the first instance, lent authority to the administration of quarantine (Slack 1985: 48). On this reading, Calvinist Protestantism appears as an unwitting accomplice in the creation of social conditions that undermine the plausibility of its own intellectual frame of reference. Certainly, during the eighteenth century we find the rectitude of the Judeo-Christian conception of the retributive God being more intensively debated than at any other time in Western intellectual history (Hick 1966: 151). Perhaps most famously, it is in Voltaire's *Poem on the Disaster of Lisbon of 1756* (Besterman 1962: 34–7) and *Candide* ([1759] 1947) that some of the most strident attempts are made to expose the cruelty of such a doctrine when it leads people to understand every event of human suffering as part of God's perfect plan to redeem 'His' creation (Kendrick 1956; Dynes 2000). In this regard, Peter Gay depicts the Enlightenment rejection of Christian 'optimism' as not so much the result of philosophical argument or scientific discovery, but rather as a consequence of the ways in which the empirical fact of human suffering had the effect of making divine providence appear incredible (Gay 1966: 197–203). Accordingly, for Voltaire an attitude of agnostic stoicism in the face of a world in which there seems to be *too much* suffering appears more humane than one which maintains that there is sacred purpose behind every experience of misery and pain. In this setting, the speculative metaphysics of a work like Leibniz's *Essais de Théodicée* ([1710] 1969) is condemned not only on the basis of its seeming injustice, but also in moral objection to the ways in which its teachings have the effect of intensifying the cognitive and emotional distress of those thrown into a world of suffering.

Indeed, Max Weber is of the view that, more often than not, faith in divine providence is abandoned not so much as a result of a process of scientific reasoning, but more as a consequence of the ways in which the apparent injustices and imperfections of the social order make the idea of God appear morally objectionable (Weber 1966: 139). Certainly, this features as the principle justification for Emmanuel Levinas's conclusion that theodicy, as traditionally conceived within the 'Sacred History' of Western societies, is no longer possible (Levinas 1988). On this view, the extremes of suffering that took place in Auschwitz, the Gulag, Hiroshima and Cambodia now ensure that there is a permanent imbalance between every attempt at theodicy and the brute fact of suffering in historical experience. Accordingly, whereas the documentary evidence of our intellectual history records a constant struggle to account for the apparent 'disproportion' between what happens 'in' human suffering and the normative assumptions of theodicy, it is only in modern times that this aporia is deemed to expose the intellectual bankruptcy of any recourse to speculative metaphysics. Moreover, in this context one might venture to identify part of the problem of representing the human *experience* of suffering as the result of the ways in which *both* the dynamics of our cultural history and the brute force of suffering upon/within this history have worked themselves out to a point where all forms of expression are liable (for the time being at least) to appear inadequate to account for the existential reality of this phenomenon.

Nevertheless, once again I would emphasize that, under the direction of such sweeping acts of hermeneutical recovery we should anticipate a variety of interpretations to be given to the documentary evidence of our cultural history. In the above examples, I hope to have illustrated that there is no agreement as to the judgements we should place upon the positive or negative value of these world-views within the cultural dynamics of human suffering. Moreover, where symbolic forms of culture are always conceived to have an *incisive* bearing upon the social experience of suffering, far more controversy surrounds the extent to which these should be taken as a *decisive* cause of this distress. Viewed as a whole, there is clearly no consensus when it comes to identifying the distinctive attributes or essential humanity of 'pre-modern' conceptions of suffering, or for that matter, those of the 'modern' age. Furthermore, in so far as the textual analysis of historical manuscripts provides us with no direct insight into the ways in which people experienced and applied their meanings to the social contexts of day-to-day life, their real social significance is always left as a matter for speculation. Indeed, on these grounds it may well be the case that where researchers work to expose the definitive character of human suffering through the 'voice' of our forebears, they will always be immersed in analytical controversy.

Questions upon questions

It seems that in making 'the problem of suffering' a topic of sociological investigation, commentators are always liable to be brought back to debate the ways in which they approach the task of questioning this phenomenon. While working to make the experience of suffering a topic of social science, researchers are always burdened by the effort to establish an adequate conception of their main object of study. It seems that at the very point of its departure, this venture falters upon the intrigue of its own making. The great urgency with which writers strive to make clear what suffering actually *does* to people always appears to be accompanied by open expressions of frustration in face of the perceived inadequacy of our categories of thought for making sense of the reality of pain in human experience. In this context, perhaps most progress is made when we renounce the attempt to render this 'knowable' and, instead, concentrate on making sense of the 'senselessness' with which we are confronted: that is, to make it our goal to understand the great difficulty of understanding what happens 'in' suffering (Arendt 1994a; Fine 2001: 19–22).

In current debates, a substantial part of these analytical frustrations arises in connection with efforts to make clear what actually takes place within the personal trauma of human suffering as embodied experience. In this context, commentators are always questioning how it may be possible to 'put into words' a greater part of the embodied sense of violation that takes place 'in' suffering. As observed by Arthur Frank, here language appears to be embroiled in 'a perpetual struggle for authenticity' (Frank 1996: 64). The essential part of the embodied experience of suffering always appears to resist articulation; the inner sense of suffering as lived experience seems to remain consistently 'unspeakable' (Frank 2001: 355). Indeed, on this evidence we may well be faced with the paradox that, at the same time as suffering makes itself known to all, its proper identity is kept most painfully obscure. Moreover, while our common humanity may be affirmed in our shared vulnerability to suffering, it seems that the absence of a language which is *sufficient* to externalize the contents of this experience always leaves those 'outside' in a position where it is all too easy to withhold acknowledgement of what happens 'in' the suffering of others (Das 1997b). Here some part of the agony of suffering appears to *consist* not only in the extent to which it is encountered as irredeemably 'alien' to personal experience (Frank 1996: 56), but also, through its defiance of language, in being an experience that is utterly 'unsharable' (Scarry 1985: 4–5).

It is with this emphasis, that Elaine Scarry argues that, in its undiluted form, the pain of suffering amounts to an experience of pure negation. Accordingly, she maintains that the annihilating force of suffering is such that it destroys not only the contents of complex thought and emotion, but also the most elemental modes of perception and human interaction. On this understanding, suffering aims to dominate all sensibility with an 'objectless' experience of 'sheer aversiveness [*sic*]' (Scarry 1985: 52–3). For this reason she contends that, where a person has the cultural resources to work at 'objectifying' their experience of suffering in language, they are to some extent 'removed' from the full force of their affliction. Here the faculty of language, in so far as it thrives upon our imaginative capacity to adopt a meaningful relationship to objects in our world, is conceived to always work in opposition to suffering (Scarry 1985: 161–80).

However, while Scarry proposes that there is a fundamental dichotomy between the pain of suffering and the work of imagination, others place an emphasis upon the extent to which suffering does not so much work to annihilate our capacity for creative thinking but, rather, thrives upon the ways in which this might add to our torment. For instance, Arthur Schopenhauer conceives the agony of suffering to be greatly intensified by the extent to which it leaves us 'thinking about future and absent things' (Schopenhauer 1970: 44). For Schopenhauer, our cultural disposition to imagine life without suffering is precisely what makes the sensation of suffering so difficult to bear. In an extreme example of this, Primo Levi reports that, contrary to expectations, his experience of Auschwitz was made all the more unbearable when for a brief period he was made to work in the relative comfort of a chemical laboratory, for here he was given the time and space in which to reflect upon the life he had lost and the repugnant state to which he had been reduced; it was the 'pain of remembering' which made his suffering even more 'ferocious' (Levi 1987: 142–50).

Indeed, time and again the literature on 'social suffering' is brought back to the intrigue that surrounds the apparent ways in which the lived experience of this phenomenon may be moderated by the social dynamics of cultural reproduction and exchange. While the essential part of the embodied experience of suffering may remain perpetually 'unspeakable', many would testify to the extent to which the intensity of this bodily feeling is either heightened or diminished within culture. It is through a process of cultural inscription that a major component of the pain of suffering appears to be brought to bear down upon the body, and conversely, it seems possible to achieve some manner of relief from this experience by modifying the cultural significance that it holds for a group or individual. Accordingly, in the sociology of health and illness we now have a wealth of documentary evidence to highlight the negative impact of forms of biomedical discourse upon the traumatic experience of injury and disease, and conversely, the potential for 'illness narratives' to perform a work of healing at the level of personal meaning (Hydén 1997). Similarly, the work of anthropologists such as Nancy Scheper-Hughes (1998) and Veena Das (1995) bears powerful testimony to the extent to which the pain of suffering in the context of the violence of South African apartheid and India's ethnic wars is borne by people as a form of cultural violation that demands redress at the level of social meaning. Moreover, it is with the ambition of bringing these cultural dynamics of suffering to public consciousness that increasing sociological attention is being given to the potential for news media to draw politicians and policy-makers to address the lived experience of human affliction (Boltanski 1999; S. Cohen 2001; Kleinman and Kleinman 1997; Tester 2001).

Nevertheless, while this focusing upon the cultural dynamics of human suffering may be identified as having the potential to bring the analysis of this phenomenon within the domain of sociology, at this stage it seems merely to have the effect of leaving commentators still more frustrated by the difficulty of the questions that this brings to the study of culture. The effort to expose the cultural embeddedness of this experience appears to have the effect of drawing researchers into a critical confrontation with the established ways in which social science purports to explain the interrelationships between culture, experience and meaning. In almost every instance where some vital element of the cultural constitution of human suffering appears to remain resolutely opaque to the light of sociological understanding, this is understood to demand a radical re-evaluation of the conduct of social science (Graubard 1996).

Vieda Skultans provides one of the most reflexive accounts of the ways in which this takes place. In her ethnographic study of the ways in which Latvians use narratives of suffering to make sense of their traumatic experience of Soviet rule, she makes an explicit attempt to highlight the nature of 'the mismatch' between the conceptual frameworks of social science and the 'cultural grammar' of suffering at the level of personal experience (Skultans 1998: 17–34). For Skultans, what is most important to recognize here is the extent to which people 'in' suffering are beset by an experience which essentially takes place as a persistent struggle to construct a positive meaning out of what is happening to them. On this reading, a most distinctive attribute of human suffering consists in the compulsive struggle to 'reconstitute' a proper sense of cultural identity and social purpose under the brute force of events in which these are violated and destroyed (Skultans 1998: 26). In such circumstances, she advises that the effort to translate the content of this semantic agony into the traditional frameworks and ready-made categories of social science may well be akin to 'the impossibility of the well-fed anthropologist carrying out a participant observation study of famine' (Skultans 1998: 21).

Moreover, in documenting the language of her respondents as they struggle to bring their cultural resources to the task of narrating the trauma of personal experience, Skultans also writes about the ways in which her involvement in this work made her reassess her own understandings of the narrative construction of our humanity. She attests to the extent to which her attempts to describe the ways in which these people struggle to make sense of their suffering seems to constantly bring her to reflect anew upon the nature of language and the foundations of human meaning. In this regard, Skultans alights upon the suggestion that research in this area may always be liable to disrupt and challenge researchers' founding principles of understanding and methods of inquiry. Accordingly, in venturing to conduct research on the lived experience of suffering, we may well expect to be brought to question the basis of our cultural formation as human beings and the parameters of personal and social meaning.

Certainly, to date, it appears that those seeking to define the agenda for research on social suffering are always left with an abundance of questions that they identify as having the potential to radically revise the established ways in which we conceptualize the nature of human experience and the project of social science. While doubting the capacity of social science to provide a sufficient account of human suffering, writers appear convinced of the potential for this problem to direct social science toward new ways of understanding our humanity (Kleinman et al. 1992). Indeed, almost without exception, it seems that from the perceived failure of their terms of analysis writers are moved to debate the standards of rationality that frame their conceptions of 'truth' and 'meaning'. Here research on 'social suffering' leads to demands for the rewriting of human history in terms of 'the hurts we inflict on each other' (Graubard 1996: p. viii); the reconfiguration of disciplinary boundaries so as to fashion a more adequate conception of the lived reality of human suffering (Kleinman and Kleinman 1991); new forms of ethical discourse which bring the moral meaning of the pain experience to the fore of public debate (Bourdieu et al. 1999; Das 1997a); and calls for a greater understanding of the political significance of cultural representations of 'trauma', 'violence', 'atrocity' and 'abuse' (Amato 1990; Kleinman and Kleinman 1997; S. Cohen 2001).

Perhaps the repeated documentation of these analytical demands should be identified not so much as a sign of our consistent failure to make adequate sense of the phenomenon of human suffering, but rather as instructive for all attempts to frame this component of our experience with sociological meaning. It may be that the significance of the fundamental questions that initiate and flow from this research lies not only in the agenda they set for the (re)development of sociological thinking, but also in what they reveal about an essential part of the substance of suffering: namely, that it takes place within a cultural struggle to constitute our lives with positive meaning. Where researchers remain analytically frustrated under the attempt to come to terms with the enormity of the questions inspired by their encounters with suffering, do they share in an essential aspect of what suffering *does* to people?

The innovative force of this 'terminal aporia'

I am suggesting that the perceived failure of social science to provide a sufficient account of suffering may be useful for gathering a better understanding of what suffering 'is' in human experience. On these grounds it may be entirely appropriate for research on social suffering to remain immersed in fundamental questions of origins and purpose. Perhaps it is always necessary for researchers to bear the analytical frustration of failing to provide a sufficient account of human suffering in order to advance their understanding of the lived reality of this phenomenon. On this view, it may be by working to give voice to the apparent intractability of the questions that initiate and flow from their research that writers are best placed to involve us in the substance of their object of investigation.

Indeed, while this is not usually represented in terms of the explicit task of sociological research in this area, it is already the case that, more often than not, commentators rely on representing the problem of suffering as something 'more than we can say or understand' (Kleinman and Kleinman 1991: 278), so as to bring the full *gravitas* of their project to bear upon their readers. The problem of suffering is being brought to the attention of sociology, not so much through the detailing of what happens *in* suffering as human experience, but rather, through the increasing numbers of publications that make it their ambition to expose the failure of social science to devise languages for conveying the existential reality of violence, injury, deprivation and loss (Das 1997a; Kleinman et al. 1997; Morgan and Wilkinson 2001). It is already the case that by appealing to our sense of what is 'unspeakable' in suffering, writers 'speak' of suffering (Frank 2001).

We may also recognize this as an essential part of the process of arriving at 'solutions' to the problems which suffering brings to people's lives, and as such, a process which draws researchers to share in a further component of suffering in human experience. As Drew Leder observes, for those *in* suffering the constant return to questions of 'origin, extent, and significance' takes place under the *compulsion* to be free from the pain of their experience (Leder 1990: 78). Indeed, he goes so far as to suggest that this is most precisely how pain impacts upon human consciousness; the great discomfort and distress of this experience take places in a desperate search for interpretation and understanding in an overwhelming impulse to be rid of pain. On this reading, the 'telic demands' with which the pain of suffering takes noisy possession of our consciousness are a necessary part of the process by which we are made to search for solutions to our predicament.

In a similar vein, Paul Ricoeur understands human suffering to consist in the experience of perpetually failing to make adequate sense of pain. For Ricoeur, the pain of human suffering always has the appearance of being 'contradictory', 'arbitrary', 'indiscriminate', 'disproportionate' and 'for nothing'. Accordingly, it is always expressed in the form of lamentation:

> How long? Why? ... Why me? ... Why did this person die of cancer and not that one? Why do children die? Why is there *so much* suffering, *far beyond* ordinary mortals' capacity for suffering. (Ricoeur 1995: 252, emphasis original)

Moreover, Ricoeur understands this to expose a further characteristic of human suffering: namely, that it takes place under the compulsion to render its antagonism accountable to reason and open to solution. While failing to know how to make proper sense of suffering, we are scandalized into working to make this 'terminal aporia' *productive* for thought and action. Once again, there is an emphasis here upon the extent to which the utter intolerability of the negative force of suffering upon our humanity demands that such experience be 'fought against' (Ricoeur 1995: 259). For Ricoeur, whatever else it might be, 'the problem of suffering' is most emphatically 'what ought not to be', and the vigour with which this experience is questioned is sustained by the overwhelming conviction that it must be combated and opposed.

On this emphasis, there is the possibility of identifying research on social suffering as participating in or, rather, bearing the marks of its object of investigation. In almost every instance, the analytical frustration of failing to provide a sufficient account of suffering is borne with the overriding objective of eliminating its deleterious effects upon human life. This work takes place not so much for the sake of attaining a better intellectual understanding of what suffering 'is' in human experience but, rather, to discover more effective ways of responding to, and taking action against, what 'it' does to people. While consistently lamenting their failure of understanding, those engaged in the struggle to understand human suffering are sustained by the impulse to take action against what suffering does to people. In the continual questioning of this phenomenon, the aim is to achieve more effective forms of pain care, the protection of human rights, justice for the oppressed, and the end of cruelty and hardship.

I propose that we take the ongoing difficulty of 'making sense' of human suffering not as an indication of the requirement for a more coherent rationalization of the specific components of this experience, but rather as an involvement with what suffering 'is' in human experience. This failure of understanding is, paradoxically, an opportunity for understanding. Moreover, the intellectual frustrations and ethical tensions borne in face of this aporia have a further value in terms of the ways they heighten the need for taking action against suffering. On this view, what may be most important to recognize are not only the ways in which the apparent insufficiency of social science to address 'the problem of suffering' may produce a greater empathy for what suffering does to people, but also how this evident failing serves as an innovative force in efforts to combat its ruinous effects upon human life.

Conclusion

This chapter has presented a critical overview of some of the ways in which social scientists have sought to account for the *experience* of human suffering. In this context, I have focused particular attention upon the understanding that the agony of suffering takes place as a form of cultural embodiment. I have sought to identify and explain the analytical concerns that comprise the agenda for research into the cultural constitution of the embodied experience of pain and its conception as 'a problem of suffering'. I have also outlined some of the new directions in which researchers are seeking to advance this field of study.

Throughout this discussion I have drawn attention to the ways in which the effort to conceptualize the existential components of human suffering draws researchers to debate the adequacy of the language of the social sciences to address the reality of this phenomenon. Without exception, researchers labour under the conviction that something vital is always being left out of their accounts of what suffering *does* to people. They are repeatedly brought to the conclusion that they are both conceptually and methodologically ill-equipped to make human suffering their object of investigation. While there is no doubting the necessity of establishing a proper account of the destructive force of suffering upon our humanity, there certainly appears to be good cause to doubt the capacity of social science to create an adequate framework for this endeavour. In this context, I have highlighted some of the phenomenological attributes of suffering and the characteristics of our cultural approaches to it that are understood to perpetuate this analytical frustration.

The most common response to this evident aporia has been to propose a radical revision of the epistemology and ethics of social science, in an attempt to bring into focus the dynamics of suffering within the interrelationship between culture, society and human embodiment. Accordingly, this research tends to be embroiled in fundamental questions of origins, significance and purpose, in an effort to clarify the constitution of suffering in human experience and identify the optimum ways in which its antagonism might be opposed. While looking to promote this endeavour, I have nevertheless worked to highlight the possibility that, not only might a burden of analytical frustration always remain to obstruct these aims and objectives, but also that this is perhaps inevitable and even necessary if we are to arrive at a fuller understanding of what suffering *does* to people. I have argued that it is when placed under the frustration of being driven to ask such fundamental questions of origins, significance and purpose that, paradoxically, we may be in a position to share in a vital component of what suffering 'is' in human experience: namely, a cultural struggle to reconstitute a positive sense of meaning and purpose for self and society against the brute force of events in which these are violated and destroyed. Moreover, on this emphasis, I have also made efforts to highlight the potential for this 'problem of suffering' to serve as a force of innovation in the impulse to combat the experience of *too much* pain.

In this regard, a sociological response to human suffering may be conceived to require that we amplify unsettling questions of meaning and morality, that we work to expose the apparent senselessness of the experience of injustice, violence and oppression, and that we make abundantly clear the terminal failure of understanding that takes place under the attempt to render the cultural grammar of suffering accountable to the rationality of scientific analysis. What may also be vital to recognize is the extent to which this 'problem of suffering' consistently appears as a vital component of processes of cultural innovation, political reform and social change. On this view, our concern may be to identify the extent to which the 'unassumable' tensions borne in the face of what suffering does to people serve as the *motive force* in the advancement of ethical debate on the character of our times. Indeed, perhaps we should understand this as always necessary for creating the social dynamics for radical alternatives to the ways we live now.

3

OUR CLASSICAL HERITAGE

Human suffering is a primary inspiration for the work of sociology. Where every part of our experience of life may be framed as a matter of sociological concern, then, more often than not, this takes place with a focus upon the ways in which people are made socially vulnerable to some manner of injustice, injury or harm. Through sociology, modern society is exposed as comprised of individuals denied a dignified existence, communities breaking apart under the corrosive force of rapid social change, and large sections of population with no hope of fulfilling their human potential so long as they remain excluded from the wealth and opportunities of a privileged few. The tenor of sociological discourse has always been more attuned to the misery of the human condition than its occasions for joy.

Nevertheless, while human suffering inspires the work of sociology, there is no long-standing tradition of sociological debate on 'the problem of suffering' *per se*. For the moment at least, the 'sociology of suffering' is unlikely to be recognized as a distinctive field of study. While the existential character of human suffering is readily identified as a pressing concern for philosophy, theology, the arts and medical science, it is unlikely to be framed as matter in need of urgent sociological attention.

As I have already noted, there may be some good reasons for this. The majority of sociologists may well consider the concept of suffering to be so open to cultural interpretation that it holds no value as a category of 'scientific' analysis. It could be out of preference for terms such as 'alienation', 'anomie', 'injury' and 'distress' that they tend to omit direct reference to 'human suffering' from their work. In addition to this, some might argue that as a matter of ethical principle we should resist the temptation to bring sociological attention to bear upon the details of personally violating experience, on the grounds that the language of social science is bound to trivialize the 'human significance' of suffering to a point that is morally objectionable (Frank 2001; Steiner 1967).

However, in a more critical vein, Alvin Gouldner has argued that the omission of the category of 'suffering' from social theory and the absence of any well-developed agenda of sociological research on this subject are more a result of the 'dispassionate' ways in which the majority of sociologists conduct their work. As far as Gouldner is concerned, the greater danger here is that in failing to devote attention to the lived reality of human suffering, 'scientific' sociology runs the risk of becoming both morally suspect and intellectually stunted. He maintains that by distancing itself from the language of suffering, sociology leaves itself open to the accusation that it displays both a heartless disregard for humanity and ignorance of the social experience of modernity.

Similarly, Veena Das (1997a, 1997b) and Pierre Bourdieu (1999) raise the disquieting suggestion that in order to have their work resonate with a language of 'expert authority', sociologists have been all too ready to ignore, marginalize and even 'silence' the genuine voice of people who experience extremes of violence, material hardship and social upheaval. Following Gouldner, these writers argue that, by failing to devote explicit attention to the *lived reality* of human suffering, sociologists risk finding themselves both allied to the interests of those whose positions of power and privilege are maintained at the cost of doing violence to large numbers of people and conceptually blind to an experience of humanity that is vital for understanding the social character of modern times.

Nevertheless, while such criticisms may well be sustained in relation to a great deal of the work that now takes under the banner of 'sociology', I would like to argue that we should be more circumspect when it comes to the ways we relate these to the classical heritage of our discipline. It may now be the case that mainstream sociology is largely untroubled by questions relating to the existential meaning of human suffering. Yet there are passages in the writings of Marx, Durkheim and Weber where such questions are identified as of pressing concern. Indeed, I would go so far as to suggest that, despite the important differences in their respective accounts of modernity, all these theorists share in an understanding that the relevance and value of their work are related to the extent to which it may draw people into a clearer understanding of the social constitution of human suffering and its effects upon the dynamics of society. In this regard, the apparent lack of overt sociological attention to 'the problem of suffering' is more appropriately identified as a matter on which our discipline has failed to acknowledge and develop an important part of its classical heritage.

In this chapter I seek to recover the contrasting ways in which Marx, Durkheim and Weber conceptualize the existential character of human suffering and its significance for our cultural and social development. I argue that it is possible to read these theorists as all sharing a concern to debate the ways in which experiences of suffering are liable to intensify under the social conditions of modernity. Moreover, while working to produce their own distinctive accounts of modern society, at some point they all consider it necessary to give thought to how 'the problem of suffering' *in its own terms* makes a dynamic contribution towards our cultural formation, and at times serves as the motive force of social change. I maintain that each writer is inclined to develop his analysis of society with a mind to explaining a particular aspect of suffering; thereby, they all have something original and important to contribute to the groundwork for a 'sociology of suffering'.

This venture also serves to highlight some of the neglected passages of writing that present us with fresh opportunities to assess the value of classical social theory for understanding today's world. Whereas the ideological debates of 'Cold War' sociology provide us with many highly politicized and partial accounts of the works of these major theorists, I would highlight the potential for questions relating to the social character and meaning of suffering to inspire alternative visions of the classical tradition. Accordingly, this chapter may also be read as an attempt to underscore some of the ways in which theorizing the problem of suffering may lead sociology to develop new creative relationships with its history.

Karl Marx: the dialectics of suffering in capitalist society

Perhaps as a consequence of academic infatuation with issues of substantive theory, there has been a tendency to give only minimal attention to the passages in his writing where Karl Marx seeks to elucidate his arguments with reference to the empirical evidence of suffering (Jordan 1971: 67). Marx was greatly affected by Friedrich Engels's account of *The Condition of the Working-Class in England* ([1844] 1973) and this directly influenced his own attempts to detail the social degradation, physical torment and misery of industrial labour in *Capital, volume 1* ([1867] 1976) (McLellan 1977: 68). Engels provides one of the first, and certainly most passionate, attempts to describe the rank squalor of the living conditions of workers in slum districts of new industrial towns. Moreover, particular attention is given to the bodily afflictions suffered by men, women and children who have no choice but to work in conditions of brutal hardship. Large sections of his study are given over to harrowing descriptions of the physical deformities, atrophying weariness, chronic diseases and painful early deaths of mine workers, machine operatives and agricultural labourers as they struggle to exist in the direst circumstances. Likewise, in the chapters on 'The Working Day', 'Machinery' and 'The General Law of Capitalist Accumulation' of the first volume of *Capital*, Marx dwells on such details so as to emphasize the 'physical deterioration', 'intellectual degeneration' and 'moral degradation' that takes places as a consequence of capitalist exploitation of the labouring classes (Marx [1867] 1976: 340–426, 517–26, 807–70).

More than any other theorists in the 'classical' tradition, Marx and Engels worked to document the brute facts of human suffering in conditions of extreme poverty and cruel toil. In *Capital, volume 1*, Marx is not only concerned to expose and explain the law of capitalist economic organization, but also, in the most vivid terms, to detail its tragic human consequences. Indeed, perhaps we have not gone far enough to recognize the extent to which Marx presents suffering not only as the result of the logic of capitalist accumulation, but also as necessary for making people into docile bodies for exploitation (Das 1997b: 566). His extensive cataloguing of experiences of suffering are intended to provide analytical insight into the methods of capitalist production, as well as to cast their oppressive tendencies in moral perspective. As Marx explains:

> [W]ithin the capitalist system all methods for raising the social productivity of labour are put into effect at the cost of the individual worker; that all means for the development of production undergo a dialectical inversion so that they become means of domination and exploitation of the producers; they distort the worker into a fragment of a man, they degrade him to the level of

an appendage of a machine, they distort the actual content of his labour by turning it into a torment; they alienate (*entfremden*) from him the intellectual potentialities of the labour process in the same proportion as science is incorporated in it as an independent power; they deform the conditions under which he works, subject him during the labour process to a despotism the more hateful for its meanness; they transform his life-time into working-time, and drag his wife and child beneath the wheels of the juggernaut of capital ... the law which always holds the relative surplus of population or industrial reserve army in equilibrium with the extent and energy of accumulation rivets the worker to capital more firmly than the wedges of Hephaestus held Prometheus to the rock. It makes an accumulation of misery a necessary condition, corresponding to the accumulation of wealth. Accumulation of wealth at one pole is, therefore, at the same time accumulation of misery, the torment of labour, slavery, ignorance, brutalization and moral degradation at the opposite pole, i.e. on the side of the class that produces its own product as capital. (Marx [1867] 1976: 799)

In the history of Western Marxism, controversy has always surrounded the extent to which Marx held the immiseration of the proletariat to be a determining factor in the generation of class consciousness and as necessary for the revolutionary transition towards communism (Wilks-Heeg 1998: 124–9). Indeed, following the unprecedented rise in absolute standards of living among the majority of populations in advanced industrial societies through the twentieth century, this is certainly one of the points on which critics have worked hardest to discredit his theories (Conway 1987: 130–3). Given the analytical weight that Marx accords to the 'doctrine of increasing misery' in the first volume of *Capital* when explaining how the historical tendency of capitalist accumulation is bound to arrive at a point where 'the expropriators are expropriated' (Marx [1867] 1976: 929), some would argue that a most essential component of his account of the 'laws of motion of capitalism' are falsified by the extraordinary fact of mass consumption (Meek 1962).

Among Marxist scholars, one of the defensive responses to this apparent discrepancy between fact and theory has been to argue that in his later writings Marx had already begun to recognize that within capitalist social relations the absolute standards of living of the proletariat might be improved, and had started to revise his earlier emphasis upon mass misery as the motive force for working class revolt. Accordingly, following Louis Althusser (1969), Mark Cowling attempts to draw a clear distinction between the young

Marx of the *Economic and Philosophic Manuscripts of 1844* ([1844] 1959), who, so it is claimed, believed that communism would emerge through a spontaneous class response to an ever-intensifying experience of material impoverishment and social degradation, and the mature Marx, who placed greater emphasis upon practical political strategy as the spur to radical social change (Cowling 1989: 27). On this reading, there is no strong line of continuity between Marx's earlier preoccupation with the material conditions of alienation and his later concern to analyse the capitalist mode of production. Indeed, Cowling goes so far as to argue that while Marx always remained motivated by a concern to abolish human alienation, we should interpret the appearance of this concept in his later works as a 'psychological hindrance' to understanding the substantive content of his mature thought, or even 'a logically contradictory theory' which should be taken more as an expression of sentiment than a matter for analytical concern (Cowling 1989: 15–17).

Nevertheless, in light of his emphasis on the theme of alienation in the *Grundrisse* (1973), others maintain that this should always be understood to have been among Marx's core concerns and, further, that in detailing the misery of workers he was seeking to expose how this might be consciously recognized in human experience (Geras 1983; McLellan 1971: 108–10; 1973: 81–8, 115–21; Mészáros 1970). Thus, while it is undoubtedly the case that his mature writings on the dynamics of capitalism contain more qualified remarks on the role of immiseration in the generation of class consciousness, there is certainly no conclusive evidence to suggest that this was reduced to the position of being only a minor component of his analysis. Indeed, on this matter Jon Elster argues that Marx always understood that for the proletariat to be motivated to abolish capitalism, it was vital for them not only to be convinced of the intellectual merits of communism, but also to be suffering under a burden of hardship and misery whereby it was made all too painfully clear that they had nothing to lose but their chains (Elster 1985: 528–31). For Elster, it is not so much the objective condition of alienation, but rather the subjective experience of this as human suffering, which serves as the motivation for radical social change, for 'revolution is a costly and painful process, that will be initiated only if the situation is *experienced* as desperate' (ibid., my emphasis).

However, while there is clear evidence that Marx was always concerned to expose social conditions that produce large-scale human suffering and, further, that throughout his work he maintained the understanding that this must comprise some part of the dialectics of social change, he does not provide us with any sustained analysis of the precise ways in which the conscious *experience* of suffering works to this effect. Although his later writings display a passionate concern to detail the ways in which the dynamics of capitalist accumulation take place at the cost of hardship and misery, he never provides us with any in-depth analysis of how the distress of suffering at the level of personal experience might serve to accomplish the creation of a revolutionary class consciousness. Marx categorically states that the tendency of the working class to revolt will grow in proportion to 'the mass of misery, oppression, slavery, degradation and exploitation' (Marx [1867] 1976: 929) experienced within capitalist relations of production; but he does not venture to explain precisely *how* suffering contributes to such strength of solidarity and purpose. Moreover, on this matter, it is possible to highlight an ambiguity that is largely neglected within the domain of Marxist scholarship.

How is it that *through* their 'physical deterioration', 'intellectual degeneration' and 'moral degradation' the working class might become a united force in pursuit of communism? How can experiences that are so painfully negative and essentially dehumanizing be made into a positive force for the construction of social conditions for realizing our 'essential powers'? What are we to make of the apparent paradox that, while on the one hand Marx would alert us to the oppressive force of suffering upon the physical and social body, on the other he would have us understand this as a necessary constituent of the historical process whereby people are physically and socially empowered to fulfil their human potential?

It is only in the *Economic and Philosophic Manuscripts of 1844* that Marx begins to sketch some possible answers to these questions. But by no means are we presented with an unequivocal point of view on how people are liable to experience and relate to their suffering. Indeed, in these essays he provides some arguments to highlight the potential for suffering to heighten the condition of alienation and obstruct the realization of class consciousness, as well as reasons for us to identify this as a potential spur for the struggle for human freedom. For example, on the negative side, in the introduction to the critique of Hegel's *Philosophy of Right*, human suffering features not so much as a force of radical social change, but rather as a contributing factor to the maintenance of the *status quo*; for it is this which guarantees the psychological appeal of religion, and leads people to ignore 'the truth of the here and now' in favour of the 'illusory happiness' of life in the hereafter (Marx 1977: 63–4). However, in a more positive vein, in a section of manuscript where he attempts to outline the 'essence' of human nature, he maintains that 'suffering, humanly considered, is a kind of self-enjoyment of man' (Marx 1959b: 101). Indeed, in the essay where he offers a 'Critique of the Hegelian Dialectic and Philosophy as a Whole', he appears to hold to the view that suffering is always necessary for us to engage in 'passionate' pursuit of the 'objective' truth of our human condition (Marx 1959a: 146). Accordingly, in this context Marx may be interpreted as holding two contradictory points of view on the relationship of humanity to suffering; while on one hand there is the suggestion that suffering works to obstruct the realization of human potential, on the other it is conceived to be an integral part of the process whereby we might attain full 'enjoyment' of self and others.

Andy Merrifield (1999) provides one of the most considered attempts to draw out the meaning of these passages, and suggests that Marx outlines an ideal image of humanity which is akin to that presented by Dostoevsky's 'paradoxicalist' in *Notes from Underground* ([1864] 1972). On this view, the existential encounter with suffering is deemed necessary for people to gain clarity of insight into their essential nature and to engage in passionate pursuit of human freedom; suffering serves as a kind of sensuous 'knowledge' for attaining intellectual, emotional and physical fulfilment (Marx 1959b: 100–1). However, what separates Marx from Dostoyevsky is the former's recognition of the moderating force of the social context upon this potentiality. Merrifield is concerned to emphasize the extent to which, unlike Dostoyevsky, Marx believed that 'it is *precisely because* we suffer and feel pain that it behoves us to seek ways of reducing and abolishing *certain kinds of pain and suffering*' (Merrifield 1999: 85, emphasis original). For Marx it was all too clear that the misery and toil experienced within social relations of capitalist accumulation obstructed the development of the 'total person'; it was only under the right kind of social system that people might be equipped with the 'vital powers' to attain freedom through suffering.

Nevertheless, the ambiguity remains. Marx never ventures to detail the distinction between what might be referred to as the 'right' and the 'wrong' kinds of suffering. Moreover, there is never any sustained attempt to illustrate how, as a possible consequence of the dialectical relationship between these phenomena, we might finally work towards the fulfilment of our individual and social potential. Indeed, as Merrifield notes, given the emphasis that Marx places on this process in the manuscripts of 1844, and furthermore, the possibility of identifying this vision as 'the central philosophical tenet upon which [his] mature critique of political economy is founded', it remains a mystery why Marx never sought to develop his thoughts on these matters and draw out their political implications (Merrifield 1999: 75 and 85).

However, for the purposes of this project, the points that I wish to emphasize are fourfold. In the first place, in light of the above, I suggest that Marx's conception of the force of suffering upon the development of self and society presents us with new opportunities to re-evaluate his overall contribution to our understanding of conditions of modernity. Moreover, in addressing the relative neglect of his contribution to the development of empirical sociology, it may be appropriate not only to reflect anew upon the role of documentary evidence of human suffering in our assessment of Marx, but also for any sociological attempt to unmask the essential character of modern society. In short, by questioning the impact of suffering upon human experience and the dynamics of social institutions, we may be inspired to re-assess his legacy to both our theoretical understandings of contemporary society and our methods of empirical inquiry.

Second, in this context, one of the basic insights that may be identified as part of his challenge to our thinking concerns the extent to which *through* their anguish, grief and misery people may be observed to reveal essential components of the character of society. Marx's efforts to detail the hardships experienced during 'the working day' are intended not only as a moral denunciation of capitalist social relations, but also as part of the explanation of how, in this context, power is exercised and exploitation takes place. In questioning how experiences of suffering take place, Marx appears to hold to the understanding that this is essential for the proper analysis of political economy. His documentation of human suffering is far more than a catalogue of the unfortunate 'side-effects' of particular social relations of production; rather, it has the analytical purpose of exposing some of the core attributes of self and society.

Third, in developing this line of inquiry Marx displays a tendency to conceptualize the dynamics of the social body and the physical body as one; the 'subjective' experience of suffering is at the same time an expression of a society in pain, and it is only by addressing the social constituents of this experience that some manner of personal healing can take place. This point may be particularly important to raise as part of the critical response to writers such as Arthur Kleinman, who, in the attempt to advance the topic of 'social suffering' in contemporary social science, complain of the absence of any developed sociological theory of 'sociosomatic' experience (Kleinman 1996: 204). On this view, if Kleinman is correct in his prediction that future ethnographies of suffering are likely to be preoccupied with 'the search for social theories of the human misery of violence, poverty and oppression that connect the social and the corporal' (Kleinman 1996: 206), then it may be that this is best achieved through Marx. At the very least, we might credit Marx with having been among the first to recognize this as a matter for sociological concern.

Fourth, whatever ambiguities remain with regard to his conception of the role of suffering within the positive transcendence of human alienation, what may be of lasting significance here is the fact that he identifies this as a key variable within the dialectics of social change. Accordingly, the problem of suffering *in its own terms* is conceived to be a dynamic factor within the dialectical formation of modern society that sets the parameters for its future trajectories. There is plenty in Marx that may draw us to reflect upon the extent to which human societies are created and transformed under a perpetual compulsion to manage and resist the negative force of suffering upon body, mind and spirit. Moreover, on this point at least, he raises matter for analysis that can also be found in the works of Emile Durkheim and Max Weber, although, as we shall see, they by no means all hold to the same interpretations of the sociological significance of this process.

Max Weber: the irrational force of suffering within the culture of modernity

Now, more than ever before, there is little agreement on how we should read Weber's sociology. This may be viewed largely as the result of the declining influence of Talcott Parsons and the 'Marx versus Weber' debate upon the ways in which contemporary exegesis makes sense of his writings (Turner 1999: 1–71). Talcott Parsons has been widely criticized for promoting an interpretation of Weber as primarily a theorist of social action and for championing a highly selective and somewhat misleading account of his core interests in terms of a project to establish a natural science of society (Tribe 1989; Burger 1993). Moreover, where Weber's sociology has traditionally been received in terms of a debate with 'the ghost of Marx' (Salomon 1935), there is now a fuller recognition of the extent to which this comprises just a part of his project that is by no means his presiding concern. Indeed, not only does it now appear that the differences between Marx and Weber have often been unduly exaggerated (Sayer 1991; Löwith 1993; Turner 1996), but also that the fascination with this topic may be explained more as a reflection of the ideological concerns of Cold War politics than a proper account of Weber's historical outlook and political orientation.

In place of these dominant influences upon our reception of Weber, there is now a far greater emphasis upon the need for us to take our interpretive cues from the ways he conceived the political and cultural crisis of *fin-de-siècle* German liberal bourgeois society. In this context, the last twenty years of critical 'recovery' and 'reconstruction' of Weberian sociology has brought writers to a fuller recognition of the extent to which Weber's personal concern with the possibility of establishing and sustaining a 'meaningful' existence under conditions of modernity may well provide us with the key to interpreting his life's work. While there are some clear differences of emphasis in the works of writers such as Wilhelm Hennis (1988), Laurence Scaff (1989, 2000), Harvey Goldman (1993), Alan Sica (1988, 2000) and Ahmad Sadri (1992), and certainly they are not all concerned to address the same audience, nevertheless, there appears to be a basic convergence upon the understanding that 'one gains access to his sociology as one grasps his outlook on the problem of meaning in life' (Burger 1993: 835).

On this view, it is not so much Weber's debate with Karl Marx but, rather, his struggle to come to terms with Friedrich Nietzsche's pronouncement on 'the death of God' that leaves its mark all over his sociology. For instance, the influence of Nietzsche is held to rest heavily upon the ethics that run through Weber's political sociology (Turner 1992: 184–208). Moreover, his methodological writings are understood to have been developed in close correspondence with a Nietzschean critique of the philosophical foundations of knowledge (Scaff 1989). Perhaps most important of all, it is with reference to the portent of nihilism that haunted Weber, that scholars have sought to reveal the logic that runs through his sociology of culture. Indeed, in this context it is the debate with Nietzsche that is held to expose the full *gravitas* of Weber's abiding concern with Leo Tolstoy's question: 'What shall we do, and, how shall we arrange our lives?' (Scaff 1989: 101–2).

There are a number of different ways in which one might retrace the steps towards this 'quiet revolution' (Turner 1992: 211) in the interpretation of Weber. However, in almost every instance Frederich Tenbruck's article on 'The problem of thematic unity in the works of Max Weber' (1989) is at some point identified as a seminal event that provoked scholars to reread Weber so as to arrive at new understandings of his work. Indeed, with the benefit of hindsight Bryan Turner goes so far as to maintain that 'it is the argument with Tenbruck's interpretation which has established the contours of recent Weberian scholarship' (Turner 1999: 14).

This 'argument', if indeed one is correct to label it as such, has branched out in a number of directions. Tenbruck's article is famous for stoking the flames of debate over the extent to which Weber's 'central question' may be appropriately identified as focused on the meaning of modern rationality (Hennis 1983: 137; Turner 1996: p. xix; Whimster and Lash 1987: 1). Moreover, in this context he has provoked scholars to question the relative status of those essays published posthumously in various forms as *Economy and Society* ([1921] 1968) as compared to the writings on religion that comprise his *Gesammelte Aufsätze zur Religionssoziologie* (1920–1), and whether it is more in terms of the former rather than the latter that we 'see' Weber at work on his core concerns (Turner 1992: 225). In addition to this, Tenbruck's article is identified as a seminal contribution to debates surrounding Weber's allegedly 'evolutionary' view of the rationalization process (Schluchter 1981; Mommsen 1987; Love 1993). However, in the final analysis, for writers such as Wilhelm Hennis (1983, 1988) and Bryan Turner (1992: 226; 1999: 16), Tenbruck's greatest achievement may have been to have inspired researchers to inquire into the essential character of Weber's philosophical/cultural anthropology and, further, the extent to which this is fundamental to any claim to an understanding of his work (Hennis 1988; Goldman 1993; Scaff 1989; Schluchter 1996; Turner 1999: 16).

For my purposes, what is most interesting here is the fact that in drawing attention to the anthropological principles that underpin Weber's conception of the cultural development of modern rationality, Tenbruck also provides us with a fresh opportunity to explore the relative importance of his thinking on 'the problem of suffering' for his assessment of 'the fate of our times'. Indeed, although this provides the context for Tenbruck's identification of Weber's conception of the cultural/psychic needs of personality, to date no attempts have been made to dwell directly upon the significance of his concern with human suffering for evaluating the relevance of his theory for today's world. Here I am interested in the extent to which Weber appeared to recognize 'the problem of suffering' as a constant and dynamic factor in the social definition of our cultural reality and as always liable to shape the ways in which people act upon the environments in which they are forced to live.

As far as Tenbruck is concerned, the distinctive components of Weber's cultural anthropology are most clearly revealed in the context of his reflections upon the problems of theodicy in face of 'the brute fact that suffering exists' (Weber 1948c: 354). In this regard, the essays translated by Hans Gerth and C. Wright Mills (1948) as 'The social psychology of the world religions' and 'Religious rejections of the world and their directions' are held to be particularly significant. In the former Weber conceives the 'rational construction' of religion as a universal form of culture that evolves under the driving force of 'the experience of the irrationality of the world' (Weber 1948b: 125), while in the latter this is developed in terms of its practical and ideal consequences for social life as a whole. Here we find Weber not only concentrating upon the extent to which it is possible to consider the historical development of religion as a result of the different ways in which people use their culture to cope with the experienced reality of suffering, but also reflecting upon the potential for the 'social character' (Fromm 1942: 239–53) of entire societies to come under the influence of this process (Bowker 1997: 361–3).

Weber's anthropological theory develops according to the premiss that the majority of people adopt a basic 'pragmatist orientation' towards the business of everyday life, but on occasion they are thrust into painfully 'irrational' experiences that leave them in a position of not knowing how to think or act in their world. Weber appears to hold to the view that our cultural perspectives on everyday life are always liable to be found wanting when called upon to make sense of acute experiences of personal suffering and social injustice. In these extreme circumstances we are left struggling to find sufficient meaning for our experience of the world and are made agonizingly aware of our inability to act effectively so as to overcome the apparent causes of our affliction or, indeed, that of others. In Tenbruck's words, such experiences 'shatter the purely purposive-rational categories of a pragmatic orientation to things; they can neither be explained nor overcome by technical or artificial means' (Tenbruck 1989: 69).

It is as a result of such shattering experiences of suffering that we come to have a yearning for some kind of charismatic release: that is, some extraordinary (in many instances 'magical' or 'supernatural') means of breaking with the harsh reality of a world in which there is too much suffering. The sheer brutality of extreme affliction is liable to cause us to reach out for solutions beyond those of an everyday pragmatic orientation to things, for in these contexts such solutions are bound to be found wholly inadequate to address the severity of our plight. Herein Weber identifies some of the most vital social and psychological functions of religions and, in the final analysis, the origins of these phenomena (Weber 1948d).

Throughout most of our history, humanity has commonly looked to religion to offer a means of transcending the mundane horizons of our everyday cultural reality. When overwhelmed by the sheer 'aversiveness' [sic] (Scarry 1985) of too much suffering, 'sacred' forms of culture have most often provided people with a means of imagining/experiencing some manner of charismatic release from their affliction; the extraordinary power of religion is encountered in its capacity to provide the hope of salvation. Yet at this point in Weber's theory we also come across an instance of his ultimately ambivalent attitude towards this component of our humanity (Dow Jnr. 1978). For while on the one hand he identifies the search for the 'emotional life-force' (Dow Jnr. 1978: 85) of charisma as an inevitable and even necessary response to the problem of suffering, on the other he appears to hold to the view that this will never be wholly sufficient for people to achieve a satisfactory solution to the intellectual and pragmatic dilemmas that comprise this experience. In this context, we witness the development of a further 'religious' and what Weber at one place refers to as 'pharisaical' (Weber 1948d: 271) need: namely, a comprehensive rationalization of the problem of suffering. This is manifested in questions of theodicy.

Tenbruck dwells particularly upon the extent to which Weber understood the development of modern rationality to have been conditioned by the repeated attempts of particular forms of theodicy, while 'always under the spur of charismatic needs' (Tenbruck 1989: 70), to articulate systematic explanations of events of suffering that enable people to realize a unified standpoint for action. The world images provided by religious ideas, while at one point being oriented towards the fulfilment of charismatic needs, are also placed under an intense pressure to satisfy people's irresistible longing for a comprehensive intellec-tual/rational meaning for their suffering, as well as a means to practically overcome the ravages of their affliction. Tenbruck would have us understand that:

> What characterises the distinctiveness of Weber's approach is that world images, the product of irrational circumstances, succumb to a double pressure of rationality. First, the image of the world has to satisfy the structure of theodicy; that is those obscure aspects of existence that are perceived as unfathomable have, at their own level, to be explained theoretically and, at a practical level overcome. Second, in meeting this demand, they have to contribute to a more unified and comprehensive explanation of the world from the standpoint of a rational theodicy. (Tenbruck 1989: 67)

While Weber appears to hold to the view that this double pressure of rationality is a universal constant in the cultural experience of humanity, nevertheless, it is important to recognize the extent to which he understands its psychological intensity and social consequences to be moderated through the different types of religious ideas that are adopted around the world as solutions to the problem of theodicy. In *The Sociology of Religion* (1966) he concentrates his attention on three 'pure types' of theodicy in order to trace the contrasting intellectual and practical con- sequences of different concepts of God and doctrines of salvation as these confront the problem of suffering.

First, he identifies 'the most complete formal solution' to the problem of theodicy in the doctrine of karma, for here, at least in theory, the problem of unjust suffering does not arise. On this view, all present suffering, no matter how acute, may be regarded as atonement for wrongdoings committed in a previous existence. There is no such thing as uncompensated guilt or evil; to think in such terms betrays a failure to recognize the limitations of one's finite perspective on life. Indeed, within some forms of Buddhism we even find such ethical notions as good and evil being identified as no more than 'an illusion of the ego' locked in an eternally helpless struggle for life. Weber identifies the logic of such a doctrine to encourage a practical response that aims 'when most modestly conceived' to reduce the experience of suffering in one's next reincarnation or, most ideally, to end the cycle of suffering altogether via the elimination of rebirth as such (Weber 1966: 145–7).

Second, there are various religions that hold to a 'dualistic' outlook on suffering as a consequence of a struggle between the forces of good and evil or light against darkness, such as in

Gnosticism and Manicheism. Weber suggests that in so far as humanity is involved in this process, then those who suffer are liable to be identified as contaminated in some way by dark forces and, as a result, those who are perceived as not so 'soiled' are likely to develop an 'aristocratic feeling of prestige' (Weber 1966: 145). He suggests that it is particularly within such religious frameworks that one is likely to encounter more 'tabooistic' approaches towards ethics, with certain behaviours (most often in connection with the material and corporeal dimensions of our existence) being identified as contaminating, and thereby reprehensible.

Last, Weber devotes the most detailed analysis to those religious outlooks that hold to some strictly monotheistic belief in the doctrine of predestination, as in Islam, Judaism and Christianity (Weber 1966: 138–43). At one level he is inclined to identify these religions as all sharing in a similar type of theodicy in so far as they are all liable to be confronted with the task of explaining how their belief in the existence of an all-powerful, unitary God who is 'righteous' and 'cares' for his people can be justified in the face of a world in which there appears to be too much useless suffering. Yet he would also have us recognize that, in accordance with differences in the forms assumed by this particular God-concept and in the doctrines of sin and salvation found in these religions, we shall find believers with sharply contrasting ethical orientations towards their affliction. In this context, the differences between the social actions of those with a more 'mystical orientation' towards their suffering, which leads them to seek their salvation in a 'contemplative flight' from this world in the hope of redemption in the world to come, as opposed to those who react against suffering with an 'active asceticism' that conceives individuals as tools designed for the purpose of bringing about God's kingdom on this earth, are identified as particularly significant (Weber 1948c: 324–6). Indeed, it is especially in relation to the latter that Weber conceives the problem of suffering to have the most far-reaching consequences for the institutional organization and cultural dynamics of modernity (ibid., 327).

Where people are confronted with the intellectual problem of, on the one hand, reconciling their belief in a unitary God as *Summum Bonum* with the evidently unjust suffering of his creation, and, on the other hand, of upholding an 'active asceticism' as the God-willed response towards affliction, Weber appears to hold the view that the double pressure of rationality is liable to be encountered in its most psychologically intense and socially dynamic forms (Weber 1966: 139; 1948c). It is this particular type of theodicy that he identifies as most significant for the overall development of modern rationality, and in the essay entitled 'Religious rejections of the world and their directions' he makes the most explicit attempts to analyse some of the ways in which this appears to have had a decisive impact upon the prevailing social character of his age.

Of most importance here is Weber's conviction that the unintended consequence of the concerted efforts of a 'rationally active asceticism' to work towards the establishment of God's kingdom on earth would ultimately give rise to a cultural situation in which it becomes ever more difficult to uphold 'the claims of the ethical postulate that the world is a God-ordained, and hence, somehow meaningfully and ethically oriented, cosmos' (Weber 1948c). He would have us recognize the paradox that it is precisely as a long-term consequence of the efforts to uphold faith in the goodness and meaningfulness of the divine order, and by actively working to extend the reign of God's kingdom on earth, that believers unwittingly contribute to the creation of cultural conditions in which religious postulates are less likely to be identified with the possibility of expressing 'the truth' about the meaning of our situation. On this view, it is the very attempt of a particular type of theodicy to indicate and explain the way towards overcoming the excessive suffering of humanity that lends a vital dynamic to the development of cultural conditions that render theodicy both intellectually incredible and practically irrelevant (Weber 1948c: 353–7).

Weber argues that the response of 'active asceticism' cultivated 'a rationally ordered mode of conduct that had to prove itself free from the influence of magic' (Tenbruck 1989: 73). He suggests that within this world-view, believers are bound to understand that it is a matter of God's will that they should make every effort to bring ungodly 'disorder' under the powers of human control; for suffering highlights the presence of sin, and God has ordained that we must do all we can to act against sin so as to work towards the institution of his kingdom on earth. Such action is held to intensify a process of rationalization that leads to the different spheres of life being detached from each other to the point where the technical sophistication of our intellectual understanding in one realm is ultimately bound to lack sense in terms of its meaning for the whole. Moreover, in so far as this action consolidates the drive to render the forces of nature subject to the powers of empirical science, then it is identified as having 'worked through to the disenchantment of the world and its transformation into a causal mechanism' (Weber 1948c: 350–1). Weber would have us recognize the extent to which this process is liable to push 'religion from the rational into the irrational realm', and thereby have the unintended consequence of rendering the original (at one time rational) response of theodicy formally devoid of meaning and practically irrelevant to the immediate task of opposing the forces of affliction (ibid.).

A historical example that illustrates some of the components of Weber's thesis can be found in Paul Slack's study of *The Impact of Plague in Tudor and Stuart England* (1985). In this work, Slack is concerned to trace the early development of 'secular' approaches to combating epidemic disease that stress the natural origins of contagion and the requirement for public health measures to treat plague as a predominantly social problem. While alerting us to the material and class interests that pressured local governments into enforcing the rule of quarantine upon the poorest and most disease-ridden sections of the population, he is also adamant that this could only have taken place in so far as the majority of people believed that the authorities were acting in accordance with God's will for his people. In this context, Slack argues that over these centuries, the intensive suffering experienced under repeated outbreaks of plague had the effect of extending a particular line of logic *within* the prevailing religious world-view towards the institutionalization of a secular approach towards combating epidemic disease.

Slack explains that while it was commonly understood that God was the primary cause of all events that took place in the world, it was also accepted that his will was exercized through secondary natural causes and that, with God's guidance and blessing, these could be rationally apprehended and brought under control. Indeed, where the majority of people believed that events of acute suffering were a sign of God's judgement upon the sin of humanity, then it was as a point of sacred duty that they sought to actively 'reform' their society on the understanding that they were working with God to appease his wrath. But, as to precisely what this required in terms of action, considerable disagreements remained.

Throughout this period of history, when it came to explaining the natural causes of plague, the miasmatic theory held sway. The sinful corruption of either the spiritual or the earthly realm was understood to pollute the air with foul-smelling vapours that were the natural cause of plague. On this view, the symbiotic nature of the relationship between the heavenly and earthly realms was largely beyond doubt. Nevertheless, the precise mechanics of this relationship remained shrouded in mystery. Written documents of the time record a great amount of confusion as to precisely what should be addressed as the most immediate cause of the stench of corruption and, further, what should be done to make it go away (Slack 1985: 22–50). This produced centuries of debate over the question: 'What should we do, and how should we live, when plague wreaks havoc among us?'

Over time, the regular incidence of plague provided people with many opportunities to observe and gauge the effects of various actions taken to halt the spread of epidemic disease, and the accumulated empirical evidence pointed to the conclusion that quarantine was by far the most effective means of combating plague's deleterious effects upon society. However, for many it appears that this was extremely difficult to accept in so far as they were unable to reconcile the logical implications of observed results with certain components of the intellectual outlook and ethics of received tradition. Most notably, the gradual spread and stricter policing of quarantine laws came into direct conflict with the religious beliefs of those who held the view that it was by encouraging acts of charity towards the sick and the poor that God would be most pleased to halt the spread of plague. Accordingly, plague intensified a profound tension within the prevailing religious world-view between, on the one hand, an emphasis upon the divine command to flee and cleanse ourselves from sin and, on the other, the gospel injunction to practice compassion towards those in affliction. The question of whether plague was a sign of God's displeasure with regard to our collective failure to faithfully carry out our duty to either the former or the latter command returned with each outbreak of disease (Slack 1985: 227–54).

With the benefit of hindsight, given the economic and political considerations in favour of quarantine, perhaps the majority of disputes were always liable to be resolved in this direction. Slack is convinced that it was not just the empirical evidence in support of the effectiveness of quarantine, but also the fact that this appealed to the social prejudices of the ruling élite and aspiring middle classes, that ensured that this would eventually be adopted as the most common solution to the dilemma. But, in addition to all this, Slack is adamant that these developments could only have taken place in so far as they were at the same time 'nourished by Calvinist Protestantism' (Slack 1985: 48). He argues that it was the 'active aceticism' inspired by the particular injunctions of

Protestant theodicy that enabled people to conceive divine purpose at work in the secular enforcement of quarantine, and that without this ideological support, such actions would have been inconceivable. Indeed, when compared to the largely fatalistic responses to plague among Turkish Muslims, he maintains that it is in these religions' contrasting conceptions of divine providence that we find an important part of the explanation for why quarantine was first adopted as the distinctively Western European response to plague (Slack 1985: 49–50). All other considerations aside, Slack maintains that it was as the unintended consequence of a protracted attempt to solve the particular problems of Protestant theodicy that, by the end of the eighteenth century, there was 'a far more secular approach to epidemic disease than most Englishmen in 1500 would have found acceptable' (Slack 1985: 48).

While apparently working with no thought of Weber in mind, Slack may be interpreted as providing us with a possible illustration of Weber's conception of the dynamic force of human suffering within the social development of modern rationality. Through the historical record of these cultural responses to plague, it is possible to attain some insight into the potential for the problem of theodicy in the context of Protestant asceticism spurring the process of rationalization towards the 'disenchantment of the world'. Moreover, in this context Slack also shares Weber's concern to highlight the disjunction between original purposes and end results when assessing the impact of human action upon the course of history. However, this still leaves us with much work in relation to the task of interpreting the significance of Weber's writings on the problem of suffering for discerning the cultural character of our times.

Here I would emphasize that by no means am I attempting to present this as the vital clue for unmasking the essential theme that unites his sociology; rather, I am of the mind that on this matter we shall always be faced with a conflict of interpretations. There is too much in Weber that remains incomplete and obscure. Accordingly, rather than propose a systematic approach to reading Weber, I am inclined to follow Dirk Käsler in celebrating him more as an essayist who provides us with a 'huge quarry' of suggestive concepts and intriguing hypotheses that remain to inspire new reflections upon the ways in which people create meanings for and out of their social experience of the world (Käsler 1988: 211-16).

It is perhaps of interest to note that while Talcott Parsons is criticized for promoting a distorted account of Weber's substantive concerns, nevertheless, in his 'Introduction' to some of the essays on *The Sociology of Religion* (1966) he provides us with one of the most considered attempts to outline the significance of Weber's writings on the problem of suffering for understanding his conception of modern culture. Moreover, in this context I understand him to outline two of the most important reasons for treating this problem *in its own terms* as a topic worthy of more detailed sociological analysis.

First, prefiguring some of the remarks of Tenbruck, Parsons draws attention to the extent to which Weber conceives of the universal experience of 'the problem of suffering' as a constant factor in the development of processes of rationalization. What Parsons holds to be of particular significance here is the stress that Weber places upon the potential for this experience to lead people to *break* with their normative assumptions about the meaning of reality and radically change the ways they relate to self and society. As in Marx, there is the understanding that through the pain and in face of the horror of human suffering, people are *compelled* to change the ways they think and act. However, in Weber our focus is directed not so much towards the sensuous knowledge of human affliction, but more to the psychic turmoil induced by the apparent 'meaninglessness' of extreme suffering, as the motive force that propels people in this direction. Accordingly, he calls us to reflect upon the extent to which, above all else, it is the devastating sense of meaninglessness that arises in face of 'the brute fact that suffering exists' which is always bound to feature as a pressure towards cultural and social change.

Second, in developing this theme, Parsons raises the suggestion that Weber considered this to hold *increasing* significance for the cultural experience of humanity under conditions of modernity. What is important to note here is that Weber appears to hold to the view not only that people's pragmatic orientation to the world is constantly vulnerable to the irrational force of suffering but, further, that this vulnerability is liable to intensify where society is increasingly brought under the discipline of rationalization. He contends:

> Weber takes the fundamental position that, *regardless of the particular content of the normative order*, a major element of discrepancy [between normative expectations and actual experiences] is inevitable. And the more highly rationalized an order, the greater the tension, the greater the exposure of major elements of a population to experiences which are frustrating in the very specific sense, not merely that things happen and contravene their

'interests', but that things happen which are 'meaningless' in the sense that they *ought* not to happen. Here above all lie the problems of suffering and evil. (Parsons 1966: p. xlvii, emphasis original)

However, at this point in his discussion, Parsons does not dwell so much upon the potential for this tension to expose the internal contradictions and paradoxes of rationalization as on its capacity to drive people to make society and nature still more subject to the discipline of calculable rules. As with Tenbruck, the emphasis is on the extent to which our psychological need for 'rationality, in the sense of logical or teleological consistency, of an intellectual-theoretical or practical-ethical attitude' (Weber 1948c: 324), when brought into conflict with the irrational force of suffering, is liable to intensify the social pressure towards a comprehensive rationalization of reality. Parsons's overriding concern is to highlight the extent to which Weber viewed the influence of ascetic Protestantism on Western culture as the decisive factor in the development of 'rational bourgeois capitalism', and, to this end, no attempts are made to explore the full range of interpretations that might be given to this peculiarly socio-cultural conception of the problem of suffering.

In the context of recent concerns to emphasize the extent to which Weber's research was motivated by a concern to explain the historical development of the cultural pessimism of German *fin-de-siècle* society, it may be interesting to explore the influence of his conception of the cultural dynamics of suffering upon his assessment of 'the fate of our times'. Accordingly, it may be worth investigating the extent to which Weber's diagnosis of our cultural situation was developed not only under the direction of Nietzschean philosophy, but also through a peculiar conception of the force of suffering upon the historical development of the social conditions through which 'the death of God' became all too conceivable. Indeed, at one point he remarks that it is not so much as a consequence of scientific argument that the majority of German workers are inclined to reject the 'god-idea', but rather, 'by their difficulty in reconciling the idea of providence with the injustice and imperfection of the social order' (Weber 1966: 139). To what extent may this also have proved decisive for Weber's own ethical orientation towards the world?

But what is perhaps still more noteworthy here is that while Weber is inclined to emphasize 'the irresistible force' of rationalization upon social conditions of modernity, nevertheless, his analysis of the cultural dynamics of suffering presents us with an opportunity to identify occasions on which the alleged irreversibility of this process may be brought into question (Weiss 1987). If Parsons is correct, Weber seems to suggest that it is not just the case that suffering will always retain the power to shatter our basic 'pragmatist orientation' towards reality, but also that this power is liable to increase along with the extension of the rational conduct of life into every sphere of our activity. Accordingly, there is the possibility of understanding this as always working to increase the potential for people to be forcefully confronted with the irrationalities of rationalization. In this regard, it may be with a sociological focus upon people's experiences of 'the problem of suffering' that we are best placed to expose rationalization as fraught with tensions and conflicts 'that stretch to the limits what we can bear in our capacity as individuals and as members of groups and societies' (Weiss 1987: 163). Perhaps along with this we may witness the intensification of the yearning for some manner of charismatic release from a world in which there consistently appears to be too much suffering, and thereby glimpse some of the latent possibilities within our culture for people to imagine and practice radically new ways of relating to self and others.

In summary, while a focus upon the problem of suffering in the works of Max Weber serves to elaborate upon the details of recent interpretations of his cultural sociology, more generally, this may also be valuable for outlining further components of a distinctively sociological conception of what suffering does to people. As with Marx, there is an explicit recognition of human suffering as an independent variable in the dynamics of social change. However, where for the most part Marx develops his analysis with a focus upon how this takes place in relation to the physical dimensions of this experience, Weber is predominantly concerned with the potential for suffering as an intensive form of cognitive dissonance to drive people to break with previously taken-for-granted intellectual orientations and ethical modes of conduct out of a compulsion to sustain a rational world-view. Moreover, the intricacy of his approach also requires us to reflect upon the extent to which the cultural moderation of the experience of suffering is liable to change according to the inner logic of ideal concerns. In this context, Weber presents us with sociological/ historical insight into the extent to which the experience of suffering as 'meaninglessness' takes places *within* distinctive forms of culture that are always open to change.

Emile Durkheim: collective suffering under the poverty of morality

Emile Durkheim is also concerned to expose the moderating force of culture and society on the experience of human suffering, albeit once again with an interest in developing a distinctive account of modernity and its possible futures. As with Marx and Weber, it is particularly with a focus upon the potential for society to undergo processes of rapid social change that he turns to address the peculiar components of this experience. But, while, arguably, Marx is predominantly concerned to highlight the material determinants of the sensuous bodily experience of suffering, and Weber is interested in reflecting on the cultural dynamics of suffering as 'meaninglessness', in Durkheim, the focus is on the extent to which human suffering is constituted as an emotionally charged response to transformations in the experience of social solidarity.

On this topic there are also some interesting similarities to be drawn between Durkheimian and Weberian scholarship; for it is particularly with efforts to reappraise Durkheim in critical response to the distorted accounts of his sociology developed under the aegis of Parsonian structural functionalism, that attention is drawn to the passages in his writings where he ventures to comment upon the sociological significance of human suffering. In place of the 'vulgar Durkheimianism' that portrays him as a conservative patriarch whose affiliations with positivism are displayed in an anti-individualistic and overly deterministic account of human behaviour, following the seminal interventions of Alvin Gouldner (1962) and Steven Lukes (1973), contemporary scholarship is concerned to highlight his support for socialism (Gouldner 1962; Pearce 1989; Giddens 1995b), his radical humanism (Pickering and Miller 1993), and in particular the extent to which his earlier interest in the social determinants of 'conscious strategic action' gave way in his later 'religious sociology' to a greater emphasis upon the ways in which social interactions take place as 'motivated expressive behaviour' (Alexander 1988). However, it should be added that, for some, it is not simply the case that the 'Durkheimianism' of mainstream sociology neglects to take up the challenge of his later writings, but also that its selective reading of his work has obscured his legacy to the point where we are only now beginning to rediscover the intellectual provocation of his conception of the moral condition of humanity in the age of industrial modernity (Stedman Jones 2001).

Stjepan Meštrović, in one of the more controversial of these new interpretations of Durkheim, has worked the hardest to draw attention to the sections of his work where he gives explicit attention to the social dimensions of human suffering (Meštrović 1989, 1991; Meštrović and Brown 1985). Leaving aside the debate as to whether these passages amount to evidence in support of Meštrović's argument that Durkheim should be read as a disciple of Schopenhauer, they at least serve to underline the extent to which the social dimensions of suffering can be identified as among the most persistent of his sociological concerns. From *The Division of Labour in Society* (1964), through to the later development of his conception of the duality of human nature (Durkheim 1973a), Durkheim makes repeated efforts to diagnose and explain the social psychology of human suffering.

In the section on 'The progress of the division of labour and of happiness' in *The Division of Labour in Society* (1964: 233–55), in answer to the question of whether happiness grows with civilization, Durkheim declares:

> Nothing is more doubtful ... there is a host of pleasures open to us today that more simple natures knew nothing about. But, on the other hand, we are exposed to a host of sufferings spared them, and it is not at all certain that the balance is to our advantage ... If we are open to more pleasures we are also open to more pain. (Durkheim 1964: 241–2)

At this stage in the development of his theory, some of the factors that Durkheim identifies as the causes of this excess of social suffering are akin to those found in Marx. Durkheim directs our attention to the degrading and meaningless toil experienced among the labouring classes of industrial society (Durkheim 1964: 371–3). He identifies the working conditions that force individuals to behave as regimented machines, and that keep them separated from their family throughout the entire day, as a social injustice that amounts to an act of violence against humanity (Durkheim 1964: 383). But the greater part of his analysis is devoted to the suggestion that the accelerated level of social interaction among a population undergoing a rapid division of labour is liable to make individuals suffer from a profound sense of inner loneliness and moral disorientation. His emphasis is on the extent to which our psychological health is bound to deteriorate as a consequence of the loosening of traditional social ties and the absence of moral rules sufficient to regulate the social order of industrial society.

Here the suffering of humanity is understood to be as a result of the strain placed upon the nervous system by social conditions in which individuals feel themselves to lack a sufficient sense of moral purpose and social harmony. Already in *The Division of Labour in Society* (1964), he argues that this is expressed in the increased rate of suicide that takes place under conditions of modernity (Durkheim 1964: 245–50).

In this context, Stjepan Meštrović and Hélène Brown (1985) argue that Robert Merton's (1957) 'bland' and 'essentially painless' interpretation of anomie as 'normlessness' fails to convey the passionate emphasis upon the qualitative experience of social injustice evoked by Durkheim's original use of the term; for Durkheim, anomie is tantamount to an 'evil'. They contend that Durkheim always understood the meaning of anomie (and its synonym, *dérèglement*) to refer not only to a lack of moral regulation in social life, but also to the inner feelings of pain and suffering that this is liable to engender. Indeed, in *Suicide* (1952), at the same time as this concept features in discussion of the 'alarming poverty of morality' in the modern world, it also appears in reference to the 'currents of collective sadness' and 'morbid effervescence' that aggravate 'a people's mental system' to a point where individuals may be driven to take their own lives (Durkheim 1952: 361–92).

It is in one of his final essays, on 'The dualism of human nature and its social conditions' (1973a), that Durkheim provides us with some of his most detailed reflections upon the ways in which the quality of the moral relationship between individual and society is liable to aggravate a mental state of suffering. Here suffering in the form of a 'chronic state of malaise' is conceived as endemic to the human condition in so far as in all times and places we are made to experience an inner tension between, on the one hand, 'our personal sensations and ... sensory appetites' and, on the other, the demands of 'the intellectual and moral life' (Durkheim 1973a: 162). At the same time as we are held in bondage to biological/instinctual needs, a great pressure is placed upon us 'to do violence to certain of our strongest inclinations' in order to fulfil our moral obligations to the life of society. He suggests that our essential nature as *homo duplex* guarantees that we will always feel divided against ourselves; it is this above all else which he identifies as the root cause and character of human suffering. On this view, the passions and needs of our individual organic nature can never exist in harmony with the interests of society and civilization. Durkheim states:

[W]e are never completely in accord with ourselves for we cannot follow one of our natures without causing the other to suffer. Our joys can never be pure; there is always some pain mixed with them; for we cannot simultaneously satisfy the two beings that are within us. It is this disagreement, this perpetual division against ourselves, that produces both our grandeur and our misery: our misery because we are thus condemned to live in suffering; and our grandeur because it is this division that distinguishes us from all other beings. The animal proceeds to his pleasure in a single and exclusive movement; man alone is normally obliged to make a place for suffering in his life. (Durkheim 1973a: 154)

As far is William Pickering is concerned, it is in this essay that Durkheim comes closest to presenting his work as a secular theodicy (Pickering 1984: 494); for in explaining the social formation of human nature, his overwhelming concern is to develop a sociological account of why we are always mentally disposed to suffer. At one point Steven Lukes goes so far as to suggest that this conception of the duality of human nature is so important for interpreting Durkheim's sociology that it should be considered as 'the keystone of Durkheim's entire system of thought' (Lukes 1973: 22). Indeed, he goes on to comment that in this regard there is a strong affinity between Durkheim's account of the quality of the relationship between the individual and society and that proposed by Freud in 'Civilization and its Discontents' ([1929] 1985) (Lukes 1973: 433–4); for not only do they both share the basic understanding that society always requires us to restrain our individual sensory instincts to a point that guarantees that we shall inevitably be made to exist in a psychic state of suffering, but also that this is liable only to intensify with 'the growth of civilisation' (Durkheim 1973a: 163; Freud [1929] 1985: 274–87).

Yet, in contrast to the unremitting pessimism of Freud's account of the psychic consequences of our cultural development, in Durkheim there is recognition of the potential for this, under the right social conditions, also to work towards the alleviation of suffering. While reading his late essay on the dualism of human nature in isolation from the rest of his work may well leave the impression that Durkheim conceived of the tension between individual and society in entirely negative terms, elsewhere he is to be found reflecting upon the possibility of there being social occasions on which this provides people with the means to achieve some manner of relief from intensive experiences of mental/ emotional distress, as well as to inspire them with concern to behave compassionately towards the suffering of others. More-over, in this context, he identifies social settings in which suffering itself may have a psychologically redemptive purpose as well as cultural processes in which it serves the interests of moral solidarity.

In his discussion of piacular rites in *The Elementary Forms of the Religious Life* ([1912] 1915), Durkheim observes that 'every misfortune, everything of evil omen, everything that inspires sentiments of sorrow or fear necessitates a *piaculum*': that is, 'a ceremony of mourning'; and in this particular context, he identifies a potential for suffering to serve as the stimulus for social healing and solidarity (Durkheim [1912] 1915: 389). While noting that people often experience an intensification of painful and sorrowful feelings when they come together to mourn the loss of a loved one or lament some form of tragedy, Durkheim highlights the ways in which this appears to 'neutralize' or 'discharge' sentiments of grief so that people attain a measure of relief from their distress (Durkheim [1912] 1915: 401). He suggests that 'the group is re-calmed by the mourning itself' (ibid. 413). Moreover, he contends that such a 'communion of mourning' is also a form of 'moral communion' that functions to affirm people with a clear sense of social belonging and purpose. Thereby, William Ramp notes that Durkheim appears alert to the paradox that it is precisely on occasions when people feel most tormented and threatened by danger that, as a group, they are most likely to express their sense of collective loyalty and mutual concern (Ramp 1998: 141–2). While in Ramp's view the 'vivacity' of Durkheim's descriptions of these rites is not matched by analytical rigour, nevertheless, there is no doubt that Durkheim conceived of the emotional intensity of such 'effervescent assemblies' as serving as a force for the recovery of social order, or even for the creation of wholly new ways of relating to self and others (ibid., 147).

Furthermore, it may be judged somewhat paradoxical that Durkheim conceives of the social forces that produce egoism and anomie as also having the potential to inspire a new form of moral sentimentality that makes people more sympathetic to the suffering of others. He contends that the 'morbid fever' we experience in the process of individualization is at the same time liable to be accompanied by greater feelings of sympathy towards one another as distinct individuals. In *Suicide* he contends:

> [P]ity for another and pity for ourselves are not foreign to each other, since their development or recession is parallel ... What they

express is the moral value of the individual in general. If the individual looms large in public estimation, we apply this social judgement to others as well as to ourselves; and we become more sensitive to whatever concerns each of them as well as what concerns us particularly. *Their griefs, like our own, are more readily intolerable to us.* Our sympathy for them is not, accordingly, a mere extension of what we feel for ourselves. But both are effects of one cause and constituted by the same moral state. (Durkheim 1952: 359–60, my emphasis)

In his essay 'Individualism and the intellectuals' ([1898] 1973b), 'moral individualism' is celebrated for the extent to which it may lead to 'sympathy for all that is human, a broader pity for all sufferings, for all human miseries, a more ardent need to combat them and mitigate them, a greater thirst for justice' (Durkheim [1898] 1973b: 49). Natan Sznaider goes so far as to celebrate this insight as Durkheim's most valuable contribution to our understanding of the historical peculiarity of modern liberalism (Sznaider 2001: 22–3); for in Durkheim we are presented with an opportunity to revise the distorted account of modernity as a *Gesellschaft* society (Tönnies [1887] 1955), and instead recognize the extent to which it is *only* in societies where there is an advanced division of labour that people may be socially conditioned to give full expression to their 'compassionate temperament'. While it may appear all too readily apparent that conditions of modernity leave large numbers of people more vulnerable to the sensation of suffering, as far as Sznaider is concerned, Durkheim's greatest achievement was to recognize the potential within the moral conditions that gave rise to the torment of egoism at the same time to serve as the well-spring for compassion.

However, at this point it should be added that this is an area of his theory which may be most heavily criticized for its conceptual obscurity, for, as Anthony Giddens points out, Durkheim is never entirely consistent in the ways in which he accounts for the interplay between egoism, anomie and moral individualism. While he repeatedly affirms that these all originate in the same moral conditions, the precise nature of their social and psychological constitution is never worked out with analytical rigour (Giddens 1995a: 127). Moreover, the rather crude teleology that characterizes his account of the social evolution of the state and his failure to give adequate attention to the *realpolitik* concerns of civil society may be judged to leave us with many more questions than answers when it comes to specifying the precise combination of social circumstances in which 'moral individualism' may serve as a *sufficient* counterbalance to egoistic instinct (Giddens 1995b).

Nevertheless, it is not my intention to embark upon a systematic critique of his entire theory, but rather, to highlight the ways in which his analysis of the moral relationship between the individual and society is at the same time designed to account for the social dynamics of human suffering. As with Marx and Weber, so it is possible to read Durkheim as having a particular concern to explain the social constitution of painful experience and why this is liable to intensify under conditions of modernity. Moreover, along with these theorists, he would also direct our attention to the extent to which the cultural and psychological dynamics of suffering contribute not only to the formation of modern society, but also to the social pressures for this to change. Once again, the problem of suffering is identified as a significant variable within the social development of modernity that may be analysed *in its own terms* as a dynamic factor within the cultural realities in which we are made to live.

Durkheim shares Weber's negative emphasis upon the extent to which the problem of suffering is endemic to the human condition as such. Accordingly, the psychological theory developed through his account of the dichotomy between the individual and society presents us with a thoroughly pessimistic view of the ways in which the social conditions of modernity are liable to generate more intense experiences of psychic/emotional pain. But, he also stands with Marx (albeit for quite different reasons) in recognizing the potential for such aggravated states of suffering to serve a positive purpose in the creation of more humane forms of society. Indeed, among these three, Durkheim arguably provides us with the most developed account of the *variety* of individual responses to this experience and the social circumstances in which they are most likely to take place.

For the purposes of this chapter, I have done no more than introduce the reader to the basic components of Durkheim's sociological conception of suffering. At best, I have merely hinted at some of the directions we might take in order to reappraise his theory. Certainly it may inspire us to reflect anew upon the psychological premises that comprise his account of the social determination of human nature. Moreover, here there may be cause to reconsider the nature of modern sentimentality and its contribution to the political organization of contemporary societies. Indeed, perhaps it is in terms of such an inquiry that we are best placed to rediscover the 'humanitarian Durkheim' and better appreciate the heartfelt concerns that motivate his radical programme for the moral reform of society.

Conclusion

In this chapter I have sought to recover the distinctive ways in which Marx, Durkheim and Weber conceptualize 'the problem of suffering' and to apply these to their respective accounts of society. I have sought to highlight their shared understanding of modernity as comprised of social conditions in which experiences of suffering are always liable to intensify. In this regard, the quantity and quality of human suffering *in their own terms* are held to warrant sociological attention in so far as this amounts to a dynamic element within our social relationships that may lead us to radically change the ways we relate both to others and to ourselves.

Each writer applies his own distinctive set of questions to the analysis of this phenomenon. In each case we find an emphasis placed upon a distinctive attribute of suffering as holding significance for exposing a definitive part of the character of modern society. However, it may also be appropriate to consider this as providing us with a range of insights into how different aspects of society are liable to condition particular components of suffering. I hold the view that drawing upon the essential concerns of one writer does not necessarily require that we deny the relevance of the concerns of others to the sociological study of this experience. I suggest that each theorist has something original and important to contribute to the agenda for research into the problem of suffering for contemporary societies.

In Marx our concern is mostly directed towards the ways in which suffering takes place as a physical experience of social degradation and material deprivation. In the first place, Marx would have us identify this as an essential aspect of the ways in which power is exercized and exploitation takes place in capitalist society. In this regard, the debate over the extent to which the accumulation of misery under capitalism *necessarily* corresponds to the accumulation of wealth may be judged to be more pertinent than ever before in a global society where the gap between rich and poor stands greater than at any other time in human history (see chapter 4). Second, he leaves us with the troubling suggestion that within the dialectics of social change, such suffering may be necessary for our future progress in so far as, above all other considerations, it drives people collectively to oppose the social conditions that perpetuate their diminished state of humanity. Accordingly, he would also have us reflect upon the ways in which suffering has the potential to serve as a kind of sensuous knowledge to awaken people to their class position within the capitalist mode of production and the possibilities for this to change.

In Weber, we are presented with a theory for explaining how suffering acquires its character of being 'meaningless'. Accordingly, attention is focused upon the ways in which this takes place as a heightened state of cognitive dissonance. Weber would also have us reflect upon the extent to which this contributes a vital dynamic to a process of rationalization that has come to dominate almost every aspect of our lives. Here the suggestion is that it is under intensive experiences of suffering that we are most likely to express our basic psychological need for 'rationality, in the sense of logical or teleological consistency, of an intellectual-theoretical or practical-ethical attitude' towards reality. However, as part of his bleak assessment of 'the fate of our times', he also highlights the potential for this to increase yet further the likelihood that normative expectations for reality will fail to match the content of lived experience. Weber would have us understand that it is as an inevitable part of the cultural reality in which we are made to live, and which through history was created in part as a response to suffering, that we are likely to become greatly distressed by the apparent senselessness of the content of painful experiences.

In Durkheim, we are provided with insight into how the emotional components of suffering may be conditioned by the quality of the moral dichotomy between individual and society. Here we are presented with a sociological theory which accounts for why suffering is experienced as a profound sense of inner loneliness and/or as the morbid feeling of being divided against oneself. But in this context he also raises the intriguing suggestion that this may at the same time be accompanied by a greater sensitivity to the suffering others. While on the one hand he offers us an explanation of why 'currents of collective sadness' are liable to intensify under the social pressure of individualization, on the other, he outlines the potential for this to inspire us with feelings of compassion towards the plight of others as distinct individuals. Durkheim leaves us with the perhaps troubling proposition that it is only in so far as we ourselves are made socially vulnerable to a mental state of suffering that we are likely to become sentimentally oriented to the suffering of others.

By drawing attention to these contrasting sociological perspectives on human suffering, I have sought to emphasize the extent to which they might equip us with the groundwork for future inquiries into the cultural formation and social dynamics of this experience. I have also sought to draw attention to the ways in which each writer leaves us with a range of analytical dilemmas that invite further dialogue and debate over the meaning and value of their social theories. At the very least, I hope that I have done enough to illustrate the potential for a 'sociology of suffering' to inspire new creative relationships with classical sociological theory. I maintain that it is in working to retain the value of our classical heritage that 'the problem of suffering' may become more central to critical sociological debate over the character of our times and the possibilities for this to change.

4

SOCIAL SUFFERING: A CRITICAL APPRAISAL

The majority of people in industrially advanced nations are better fed, more affluent and living longer than at any other time in history. In addition to this, most are equipped with the educational and technical resources to experience a range of cultural, material and symbolic goods that were entirely unknown to previous generations. Accordingly, there is evidence on which to argue that we are living at the highpoint of human civilization (Leadbeater 2002). However, such achievements may do little to inspire faith in 'progress' when set against data that reveal that both the frequency and the scale of events of suffering have also increased. Indeed, on a number of counts there is perhaps more reason to identify us as living through the most destructive and most violent of times.

It is only in the last century that techniques of warfare have been designed for the massacre of civilian populations and that states have sought to apply industrial technologies to the task of genocide. Where over the last century the number of battlefield deaths is estimated to amount to approximately 40 million, Rudolph Rummel calculates that in addition to this, near to 170 million people have been murdered by governments (Rummel 1994, 1996). Barbara Harff records that from 1945 up to the mid 1990s there were 48 episodes of genocide and political mass murder, while during this time Ted Gurr was able to identify 80 communal and regional groups that were being subjected to some form of violent discrimination and a further 22 groups caught up in conflicts that ran the risk of genocidal outcomes (Harff and Gurr 1996). While some cautious notes of optimism were sounded in response to the appearance of a positive trend indicating a decline in the number of violent conflicts towards the end of the 1990s, it is now feared that with the escalating 'war on terrorism' this may amount to no more than a discrete aberration in the long-term trend which suggests that societal conflict and interstate conflicts have increased sixfold since the Second World War (Gurr et al. 2000; Rotfeld 2002; Seybolt 2002).

Aside from the victims of large-scale military conflict and mass politicide, each year organizations such as Amnesty International and Human Rights Watch document tens of thousands of individual cases of false imprisonment, torture and execution. The *Amnesty International Report 2002* presents evidence of the gross violation of human rights in 152 countries, while the accumulated details of earlier reports reveal that in 70 of these countries the incidence of torture and ill treatment may be adjudged to be widespread and persistent (Amnesty International 2000: 9). Moreover, Amnesty International maintains that its figures always underestimate the real extent of violence and degradation suffered by millions of people around the globe, as more often than not the full scale of such abuse is effectively concealed by the perpetrators, so that it remains impossible to maintain a reliable record of all the horrors that take place (ibid.).

Statistics on poverty, hunger and disease also speak of large amounts of human suffering. On every continent the numbers of poor are rapidly increasing. Almost half of the world's population live on less than $2 dollars a day, while a fifth – that is, close to 1.5 billion people – live in absolute poverty on less than $1 dollar a day. The World Bank calculates that the income gap between the richest and the poorest nations has effectively doubled over the past 40 years, so that the average income in the richest 20 countries of the world is now 37 times greater than that of the poorest 20. For the majority of the 85 per cent of the world's population who live in developing societies, everyday life consists of a constant struggle for existence under conditions in which a combination of hard physical labour, malnutrition and disease are liable at any time to bring their lives to a premature end (World Bank 2000).

While Sub-Saharan Africa has an infant mortality rate of 90 per 1,000 live births, the OECD average stands at 6 per 1,000. In developing societies, a third of all children suffer from malnutrition, and it is estimated that as many as 30,000 die each day from preventable causes (UNDP 2000). Where the toll of infectious disease has been radically reduced among the populations of high-income countries, in developing societies 21 per cent of all deaths are caused by diarrhoea, acute respiratory infections, malaria, measles and perinatal conditions (WHO 1999). A large proportion of these deaths are held to be directly attributable to the fact that more than 1 billion people lack access to safe drinking water, and 2.4 billion lack adequate sanitation facilities (UNDP 2000). Furthermore, the alarming spread of HIV/AIDS and tuberculosis in low- and middle-income countries is decimating populations to the point where rates of life expectancy in Eastern Europe, the former Soviet Union and Africa are now in decline (World Bank 2000: 26–7).

In addition to all this, the majority of environmental experts hold to the view that we are on the brink of a global ecological catastrophe, and that over the next 40 years many of the world's poorest countries are likely to suffer even more severe water and food shortages. While it is already the case that 800 million people world-wide are suffering from malnutrition, the World Bank warns that food production will have to double over the next 35 years if we are not to avoid famine on a scale without historical precedent (UNFPA 2001). Moreover, when detailing the greatest threats to the future of humanity, it is the scarcity of water that is set to have some of the most negative impacts upon people's health and safety. In many developing societies rapid urbanization is expected to increase dramatically the stress on diminishing water supplies and it is predicted that this will soon become a major source of conflict between nations (ibid.).

While the suffering of people in industrially advanced nations may appear as nothing when compared to the apocalyptic annihilation of human life in the developing world, nevertheless, even there, plenty of research data are being gathered which suggest that large sections of population remain greatly distressed by their experience of day-to-day life. In high-income countries with ageing populations there is now a widely reported epidemic of chronic pain. Studies suggest that at any one time anywhere between 10 per cent to 30 per cent of the population of the United States of America are suffering from disabling experiences of back pain, arthritis and migraine headaches, while in the United Kingdom it is estimated that this figure may be as high as 46 per cent (Elliot et al. 1999; Gureje et al. 1998; Koestler and Myers 2002; Harris & Associates 1999). Moreover, such experiences of chronic pain are identified as among the major factors contributing to increasing rates of psychiatric morbidity within these populations (WHO 2001: 8). In the UK, it is calculated that 11 per cent of the population are suffering from some kind of mixed anxiety or depressive disorder (ONS 2002), while in the USA a recent National Comorbidity Survey estimates the prevalence of depression to be at 17.1 per cent (Greden 2001: 5). Indeed, the World Health Organization now ranks unipolar depressive disorders as the leading burden of disease in high-income countries (WHO 2001: 19). Accordingly, there is mounting evidence to suggest that, while free from suffering caused by diseases of poverty, the populations of advanced industrialized nations are being made increasingly vulnerable to disabling experiences of pain and illness that hitherto have not been calculated among the major scourges of humanity.

The last 30 years may be distinguished as a time in which social scientists, medical demographers and government statisticians have collected an unprecedented amount of data to document formally and categorize systematically the suffering of humanity. Such metrics of suffering point to a world in turmoil, with hundreds of millions of people living under the most brutalizing conditions, which by humane standards must be judged intolerable. In 'objective' terms of measurement, we are living through the most murderous and socially divided period of history for which we have record. Never before in human history have such efforts been made to quantify the amount of suffering endured by societies.

However, in recent work on 'social suffering', writers have repeatedly made the critical suggestion that such data are by no means adequate to convey what suffering entails for people's experience of their humanity. Indeed, some go so far as to argue that more often than not this information functions only to service a technocratic demand for an 'objective' account of the cost of suffering to society, and that in this context, no thought is given to the violation of human dignity that occurs to individual sufferers (Frank 1992; Kleinman and Kleinman 1997). On these grounds, the populations of Western societies are judged to display a diminished sense for one another's value as human beings; for the level of public outcry in response to the official record of suffering is perceived to fall way short of what would be congruent with the brute facts of the matter. It is in an attempt to combat society's 'silence' towards the issue of what the experience of extreme pain, poverty, violence and terror actually *does* to people that research on 'social suffering' aims to present us with new ways of *thinking with* the suffering of others so as to bring this to the fore of public debate and have it occupy a central position in the ways in which we evaluate the progress of our times.

This chapter offers a critical overview and appraisal of contemporary writing on 'social suffering'. This takes place with reference to the terms of analysis and methodological concerns with which Hannah Arendt sought to 'dwell on the horrors' of totalitarianism. I maintain that at a number of levels it is possible to identify themes in Arendt's work that prefigure those raised by contemporary research on 'social suffering'. In this context, I am particularly concerned to have us consider the extent to which in Arendt's attempts to make sense of the 'banality of evil' and in current efforts to construct texts that convey more of the lived experience of suffering, we are presented with a new departure in the project of social science. I argue that this is characterized by the attempt to fashion a political style of writing that goes as far as possible towards involving readers in the apparent senselessness of human suffering. While there is certainly no agreement on the methods by which this is to be achieved, nevertheless, I suggest that contemporary writers such as Pierre Bourdieu, Veene Das and Arthur Kleinman share in the basic understanding that it is by bringing their readers to the knowledge of 'a seemingly unendurable reality' (Arendt 1968: 27) that they can do most to provoke public debate on the social meaning and moral purpose of our times. Theorists such as Marx, Durkheim and Weber provide us with distinctive sociological approaches to understanding how 'the problem of suffering' comes to comprise our social consciousness of modernity and, further, go so far as to identify this as a motive force for social change; nevertheless, it is only on rare occasions that they reflect upon the possibility that this may be decisive for our social development. By contrast, in the works of Hannah Arendt and in studies of social suffering, this is presented not only as the 'fundamental' intellectual challenge of our times, but also as a matter which raises the most urgent questions of humanity.

Writing on 'social suffering'

As I write, the term 'social suffering' does not have wide currency in social science, but in recent sociological and anthropological studies of human suffering it has featured as a concept intended to refer us directly to the *lived experience* of pain, misery, violence and terror. Research into 'social suffering' is addressed to a wide assemblage of both spectacular and ordinary occasions when human dignity is violated and people come to some kind of grief and harm; but in every instance an emphasis is placed upon the ways in which such events are experienced by individuals as *social* forces and *cultural* phenomena (Kleinman et al. 1997; Bourdieu et al. 1999). In this regard, there is a particular concern to make clear the ways in which people directly encounter the social meaning of their afflictions. Here commentators aim to highlight the extent to which the experience of human suffering involves far more than the bio-mechanics of pain, the sheer numbers of people killed in conflict zones, or a calculated level of disability, scarcity and want. In these writings an attempt is made to reflect explicitly upon what suffering *does* to a person's humanity and how people experience, interpret and live through the social significance and moral meaning of their injuries, pains, material deprivations and loss.

A great deal is perceived to be at stake in these endeavours. In the first place, by creating symbolic forms of culture and styles of writing to convey a greater part of the lived experience of suffering, it is hoped that it may be possible to invigorate public debate on the abuse of human rights and to evoke greater outpourings of compassion towards the pain of others. Writers who broach this topic tend to make explicit their concern to bring the standpoint of those 'in' suffering to bear directly upon the hearts and minds of policy makers, politicians and publics; for great hopes are invested in the possibility that if people can be made to *feel* more sympathy towards, and responsibility for, the suffering of others, then they will be motivated to act against the political decisions and social conditions that damage and ruin human life (Kleinman 1995; Kleinman and Kleinman 1997).

Second, a number of commentators contend that such works serve not only to draw public attention to the lived experience of human suffering, but also to provide some measure of healing at the level of social meaning for those 'in' pain. Here much intrigue surrounds the extent to which a major component of the embodied sensation of suffering takes place as a consequence of the negative meanings that people acquire and create for events in their lives, particularly where these are perceived as being fundamentally senseless and without purpose. In this context, researchers conceive their task in terms of an effort to equip people with the cultural resources to establish a means to narrate traumatic experiences that would otherwise be left in 'silence', so that they may arrive at a position such that they can resume the task of living (Morris 1997). The practice of ethnography is itself understood to make a positive contribution to the advancement of a 'politics of recognition' (Taylor 1992), in so far as it helps bring about the creation of public spaces in which sufferers may achieve a shared voice for recounting their experience and, most importantly, a social acknowledgement of the terrible events they have endured (Das 1995, 1997a, 1997b). Indeed, in many instances, it is in the knowledge that others recognize and acknowledge what the trauma of suffering actually *does* to a person that suffering individuals and communities report being able to embark upon a journey towards recovery and healing (Adelson 2001; Chuengsatiansup 2001; Scheper-Hughes 1998).

Taken together, these concerns are understood to point to the possibility of creating new interpretative frameworks for 'seeing' the world in terms of 'the hurts we inflict upon one another' (Graubard 1996) and, more specifically, for recognizing the extent to which the trauma of suffering takes place as an embodied experience of culture, politics and society (Kleinman 1986). It is claimed that on these grounds we may arrive at a position whence to relate to modern times more from the standpoint of the millions of 'ordinary' and forgotten people whose lives have been, and continue to be, ruined, wasted and swept away by violence, poverty, cruel toil and disease. Moreover, it is argued that in concentrating its attention upon the task of exposing more of the lived experience of suffering, social science is best placed to promote an understanding of our common humanity that can serve as the grounds for cross-cultural debate on the rights to global citizenship (Turner 1993, 2002).

What should we make of these developments? What do they imply for the conduct of sociological research and the task of writing about the character of society? On what basis should we evaluate the cultural and political significance of these efforts to draw society into debate on the lived *experience* of suffering? In what ways might this work contribute to or, rather, call for a 'sociology of suffering'?

Thinking with Hannah Arendt

To begin answering some of these questions, and for the purpose of highlighting an important historical precedent to these works, I would have us reflect upon the extent to which the concerns of research on 'social suffering' may be associated with the pioneering efforts of Hannah Arendt to comprehend the social psychology of totalitarianism and its implications for our humanity. I contend that at a number of levels it is possible to identify themes in Arendt's work that prefigure those raised by contemporary research in this area. Moreover, by charting the ways she laboured to make the 'evil' embodied in a figure such as Adolph Eichmann part of our 'thinking', we may arrive at a position from which better to evaluate the political and cultural significance of recent attempts to bring the brute facts of human suffering to bear upon the moral consciousness of our times.

In much of her work Arendt openly displays a struggle to articulate social realities that have been left either 'undescribed' or interpreted in fixed categories that impose strict limitations upon the possible meanings that we might read into our experience of the world (Canovan 1974: 7). It is particularly in light of events of extreme suffering that she appears most alarmed by the capacity for the 'efficient talk and double-talk' of technocratic experts to explain away the harsh realities of political oppression, economic hardship and human misery. In this context, she would alert us to the moral calamity of 'speech that does not disclose what is but sweeps it under the carpet, by exhortations, moral and otherwise, that, under the pretext of upholding truths, degrade all truth to meaningless triviality' (Arendt 1968: 8).

Arendt is never more intensively preoccupied with these concerns than in her attempt to understand the terrible truths disclosed by the Nazi crimes against humanity; for here she conceives her task to require a complete break with Western traditions of debate on the 'problem of evil' and the human motives that bring this into being (Bernstein 2002). The discovery of what took place in the death camps brings her to the firm conclusion that, in face of such 'radical evil', 'we have nothing whereby to understand a phenomenon that nevertheless confronts us with its overpowering reality and breaks all standards we know' (Arendt 1973: 459). What appears to her to be totally without precedent is not so much the shocking numbers of people massacred under these conditions but, rather, the fact that this took place as part of a systematic attempt to destroy them as juridical, moral and individual human beings. The terrible originality of the 'evil' of totalitarianism lies in its ambition to render all people equally *superfluous*, so that the very category of 'being human' is violated and destroyed to the point of utter meaninglessness. It is in this quite particular sense that she understands the Nazi crimes as crimes against humanity (Bernstein 1996).

It is as part of the effort to understand how such 'evil' is established and sustained in existence that, in her report on the trial of Adolph Eichmann (Arendt 1963a), she starts to refer to this as 'banal'. In this context, she takes seriously Eichmann's argument in defence of his involvement in the Holocaust — that is, that he was simply obeying orders and was never acting with any wicked motives in mind. According to Arendt, the 'banality of evil' is incarnated in forms of social behaviour whereby individuals such as Eichmann give no thought to the involvement of their actions within the creation of systems designed for mass murder. She maintains that Eichmann was no great 'monster' and had no 'demonic' presence. What struck her most forcibly was his complete 'ordinariness'; yet, at the same time, this was precisely what was so terrifying about this man. In the figure of Eichmann, Arendt was confronted with the shocking truth that it was only in so far as 'average', 'normal' people are prepared to act in thoughtless compliance with the logic of social processes designed for the purpose of industrial genocide, that events such as the Holocaust are made possible. The 'evil' that treats people as though they are utterly superfluous is sustained by the banality of sheer thoughtlessness (Bernstein 1996).

Arendt's efforts to disclose the radical novelty of the 'evil' of totalitarianism was widely recognized as a great advancement in the struggle to understand the nature of the violation that took place at camps such as Auschwitz. Indeed, as Steven Aschheim notes, some even held to the view that *The Origins of Totalitarianism* amounted to 'the greatest advance in social thought since Marx' (Aschheim 1997: 118). Nevertheless, when subsequently she ventured to refer to the 'evil' of Nazism as 'banal', the controversy that surrounded her work led many to dismiss her thought as essentially an act of bad faith (Rotenstreich 1984–5). Indeed, some went so far as to condemn *Eichmann in Jerusalem* as both intellectually facile and morally repugnant; for the even-handed, matter-of-fact tone of her analysis of Eichmann's personality and motives was understood to betray a lack of sympathy for the victims of his crimes, as well as to lend support to the arguments put forward in his defence. Her emphasis on the 'banality of evil' was interpreted not only as an effort to undermine the reasoning whereby the court judged Eichmann to be guilty of crimes against humanity, but also as betraying a deep loathing for her own Jewishness (R. I. Cohen 1993; Podhoretz 1964; Syrkin 1963; Whitfield 1980).

However, with the publication of some of her private letters of correspondence (Arendt and Jaspers 1992) and her final lectures on *The Life of the Mind* (1978), it has become possible to attain a deeper insight into the ethical dilemmas and creative decisions that inspired her to promote this phrase as a means to incite debate on the peculiar novelty of 'evil' in our times. Certainly in this context it is clear that Arendt was alert to the possibility that such language would appear highly inappropriate, or even offensive, to those seeking to make sense of the Nazi crimes in terms of traditional 'Judeo-Christian' conceptions of human depravity (Arendt 1978: 3–16). Moreover, on the evidence of her correspondence with Karl Jaspers, it appears that Arendt herself settled on emphasizing the 'banality' of these crimes only at the end of a protracted course of anguished thinking.

It is Jaspers who first works to persuade Arendt to the view that we should aim to 'see these things in their total banality, in their prosaic triviality, because that is what truly characterises them' (Arendt and Jaspers 1992: 62). This is written in response to an earlier letter in which Arendt poses the problem of how it might be possible to find concepts that are adequate to the task of conveying the 'monstrousness' of crimes that seem to 'explode the limits of law' (ibid., 52). With his emphasis on the 'banality' of the Nazi crimes, Jaspers is concerned to alert Arendt to the danger of bestowing a 'streak of satanic greatness' upon those responsible for perpetrating mass murder, lest any support is given to the notion that the explanation for such atrocity lies beyond the realms of human understanding. In this context, it is argued that we should resist all temptation to represent these events in a manner that obscures sociological and psychological insight into the conditions under which large numbers of 'ordinary' people will thoughtlessly lend their support to regimes that design social systems for industrial genocide. It is for this reason that, notwithstanding the many doubts and confusions that remained in her mind over how to write about the 'evil' of totalitarianism, Arendt was moved to declare: 'One thing is certain: we have to combat all impulses to mythologize the horrible and to the extent that I can't avoid such formulations, I haven't understood what actually went on' (Arendt and Jaspers 1992: 69).

It is on this basis that she works to remove all language that may be construed as 'metaphysical' or 'poetic' from her writing, so as to present her readers with an immanently rational account of the social circumstances under which the Holocaust was able to take place. Moreover, this also appears to have involved her in a concerted attempt to eliminate all elements of pathos and fury from her thinking, on the understanding that such qualities of emotion are always liable to 'distort' the ways we present 'the facts' of history (Arendt 1963a: 285). While it was made abundantly clear to her that in the figure of Eichmann she was confronted with unprecedented phenomena that defied categorization in terms of conventional notions of a 'corrupted will', 'sinful motives' and metaphysical 'evil', at the very least she appears to have been convinced that it was by thinking with the 'rational vocabulary' of social science that most progress could be made towards understanding the true nature and origins of his criminality (Aschheim 1997).

Perhaps there is some irony here, for it may be argued that such an approach has the effect of doing violence to an elemental constituent of our humanity: namely, the spontaneous gut response of moral outrage in the face of human atrocity. Accordingly, one may take the view that 'the matter of fact' tone of her analysis serves to promote a style of thinking that, elsewhere, she identifies as a core component of the very processes implicated in the creation of a social system that destroys people as juridical, moral and individual human beings. Thus, while seeking to construct a 'rational vocabulary' for exposing the 'banality' of the evil that treats people as though they are superfluous, her failure to adopt a vocabulary of moral outrage may be judged to leave us with a severely diminished account of the terrible significance of such crimes for our humanity.

However, to take an opposing and more controversial view, it may be that Arendt braved using a tone of language that was liable to arouse the moral outrage of her critics as a means to bring the 'banality of evil' within the sphere of political debate. She may have been prepared to have the 'banality' of a technical-rational language 'colour' the ways she narrated the facts of the Nazi crimes, so as to have the emotional reaction against this dispassionate frame of reference provoke us into thinking about the cultural circumstances under which 'ordinary' people will thoughtlessly act in support of social systems that treat people as though they are superfluous. On this understanding, we may be presented here with an instance in which Arendt's efforts to infect others with the perplexities of her thinking led her to take the risk of exposing her work to moral outrage. Indeed, even if at first she was only 'dimly aware' of the likelihood of causing such offence, in later years there is evidence to suggest that she looked back on the negative reaction to her report on Eichmann's trial as having served to awaken some 'thinking' on the extent to which the nature of his criminality confounded traditional ethical responses to 'the problem of evil' (Arendt 1978: 3–16).

In addition to this, in a wider reading of her works it is possible to find more carefully qualified passages in which she does not deny the need for people to have an emotionally charged and 'poetic' means of relating to the traumatic events of recent history, but rather aims to advise us on the proper cultural circumstances under which this may rightfully take place. For example, in her essay 'On humanity in dark times: thoughts about Lessing' (Arendt 1968: 11–38), she concedes that a process of lamentation is always necessary in order for people to achieve a way of living through and beyond the traumatic events of their past, and that this must ultimately feature as an authentic response to the horrors of Auschwitz. For this reason, while she herself resists using this tone of language in relating what took place in the death camps, she nevertheless understands her work to be 'constantly preparing the way for "poetry", in the broadest sense, as a human potentiality' (Arendt 1968: 29). But this concession comes with the stern warning that for the sake of 'mastering' the past, there is always a strong temptation to suppress the memory of 'a seemingly unendurable reality' so as to allow pathos to smother the truths disclosed by the brute facts of our history. Accordingly, for Arendt, there is a great danger in the extent to which the struggle to achieve some manner of emotional healing for the experience of extreme suffering leads people to surrender to the temptation to 'sweep under the carpet' the terrible reality of what took place. It is for this reason that she raises the disquieting suggestion that, when writing on the Holocaust, we may have no choice but to adopt a form of narrative that 'solves no problems and assuages no suffering'; for this may always be necessary so as to keep its terrible significance 'alive' in public memory (Arendt 1968: 29).

She leaves us with the question: 'how much reality must be retained even in a world become inhuman if humanity is not to be reduced to an empty phrase or a phantom?' (ibid.). While she found herself unable to offer a definitive answer, at the very least she appears to have been reconciled to the necessity of making herself vulnerable to suffering in order to disclose a greater part of the meaning of the 'banality of evil' for our humanity. Moreover, she appears to have written with a mind to provoke her readers into experiencing some part of the seemingly 'terminal aporia' (Ricoeur 1995) of making the knowledge of this atrocious fact productive for thought and action. Clearly, for Arendt there could be no intellectually sufficient or morally satisfying way of writing about these events, but she appears to have been alert to the potential for the paradoxical sense of 'senselessness' (Levinas 1988: 156–7) that is impressed upon us in face of extreme suffering to provoke us into taking up the task of understanding why and how the Holocaust could have taken place (Fine 2001). Indeed, in the final analysis, perhaps it is with the recognition of this potentiality that we should most sympathize with her method of writing on these matters.

From Arendt to social suffering

How might this be related to contemporary research on 'social suffering'? I would argue that it is by thinking through some of the conceptual problems whereby Hannah Arendt sought to expose the 'evil' of totalitarianism that we may be equipped to identify the key issues at stake in recent works addressed to problems of 'social suffering'. Furthermore, where these new literatures revisit and develop some of the essential concerns of Arendt's post-war work, I contend that this presents us with fresh opportunities to debate the methods she deployed for the purpose of making the problem of suffering a part of our political thinking. In this context, I suggest that where, on the one hand, Arendt provides con-temporary research with some vital terms of analysis for advancing the task of thinking about the peculiar nature of 'social suffering', on the other hand, more recent ethnographic studies of this phenomenon provide us with the opportunity to bring the details of a great variety of human experiences to bear upon our understanding of the 'radical' yet 'banal' nature of 'evil' in our times.

In the first place, I contend that Arendt identifies and conceptually delineates a core concern that lies at the heart of all research into 'social suffering': namely, social circumstances in which people are treated by others, and come to experience themselves, as superfluous. She maintains that it is in the Nazi concentration camps where individuals were manufactured as 'living corpses' that we are presented with the most extreme consequences of this social behaviour. But what is most important to recognize here is the ways in which this systematic process of human annihilation originates under social circumstances that are all too readily perceived to be part of the 'ordinary' and 'unavoidable' reality of life in modern societies. Indeed, in her analysis of how the Nazi's ultimately succeeded in expelling people from their humanity, at every opportunity she is concerned to alert us to the extent to which 'the totalitarian attempt to make men superfluous reflects the experience of modern masses of their superfluity on an overcrowded earth' (Arendt 1973: 457).

Arendt identifies the treatment of humanity as superfluous as beginning whenever people are reduced to a state of being 'homeless', 'stateless', 'outlawed', 'unwanted', 'socially burdensome' and 'unemployed' (Arendt 1973: 447). It is only under social conditions in which there is a fundamental deprivation of human rights that it becomes possible to herd people into gas chambers. On this analysis, the social processes that make possible the extermination of people as no more than 'superfluous human material' take root wherever individuals are deprived of their basic rights to life, liberty and the pursuit of happiness (Arendt 1973: 267–302). The 'final solution' could only be conceived of and put into practice at the end of a gradual process through which 'the Rights of Man' lost all validity. Arendt maintains that the first step on the road to treating people as utterly superfluous takes place whenever social circumstances are such as to place certain categories of people outside the jurisdiction of human rights legislation. It is only thereafter that social pressures can be placed upon individuals to destroy their moral solidarity and violate their personal identities.

Similarly, in the literature on 'social suffering' there are numerous studies that put their emphasis on the extent to which people become the victims of extreme acts of violence only when they are no longer seen as 'human' by their torturers and executioners (Glover 1999; Scheper-Hughes 1997). Accordingly, while venturing to interrogate the causes and consequences of such suffering, researchers are all too often made to recognize that 'human nature as such is at stake' within the details of their reports on how this takes place (Arendt 1973: 459). Veena Das and Arthur Kleinman maintain that if one compares the testimonies of survivors of acts of violence perpetrated in South African ghettos with those of people who have experienced ethnic violence in Sri Lanka or the violence of communal riots in India, what stands out in every case is 'that it is the human capacity to reduce other humans to non-humans that allows policies of mass destruction to come into play with broad consent' (Das and Kleinman 2001: 16–17). Moreover, in seeking to expose the insidious nature of these processes of 'dehumanization', attention is once again focused upon ways in which the violation of people's human dignity originates in social behaviours and cultural practices that acquire the status of being a 'normal' aspect of the ways in which individuals interpret and respond to their reality. Indeed, studies of 'social suffering' have gone much further than did Arendt in detailing the particular ways in which 'violence' is done to humanity in the social contexts of day-to-day life.

For many writers on 'social suffering', 'the violence of everyday life' is most obvious in the experiences of poor people living in developing societies (Scheper-Hughes 1992). There are numerous studies that seek to detail the variety of forms in which suffering is experienced by people as they struggle for existence under conditions of extreme poverty (Farmer 1997, 1999; Kim et al. 2000). Here efforts are made to expose the wretchedness of humanity destroyed by the ravages of material deprivation, hunger, powerlessness, illness and death, so as to bring social attention to the specific ways in which this is encountered at the level of personal experience. However, in this context, researchers often discover suffering as taking place in ways that may not be immediately apparent to 'outside' observers; for they find that it is not so much in relation to the trauma of the immediate physical experience of poverty or violence that respondents identify themselves as suffering, but more in terms of how such events subsequently leave their marks upon the meanings of self and society.

Accordingly, a number of studies seek to alert us to how some of the most intense experiences of suffering take place as people struggle to negotiate their social identity as 'witnesses of violence' (Das 2000) or as 'anonymous victims' of devastating disease and grinding poverty (Farmer 1997). Here the emphasis is on the ways in which the inner reality of suffering occurs as an 'unappeasable experience' that does not diminish with time but, rather, permanently assails the memory of 'victims' and comes to dominate the very personality of those 'violated' and 'repressed' (Langer 1997). Moreover, once again, some of the ways in which this appears to be sustained as a 'local structure of feeling' may not be readily identified as among the causes of great anguish and pain, for they reside in social practices and forms of discourse that are most likely to be perceived as an 'ordinary' part of social life.

In the literature on 'social suffering', a heavy emphasis tends to be placed upon the extent to which the personal experience of suffering is greatly intensified in relation to the dominant ways in which it is symbolically represented in the realms of public life (Das et al. 2000). Time and again, people 'in' suffering report that it is the 'everyday' language and social practices that they are forced to live by in the aftermath of painful events that make the brute facts of their affliction most violating. For example, Maya Todeschini maintains that Japanese 'hibakusha' women who survived the bombing of Hiroshima and Nagasaki report themselves as experiencing great suffering in relation to the stereotypical ways in which they are popularly celebrated as 'cultural heroines'; for this has left them constantly struggling to escape the social pressures placed upon them to exist only as 'living memorials' to the suffering of their nation (Todeschini 2001). In a similar vein, Mamphela Ramphele maintains that, while on the one hand being labelled as a 'political widow' allows the public expression of personal grief, on the other hand, it imposes social obligations upon women that prevent them from experiencing their full rights as citizens of the new South Africa (Ramphele 1997). Ramphele argues that the customary ways in which these widows are expected to conduct themselves in public, and, in particular, the social claims that are made on their bodies and identities through acquiring the label of suffering 'political' widowhood, leave them with severely restricted possibilities for defining their individual identities and voicing personal opinions.

With this emphasis upon the ways in which suffering is experienced through 'ordinary' social behaviours and 'common-sense' frames of representation, some of the most politically provocative examples of 'the violence of everyday life' have been gathered among respondents who are unlikely to be identified as the victims of any kind of great upheaval. For example, Pierre Bourdieu and colleagues provide us with a catalogue of ethnographies of French working-class life that seek to illuminate the 'ordinary suffering' experienced by large numbers of people in relation to years of feeling socially marginalized and politically powerless to effect positive change in their lives (Bourdieu et al. 1999). Likewise, in his attempts to understand the social causes of chronic pains, exhaustion and depression among the denizens of American middle-class society, Arthur Kleinman argues that much 'violence' is done to people as a consequence of them habitually having no time to spare amid the routine pressures of day-to-day life — all the more so where this is accompanied by the frustration of always being denied fulfilment in love and in work (Kleinman 2000). Indeed, it is particularly with reference to chronic pains that seem to arise in connection with the distress of work and family life that we now have an extensive literature that seeks to expose how people's suffering is exacerbated by the apparent indifference of Western medical practice and discourse to experiences of illness that cannot be readily connected to some form of physiological injury or psychiatric disorder (DelVecchio Good et al. 1992; Frank 1995, 2001; Hydén 1997; Kleinman 1988; Smail 1993).

On this basis, the literature on social suffering may be read as detailing the multiple ways in which people come to be regarded by others and experience themselves as 'superfluous'. In every study we are presented with examples of the ways in which people experience assaults upon their humanity by being denied the public space in which to bring their suffering to the attention of society (Das 1994, 1997b) and/or experiencing the erosion of moral ties (Lawrence 2000) and/or having their unique sense of individuality violated and repressed (Mehta 2000). The 'radical evil' that Arendt identifies in the context of a political analysis of 'totalitarianism' is hereby revealed as a cross-cultural component of the suffering experienced by large sections of humanity under conditions of modernity. Moreover, it is striking that in this context, respondents consistently identify a 'thoughtlessness' in other people's 'ordinary' social behaviour, forms of discourse, and institutional practices as a major source of their anguish and pain. In almost every instance, some of the most intense experiences of suffering are reported to take place in the dynamics of social relationships that may all too readily be perceived as 'banal'.

However, there is a crucial point on which studies of 'social suffering' and the work of Hannah Arendt diverge: namely, that of how to write of this experience so as to bring it to political attention and policy debate. Where Arendt sought to fashion a 'rational vocabulary' for analysing the 'evil' of totalitarianism so as to develop a 'scientific' account of the social conditions under which people come to be treated as 'superfluous human material', researchers on social suffering are inclined to adopt a quite different approach to writing on this topic. A contrasting feature of more recent studies may be identified in the efforts devoted to the task of constructing emotionally charged languages for the purpose of giving 'voice' to the personal experience of individual sufferers. One of the principle aims of writing on 'social suffering' is to go as far as possible towards involving readers in the specific ways in which painful experiences absorb the attention of individuals in their practical day-to-day engagement with local worlds. To this end, writing with 'pathos' and in genres of lamentation is understood to be a necessary part of the process of involving readers in worlds 'made strange through the desolating experience of violence and loss' (Das 1997a: 67–9, 2000; Das and Kleinman 2001: 18). Moreover, for this purpose, we are more often than not encouraged to dwell upon the personal and everyday languages that individual sufferers use to represent their existence, on the understanding that in the majority of cases this most powerfully serves to 'reach' our emotions and 'produce the shifts in thinking and seeing that are often the precondition for comprehension' (Bourdieu 1999: 619).

In this context it is argued that, so long as a 'rational vocabulary' dominates our accounts of people's suffering, we will be unable to *attend* properly to the traumatic ways in which suffering occurs in lived experience; for it is generally understood that the 'cultural grammar' through which people struggle to restore meaning to broken lives operates in a 'register' that cannot be brought to account at the level of scientific analysis (Sklutans 1998: 17–34). Moreover, some go so far as to suggest that where researchers venture to 'translate' experiences of suffering into the theoretical frameworks of social science, then the level of 'symbolic violence' that is brought to bear upon the 'reality' of people's thoughts and feelings distorts the 'truth' of lived experience to a point that is ethically repugnant (Bourdieu 1999). Indeed, in a number of studies it is argued that the disciplined process of rewriting the details of personal experience in the language of expertise effectively adds to the suffering of individuals in so far as it works to 'silence' forms of narrative expression that they hold vital for making public the brute facts of their experience. For example, Arthur and Joan Kleinman maintain that whereas economic indicators of suffering, such as the World Health Organization's metric of Disability Adjusted Life Years (DALYS), may be necessary for rationalizing the problem of distributing scarce resources to those in need, all too often this leads to people being treated in purely instrumental terms as a 'problem' to be addressed in a language of 'efficiency and cost'. Where such language comes to dominate the 'cultural rhetoric' of patient care or humanitarian concern, they argue, much violence is done to people by 'experts' who, albeit with no sinister motives in mind, reduce the traumatic significance of large swathes of human experience to purely economic considerations. Time and again, their respondents report themselves to be greatly pained by the experience of living under cultural conditions such that an official acknowledgement of the personal 'meaning' of suffering always seems to be withheld (Kleinman and Kleinman 1997).

It is with a particular sensitivity to these issues that writers such as Veena Das seek to produce 'a body of work that lets the pain of the other happen to it' (Das 1997b: 572). By using anthropological texts to record the ways in which individuals 'give voice' to their experience, she understands herself to bring to public attention some essential components of human suffering that otherwise would be left in 'silence'. In a similar vein, Pierre Bourdieu and colleagues make efforts not only to record the precise words, but also to detail the specific points of emphasis, intonation and gesture that people use to communicate their suffering, on the understanding that it is only in so far as we acquire some appreciation for the immediate 'expressive intensity' with which people talk about their experience that we can venture to 'see' the world from their particular points of view (Bourdieu et al. 1999). Where this kind of empathic witnessing takes place, it is argued that those living in horrific situations are provided not only with an opportunity to bring a portion of their experience into arenas of sociological and political debate, but also with some part of the cultural resources they require for taking up the task of rebuilding broken lives; for it is often reported that some measure of emotional healing appears to take place for suffering individuals once they understand that society is making efforts to recognize, acknowledge and 'listen' to the particular ways in which their humanity has come to grief (Das et al. 2001).

From this perspective, for us to begin to dwell upon the human embodied experience of suffering, it is always necessary to focus our attention upon the symbolic forms of expression that people use while struggling to address the social and moral meaning of what is happening to them. While such work aims to provide people with a public opportunity to speak freely about their suffering in ways that seem most appropriate to them, it also understands itself to bear testimony to an essential part of what suffering actually is in human experience: namely, an intense struggle to endow one's life with coherent and positive meaning whilst beset by experiences in which this is violated and destroyed (Skultans 1998). Accordingly, at the same time that such research presents itself as part of a political and moral struggle to bring social attention to the lived experience of suffering, it is inclined to argue that it is only by dwelling upon the specific ways in which individuals give voice to their afflictions that we can begin to grasp the significance this holds for humanity.

Such a manner of writing presents us with texts that are liable to exasperate those seeking a systematic account of the precise nature and varieties of human suffering, and certainly, in the majority of instances, researchers are unable to prescribe any complete and practicable solutions to the experiences they describe (Das and

Kleinman 2001: 16). One of the main purposes of this approach to writing is to involve readers as much as possible in people's desperate ongoing struggles to bring inadequate cultural resources to address the social meaning of what is happening to them. To this end, a particular emphasis tends to be placed upon the *insufficiency* of all that is said and done in efforts to 'assuage' and 'manage' the experiences that sufferers endure. Here there appears to be a general commitment to the view that any efforts to 'help' those 'in' suffering must begin with the acknowledgement that a substantial part of the effects of traumatic experience upon a person's humanity cannot be 'disciplined' and 'organized' so as to be brought to account within the frameworks of 'enlightened' social science, and further, that the most vital part of this does not lend itself to any bureaucratically administered 'solution' (Langer 1997).

For this reason, while seeking to fashion texts that 'bear witness' to the lived experience of 'social suffering', those who write on this topic tend to be critically minded to provoke and frustrate readers who approach their work in the expectation of finding clear guidelines for how to think and act so as to solve the problems voiced by their respondents. In this context, attempts to construct narratives of pain or record the 'broken voices' of victims of terror and atrocity are intended not only to incite debate on the social/ cultural conditions that appear to moderate the traumatic intensity of such experience, but also to bring criticism to bear upon the abstract ways in which this tends to be conceptualized as a problem for social science (Kleinman et al. 1992: 1–27). There is a general commitment to the view that in 'social suffering' we are presented with realms of human experience that have been consistently 'explained away' or ignored by experts who are only prepared to deal with people's problems in scientifically authoritative terms of 'objective measurement' and 'official diagnosis' (Das 1997b: 568–70). On these grounds, such research may be readily identified with the moral demand that social scientists revise the ways in which they conceptualize the most painful perplexities of lived experience so as to present what suffering does to people in a more 'human frame' (Morgan and Wilkinson 2001; Graubard 1996).

At this point, once again, I would draw attention to the extent to which research on social suffering and the works of Hannah Arendt display a shared set of concerns. While in these bodies of work we are presented with markedly different approaches to writing about the social conditions that render people superfluous, this nevertheless takes place with similar aims and objectives in mind. In both cases, the task of writing on these matters is identified as an ethical and political risk; for there is a basic agreement that words are always too limited to convey a *sufficient* amount of what actually happens to people 'in' suffering, and thus can all too easily have the effect of trivializing human affliction to a point that is morally objectionable. These writers appear to be constantly frustrated by the ways in which the words they use to communicate some part of what suffering does to people seem to lack the 'existential resonance' required to awaken their readers to the full significance that this holds for humanity (Canovan 1974: 1–15; Daniel 2000). Moreover, under these circumstances there seems to be a basic agreement that in writing about 'the problem of suffering' we should be aiming to involve readers at a deeper level of *experiencing* the painful reality of 'a world become inhuman', as well as alerting them to the ways in which language is used to cover up or obscure this fact (Arendt 1968: 29–30).

Arendt adopts a 'rational vocabulary' for writing about the 'evil' of totalitarianism under the conviction that languages of pathos and fury can all too easily be used to 'gloss over' or 'explain away' the banality of evil that renders humanity superfluous. She is particularly concerned to deprive her readers of the possibility of denying to themselves the harsh reality of what took place in the Nazi death camps. It is because she understands traditional narratives of tragedy and lamentation to have the effect of equipping readers with cultural resources for reconciling them-selves to the horrors of the past, so as to make peace with their history, that she resists yielding to the temptation to include such forms of writing in her work. Arendt makes a quite deliberate attempt to write about human atrocity in a manner that 'solves no problems and assuages no suffering' (Arendt 1968: 29); for it is on these terms that she understands her work to acquire the potential to provoke her readers into still greater amounts of 'thinking' about the social conditions that enable events such as 'Auschwitz' to take place.

In writing on social suffering, the greater emphasis is placed upon the extent to which the 'rational vocabularies' of Western expertise serve to divert attention away from the human significance of what suffering does to people. Time and again, it is argued that such language is not only ill-suited to convey the existential trauma of human suffering, but also that its tendency towards abstraction promotes the treatment of people in purely instrumental terms. It is in the effort to fashion narratives that, as it were, take the form of 'textual bodies' on which pain is written, that creative decisions are made to record the genres of lamentation through which individual sufferers 'give voice' to their experience. For the most part, writers on 'social suffering' are not so much concerned by the potential for such processes of mourning to appease the memory of suffering as they are impressed by the ways in which the effort to make public the ongoing struggle of people to read purpose and meaning into their experience brings social attention to the inhumanity of the world.

Accordingly, in comparing the works of Hannah Arendt to writings on 'social suffering', we are presented not only with ethnographic research to detail our understanding of the banality of evil that treats people as superfluous, but also with controversy as to the appropriate ways in which such phenomena may be addressed in writing. In this section I have only just begun to identify some of the sociological and moral issues at stake in debates over the forms of representation that are best suited to do justice to this topic. Moreover, at a theoretical level of discussion, I have only gone so far as to identify some *possible* interpretations and social responses in relation to the contrasting ways these writers attempt to provoke their readers into thinking about what suffering does to people's humanity. It is only with empirical study of the effects of such writing on reader's attitudes and behaviours that efforts can be made to assess the extent to which these possibilities comprise the ways we relate to the suffering of humanity in the social contexts of day-to-day life.

However, for the purposes of this chapter, I am most concerned to have us focus on the methodological premisses that unite these writers, rather than the questions of strategy that take them in opposing directions. Above all else, I would have us recognize the shared understanding that it is by devoting attention to the inadequacy of established categories of thought and frameworks of moral understanding for making sense of people's suffering that readers may be provoked into critical thinking about the social significance of this phenomenon. Hannah Arendt and writers on 'social suffering' are united in the conviction that it is by involving their readers in the difficulty of understanding the exact nature of the unendurable realities that violate people's human dignity that it is possible to provoke them into radically new ways of thinking about the meaning of humanity, as well as the kinds of politics that produce humane forms of society (Fine 2001).

Attending to the suffering of humanity

Arguably, the tradition of writing so as to have us dwell upon the apparent senselessness of human suffering may be traced all the way back to the Book of Job (Nemo 1998). In such writing we are encouraged to reflect upon the brute facts of intense experiences of adversity that seem to exceed the bounds of moral justification. The indignation of those seeking a rational explanation for experiences of human suffering is aroused not by a lack of reasons, but rather by the understanding that there is *too much* suffering to be explained (Sontag 1981). It is with an appeal to the ways in which excessive experiences of cruelty, violence, terror and loss seem to render reason radically questionable, and even absurd, that writing on the suffering of humanity seeks to have us debate the primal meaning and value of our cultural reality.

In modern times, perhaps Voltaire's *Candide* ([1759] 1947) stands as the archetypal literary example of this tradition of writing. In opposing the teachings of Leibniz's *Essais de Théodicée* ([1710] 1969), Voltaire does not seek to dispute the philosophical logic of Leibniz's metaphysics, but rather to have us reflect upon the extent to which the brute fact of a world that contains excessive amounts of suffering renders such notions both morally dubious and intellectually suspect. In *Candide* we are presented with a litany of terrible disasters in which human life is ruined and destroyed with reckless abandon, and it is the experiential reality of this that Voltaire would have us recognize as sufficient evidence to cast doubt upon the teaching that ultimately all things work for the good of God's perfect plan for His creation. As Peter Gay observes, for Candide, 'experience conquers doctrine' (Gay 1966: 199). Above all else, it is by involving us in the apparent senselessness of excessive amounts of suffering that Voltaire seeks to make us sceptical about Leibniz's 'optimism'.

In retrospect, such a work may be identified as among the first to give formal expression to what Emmanuel Levinas identifies as 'the most revolutionary fact' of modern cultural consciousness: namely, 'the destruction of all balance between the explicit and implicit theodicy of Western thought and the forms which suffering and its evil take' (Levinas 1988: 161). However, for Levinas, it is the Holocaust that most emphatically brings an end to such speculative metaphysics, and in this regard 'Auschwitz' has become synonymous with the understanding that there is a fundamental 'disproportion between suffering and every theodicy' (ibid., 162). In the knowledge that events like 'Auschwitz' are part of our history, he maintains that never before have we been so culturally sensitized to recognize ourselves as inhabitants of a world marred by 'useless suffering'. On this understanding, our cultural situation is such that we are particularly disposed to see human suffering as a phenomenon that has no sacred origins or providential purpose; human suffering is more likely than ever before to have the appearance of being ultimately 'for nothing'.

Certainly, there is evidence to suggest that such convictions informed Hannah Arendt's characterization of the modern world as 'a place where senselessness is daily produced anew' (Arendt 1973: 457) and where there is an unprecedented 'growth of meaninglessness' (Arendt 1994a: 314). Arendt's understanding that totalitarianism amounts to a phenomenon that 'explode[s] our categories of political thought and our standards of moral judgement' (Arendt 1994a: 310) is derived not only from the shock of discovering that it is possible for populations to act in thoughtless compliance with the logic of social processes designed for industrial genocide, but also from the sheer horror of being confronted with the knowledge that under these conditions murder becomes 'as impersonal as squashing a gnat' (Arendt 1973: 443). She maintains that the horror of social circumstances in which people are treated as utterly superfluous is of such a magnitude that it 'can never be fully embraced by the imagination' (ibid.). Moreover, she argues that such horror is made to appear all the more incredible by those who would compare this 'radical evil' to anything previously known in human history.

However, on this point, it is perhaps important to note that while theorists such as Marx, Durkheim and Weber never lived to learn of the Holocaust, nevertheless, in their writings they are troubled about theorizing social conditions that, retrospectively, can be identified as creating the institutional environment for horrors such as 'Auschwitz' to take place. Moreover, while there is no evidence to suggest that they understood this to be among the possible consequences of modernity, they clearly recognized the potential for modern societies to involve people in distinctively new and extreme forms of suffering. Indeed, in this regard, they all appear to work with an understanding that such suffering may be encountered as a radical challenge to the established ways in which people relate to the moral meaning of their world. On these grounds, it may be argued that their insights are valuable for those who would engage in a sociological struggle to understand the circumstances that make possible the 'meaningless' horror of industrial genocide.

In the first place, these theorists are certainly alert to the potential for modern societies to be comprised of social institutions that damage and destroy people's human dignity. Already in Marx's efforts to expose the brutalization of people's humanity that occurs in capitalist systems of production, in Durkheim's concern for the 'injury' and 'violence' done to people's sense of identity and belonging within the forced division of labour, and in Weber's chilling account of the necessity for bureaucratic administration 'without regard for persons', there are terrifying premonitions of the advent of social conditions in which people are treated as superfluous (Marx [1867] 1976; Durkheim 1964: 374–88; Weber 1948a). Indeed, for these writers there appears to be no doubting the fact that in the context of such suffering, the nature of humanity is at stake.

In the second place, while working to produce their own distinctive accounts of modernity, each provides us with a theoretical point of view on the potential for experiences of suffering to be encountered in terms of a radical demand for social meaning and moral purpose. In this regard, I suggest that they are all sensitive to the possibility of suffering being encountered as a phenomenon that somehow surpasses sensibility so as to have the appearance of being 'meaningless'. Moreover, they all venture to outline a sociological approach to understanding how this character of senselessness is made part of our existential reality.

Marx would have us recognize the capacity for the bodily sensation of painful toil, debilitating weariness and social conflict to drive us to put society in question. As outlined in the previous chapter, there are passages in his writing where he focuses analytical attention upon the potential for suffering to occur as a kind of sensuous knowledge of our alienated condition (Merrifield 1999). Accordingly, his analysis of class relations in capitalist society incorporates the understanding that in order for us to be awakened to the apparent 'meaninglessness' of our conditions of existence, it is necessary for us to experience physically the negative force of suffering upon our lives. On this understanding, it is as part of a struggle against the embodied sense of violation that takes place in suffering that we are driven to question what is vitally at stake in our conditions of existence and, further, are moved to oppose social structures that do violence to humanity.

Durkheim would have us consider the ways in which the intensity of the experience of suffering is emotionally charged according to the psychic tension between individual and society (Durkheim 1973b). In this context, he dwells directly upon the ways in which suffering is encountered as an intolerable sense of inner loneliness and moral disorientation. Moreover, he develops his account of the ethics of 'moral individualism' in the conviction that it is only in so far as we are socially disposed to such a sensibility that the grief of others is also made 'more readily intolerable to us' (Durkheim 1952: 359–60). Durkheim would have us understand that, along with the 'morbid fever' aroused within social processes of individualization, we are liable to be agitated into a profound sense of moral indignation towards human suffering (Durkheim 1973b). On this understanding, we should expect ourselves to be filled with an ardent desire to combat the deleterious effects of suffering upon human life, the more we are socially conditioned to experience the emotional burden of this appearing to have no moral meaning.

In Weber most attention is given to the ways in which the apparent 'meaninglessness' of suffering is derived from a cultural disposition to make the natural and social world subject to the discipline of calculable rules. On this view, we should understand ourselves to be more inclined to interpret events of suffering as 'meaningless', the more that we are culturally conditioned to expect social reality to conform to the logic of a rational world-view. In his writings on theodicy, Weber raises the disquieting suggestion that with the intensification of processes of rationalization in human society, we become more highly sensitized to the experience of having our normative expectations of reality dashed by the 'irrational force of life' (Weber 1948c, 1948d). As Parsons notes, he appears to take the 'fundamental position' that not only is it the case that we are always bound to suffer in the effort to make the world as it is conform to the world as we think it ought to be, but, further, that we are made ever more vulnerable to this experience, the more our lives become dominated by the rule of rationalization (Parsons 1966: p. xlvii). As far as Weber is concerned, we are more likely to be disturbed by the apparent 'meaningless' of suffering, the more we are culturally conditioned to desire and expect a wholly rational explanation for every experience of adversity and affliction in our world.

Accordingly, I contend that these theorists present us not only with sociological accounts of the social conditions under which people may be treated as superfluous, but also with distinct approaches to explaining how this becomes consciously identified as a 'problem of suffering'. In their respective theories of modernity, they all devote analytical attention to possible ways in which a sense of moral indignation and/or intellectual frustration is aroused in the face of the suffering of humanity. They each provide us with insights into how 'the problem of suffering' is encountered, not only as a result of us being confronted with the brute facts of extreme adversity, but also as a result of us being made subject to a process of social conditioning. They would have us reflect upon the extent to which it is under particular kinds of physical, moral and cultural conditions that this is most likely to comprise our social consciousness of reality.

However, while the direct attention that these writers devote to the nature of human suffering can be identified as a point of intrigue from which to develop new readings of their sociology, I do not want to go so far as to present this as a matter that dominates their respective attempts to discern the character of modernity. In classical sociology, 'the problem of suffering', either as an embodied experience and/or as a form of cultural consciousness, is identified as a significant force of cultural change and as a phenomenon that gives rise to questions of humanity, but it is only on rare occasions that it is recognized as being potentially decisive for our social development. Marx, Durkheim and Weber all provide us with distinctive approaches to understanding how 'the problem of suffering' is made to be part of our cultural, moral and embodied experience of modernity; but this never features as an overriding sociological preoccupation.

It is on this point that the work of thinkers such as Hannah Arendt and contemporary research on 'social suffering' may be viewed as a new departure in the repertoire of social science. In these writings we are repeatedly encouraged to attend to 'the problem of suffering', on the understanding that in this effort we will be made to address fundamental questions of human destiny, origins and purpose. For these writers it is in the context of an overt struggle to understand the difficulty of comprehending what suffering *does* to people that it becomes possible to advance radical debate on the ethics of our times and our moral responsibility towards the plight of others. The novelty of this approach lies in the particular attention devoted to generating styles of writing that involve readers as much as possible in experiencing the moral confusion and intellectual frustration in attempting to make sense of suffering. While in early periods of Western sociology, classical writers recognized the potential for 'the problem of suffering' to serve as a motive force for cultural innovation and social change, they never venture to identify writing on human suffering as a political activity that can work to bring this about.

As I have already noted, there is a long-established tradition of writing which aims to involve us at some level in the apparent senselessness of suffering so as to provoke critical thinking about the value and meaning of our cultural reality. Yet there is novelty here in having this associated with the project of social science. Perhaps it takes the experience of being confronted with the 'nightmare' reality of events such as Auschwitz for social scientists to treat this as their 'fundamental' topic of concern (Arendt 1994a). Certainly, many of those writing on 'social suffering' were also immersed for lengthy periods of time in the ethnographic study of the brute reality of extreme poverty, political atrocity and humanitarian disaster. Perhaps, it is only with direct experience of such extremes that the task of writing about the problem of suffering becomes an overriding preoccupation.

Marx, Durkheim and Weber all provide us with insights into some of the social conditions in which people are most likely to become emotionally and intellectually challenged to engage in the struggle to make sense of suffering. However, in reflecting upon the different approaches to writing on this phenomenon that are found in the works of Hannah Arendt and studies of 'social suffering', we should also consider the extent to which it is under the influence of feminist, postmodernist and non-Western frames of reference that social science is most inclined to preoccupy itself with the social meaning of distressing states of bodily feeling (Morris 1991, 1998; H. Rose 1994: 28–50; Das et al. 2000, 2001). As Richard Bernstein notes, while writing in 1945, Hannah Arendt was certainly wrong in holding the view that 'the problem of evil will be the fundamental question of post-war intellectuals in Europe'; for the majority avoided this topic (Bernstein 1996: 127). It is only now, with a generation of scholars who are more alert to the intellectual value and political importance of bodily states of feeling for generating knowledge of society and exposing the ideological construction of rationality, that increasing numbers of social scientists are venturing to attend to the suffering of humanity in their work. It is in an intellectual context that is quite different from that which informed Arendt's thinking and, further, one that she might well have approached with a measure of anxiety and suspicion, that some of her principle concerns are being formulated anew so as to perplex a wider audience. It is by engaging with the topic of 'social suffering' that social science is becoming increasingly disposed to engage in the struggle to understand the significance of the fact that it is in face of 'a seemingly unendurable reality' (Arendt 1968: 27) that the most searching questions of humanity are raised.

Conclusion

This chapter has been written with a number of aims and objectives in mind. At one level I am simply concerned to provide a summary outline of the principle concerns and political ambitions of research on 'social suffering'. However, through a critical reading of Hannah Arendt's writing on the 'evil' of totalitarianism, I have also sought to present readers with some terms of analysis for beginning the work of thinking about what is sociologically and politically at stake in the attempt to dwell upon what suffering *does* to people. This has involved me in devoting particular attention to contrasting methods of writing on the problem of suffering, so as to reflect upon the ways in which Hannah Arendt and contemporary writers on 'social suffering' seek to bring more 'existential resonance' to their work and have this provoke public debate on the morality of our times.

In this context, I have ventured to suggest that where these writers share in the basic understanding that it is possible to fashion styles of writing that serve to involve readers in the apparent senselessness of suffering, we may consider their work to amount to a new departure in the project of social science. While classical social theorists provide us with insights into the ways in which sensibility towards 'the problem of suffering' serves as a motive force of cultural innovation and social change, the works of Hannah Arendt and research on 'social suffering' are distinguished by a quite deliberate attempt to evoke this on behalf of the politics of humanitarianism. It is by writing to provoke us into 'thinking with suffering' that they seek to have us dwell upon the ethics of humanity and inspire us to take political action to create humane forms of society. Up to this point, I have only gone so far as to explore some of the basic reasoning underlying this project and the methods by which it seeks achieve its aims. There is still much work to be done when it comes to developing understandings of the significance this holds for our cultural history. Moreover, I have scarcely begun to reflect upon what this entails for the conduct of sociological research. For the most part I have sought only to expose some of the motives that inform this manner of writing. I have yet to consider the life this acquires in the domains of civil society.

5

FEELING FOR HUMANITY

The time is long overdue for sociology to revise its one-sided characterization of modernity as an age of economic rationality and naked self-interest, and rather to understand it as involving large numbers of people in feelings for humanity that impassion a desire for social justice. Under the influence of writers such as Karl Marx, Ferdinand Tönnies and Max Weber, the overwhelming emphasis has been placed upon the extent to which a society dominated by the relentless pursuit of profit and cold calculating forces of rationalization leaves no public space for the emotional warmth of community, neighbourliness and compassion. On this account, a self-sacrificing ethic of brotherly/sisterly love is held to be a purely private consideration (Bellah 1999), and at worst, may even be interpreted as amounting to no more than a sanctimonious bourgeois ideology (Horkheimer and Adorno 1972: 92–3). More recently, writers such as Michel Foucault (1965, 1977) and Zygmunt Bauman (1989, 1991) have worked to confirm this master narrative with their respective emphases upon the disciplinary technologies of 'humanitarian' reform and the totalitarian tendencies of modern rationality. Once again, it seems that prevailing wisdom contends that under conditions of modernity social relationships are impersonal, instrumental and exploitative to a point where we are left with a diminished sense of one another's individuality, dignity and value as human beings. The dominant sociological characterization of our times advances the view that not only is it the case that most humane and heartfelt concerns are eliminated from the public realm, but also that we are becoming increasingly selfish and heartless in our behaviour towards one another.

Recent work on the sociology of emotions opens the way for us to explore the possibility that human thought and behaviour may be stirred more by the force of bodily feeling than by pure reflexivity of mind. Nevertheless, it is still the case that researchers are more interested in exploring the negative experiences and consequences of emotion than in the positive involvement of this within the concerns of humanity (Barbalet 2001: 3). Accordingly, it is emotional states such as 'rage', 'shame', 'resentment', 'anxiety' and 'vengefulness' that attract most sociological attention (Ortony et al. 1990; Scheff 1988, 1994; Scheff and Retzinger 1991; Wilkinson 2001a). More interest is devoted to negative bodily feelings associated with degrading experiences of emotional labour and 'McDonaldized' forms of consumption than to the potential for us to be impassioned with desire to combat the deleterious effects of suffering upon human life (Hochschild 1983; Meštrović 1993, 1997). The emotional experience of modernity is largely debated in terms of the pathologies of self and society, rather than its significance for the development of a cultural politics of compassion and discourse on human rights.

However, there are some notable exceptions to this rule. For example, Bryan Turner maintains that 'it is because of collective sympathy for the plight of others that moral communities are created which support the institution of human rights' (Turner 1993: 489). Turner would have us recognize the extent to which, it is largely on the basis of an emotional identification with one another's human frailty and vulnerability that we are most likely to be inclined to support the politics of humanitarianism. In this regard, perhaps, Natan Sznaider has worked hardest to alert contemporary sociology to the emotive force of compassion within the development of public crusades to alleviate suffering (Sznaider 1996, 1997a, 1997b, 1998, 2001). For Sznaider, organized campaigns to oppose brutalizing social conditions are just as much among the distinctive attributes of modernity as the development of capitalism, bureaucracy and totalitarianism. Indeed, he maintains that the most interesting sociological questions arise when we focus attention upon the possibility that it may be as an unintended consequence of the intensifying force of market relations, rationalization and state control upon our lives that we are also prone to develop humanitarian sensibilities that have the potential to become an active force in the public domain. This is not to deny or defend the cruelty, moral indifference and injustice that can be attributed to egotistical calculation, authoritarianism and the pursuit of profit, but it is to recognize the potential within conditions of modernity for people to acquire moral sentiments of compassion.

On this analysis, we come to the paradox in Emile Durkheim's sociological concern to explain how the same social processes that give rise to self-centred egoism and the torment of anomie may also involve us in 'a broader pity for all sufferings' and 'sympathy for all that is human' (Durkheim 1973b: 48–9). In what follows, I seek to investigate this in more detail. However, in so doing, I do not intend to identify my work as a Durkheimian project. I hold to the view that, at least in so far as his writings on 'moral individualism' are concerned, much more is noted than is explained. Durkheim does not provide us with a substantial or logically consistent analysis of the interconnections between the 'religion of humanity' and processes of individualization (Giddens 1995a, 1995b), and for the most part he seems to work with no more than a presumption that sympathy for self and others are 'of one cause and constituted by the same moral state' (Durkheim 1952: 359–60). I am inclined to take the view that, while he may well have touched upon part of the explanation for the social origins of modern humanitarianism, it is unlikely that this can be wholly accounted for in terms of his focus upon the psychic tension between the individual and society. I consider writers such as Norbert Elias (1994), Colin Campbell (1987) and William Reddy (2001) to have made important contributions to our understanding of this phenomenon. Moreover, when it comes to the sociological study of modern feelings for humanity and the ways in which these are collectively organized, managed and expressed in the politics of contemporary society, I suspect that there is still much work to be done.

In this chapter I provide an overview of sociological, political and ethical debates on the influence of moral sentiment upon social actions taken to alleviate the suffering of others. While noting that major figures of the Enlightenment shared in the understanding that collective feelings for humanity made a vital contribution to projects of political and social reform, I outline some possible reasons for the subsequent neglect of this topic within Western sociology. Although I seek to make clear the main criticisms that can be directed towards the politics of 'sensibility', I am particularly concerned to highlight the development within contemporary social science of a renewed interest in the potential for public sentiments of compassion to serve as a motive force of social change. Accordingly, I contend that, while over the last two centuries the majority of social commentators have given little thought to the connections between moral sentiment and civil society, once again movements are being made to promote this as a serious topic of social and political concern.

I suggest that these developments provide us with grounds for re-examining Emile Durkheim's conception of 'moral individualism' and its bearing upon the political applications of his sociology. In this regard, I am particularly concerned to focus attention upon the interconnections between social representations of suffering, moral sentiment and the politics of compassion. I maintain that, while Durkheim understands 'moral individualism' to be founded upon a shared sense of outrage in face of the suffering of humanity, he never goes so far as to dwell upon the potential for political and moral debates over the social meaning of suffering to either hinder or advance this process. I argue that contemporary research on 'social suffering' provides us with opportunities to think beyond Durkheim not only to the ways in which an imagination for suffering nurtures moral sentiment, but also to the kinds of politics that advance 'sympathy for all that is human'.

Accordingly, what follows can be read as a series of critical reflections upon the ways in which public discourse on 'the problem of suffering' acquires political resonance and the powers to effect social change. By exploring the potential for public sentiments of compassion to direct the terms of moral debate and to inspire political action, I aim to gather further insights into the ways in which writing on 'social suffering' might influence people's thoughts, feelings and behaviour. Having explored some of the motives and ambitions of writers working to draw public attention to the lived experience of human suffering, I am here concerned to initiate further debates on the political value and social impact of this endeavour.

Enlightenment ethics of humanity

The majority of sociological representations of the Age of Enlightenment are inclined to emphasize the extent to which its key figures held to an unflinching faith in the power of 'reason' both to free people from the shackles of ignorance and superstition and to guide them in practical attempts to transform the natural and social world on behalf of 'civilisation' and 'progress' (Abercrombie et al. 1984; Johnson 1995). On this account there is a tendency not only to downplay the schisms that divided

Enlightenment writers, but also to represent the dominant intellectual mentality of this period as being wholly committed to the development of a rational-scientific world-view. This pays no heed to the arguments of cultural historians who maintain that 'the prosperity of reason in the eighteenth century was less the triumph of rationality than of reasonableness' (Gay 1969: 29) and that this coincided with a sentimental attachment to humanity. At this time, social commentators generally assumed that progress towards 'civilization' depended not only upon the advancement of science, rationality and social contract, but also, and perhaps above all, upon the cultivation of greater amounts of humanitarian feeling (Denby 1994; McCloy 1972; Reddy 2001; Silver 1989, 1990). Indeed, William Reddy maintains that

> The picture emerging from recent research is ... one of remarkable consensus among the educated élite about the centrality of natural sentiment to virtue, a consensus that, while encompassing some significant variations of emphasis, stretched from the highest intellectual protégés of the courts to the lowliest scribblers of melodrama, including painters, composers, and pamphleteers along the way. (Reddy 2001: 161)

References and appeals to 'humanity' are to be found throughout the philosophical and political writings of the eighteenth century. Time and again humanitarian impulses are identified as the motive force for social reform. Above all, it is on the basis of sentimental appeals to humanity that political debates are advanced on behalf of the rights of slaves, women and children (Gay 1969: 29–45). In tracing the early histories of social movements in support of religious toleration, the abolition of slavery, prison reform, child welfare and public health, Shelby McCloy notes that in every case humanitarian sentiment served to fix such matters upon the agenda of governmental concern. Indeed, he maintains that among the advocates of the Enlightenment, public displays of 'fellow-feeling' were generally recognized as 'an essential criterion of action' (McCloy 1972: 2).

When it comes to sociological accounts of this new feeling for humanity, commentators generally point to a range of factors, such as urbanization, an increasing division of labour, the extension of market relations, and the rise of artistic expressions of 'sentimentality', as all combining to create possibilities for a greater sense of inter-human identification. However, a particular focus is the extent to which the origin of modern humanitarianism is rooted in the development of a new politics of 'civil society'. Some follow Norbert Elias (1994) in emphasizing the ways in which, during this period, the state grew in its power to police public behaviour so as to impose standards of 'civility' upon an ever-broadening cross-section of society. On this account, there is a critical tendency to represent humanitarian sensibility as comprising part of a new structure of feeling in which individuals were coerced into attending more closely to the etiquette of emotional behaviour as well as to standards of personal and public cleanliness. With this emphasis, eighteenth-century humanitarianism may be interpreted as a product of a new culture of shame that inspired élite groups to make efforts to banish unwholesome spectacles of bodily pain and unruly outbursts of distressing emotion from public view (Spierenburg 1984). But others place a greater emphasis on the understanding that the cultivation of feelings for humanity took place not so much as part of an authoritarian quest for public order, but rather as a critical response to the rigid enforcement of rules of etiquette upon society. Accordingly, the sentimental novels, plays, paintings and music of this period are represented as either examples of the ways in which individuals sought 'emotional refuge' from the tyranny of 'civility' or as the means whereby social reformers sought to arouse public sympathy on behalf of a more liberal foundation for government and law (Reddy 2001: 141–72).

Certainly it is largely in terms of an emphasis upon a social requirement for liberalism, tolerance and mutual sympathy that some of the major figures in the British and French Enlightenment devoted their attention to the virtues of moral sentiment. Adam Ferguson, David Hume, Francis Hutcheson, Adam Smith, Voltaire, Denis Diderot and Jean-Jacques Rousseau were all interested in debating the possibility that sentimentality may be enlisted in efforts to build more humane forms of society. While there are significant differences of opinion between these writers with regard to the extent to which people may be morally educated into becoming more compassionately orientated towards one another, nevertheless, at the very least, they are united in understanding that human benevolence is an active force in the public realm.

It is Adam Smith who provides us with some of the most developed and forthright reflections upon the sentimental grounds of moral conduct and the possibilities for this to serve as the foundation for civic virtue. In *The Theory of Moral Sentiments* ([1759] 1976) he proposes that the strength of our natural disposition to feel sympathy towards the suffering of others is sufficient to override the moral corruption of greed and envy, so that society may be ordered above all by the 'tribute of our fellow-feeling' (Smith [1759] 1976: 9–13). While Smith recognized many occasions when our minds may be crowded by selfish concerns, he nevertheless places great faith in the power of the imagination to place us in the suffering situations of others, so that we are moved by sympathy into taking moral and political action on their behalf. In detailing numerous examples of how even 'men of the most robust make' are deeply affected by imagining themselves in the suffering of others, he goes so far as to declare:

> We sympathise even with the dead ... It is miserable, we think, to be deprived of the light of the sun; to be shut out from life and conversation; to be laid in the cold grave, a prey to corruption and the reptiles of the earth; to be no more thought of in this world, but to be obliterated, in a little time, from the affections, and almost from the memory, of their dearest friends and relations. Surely, we imagine, we can never feel too much for those who have suffered so dreadful a calamity ... And from thence arises one of the most important principles in human nature, the dread of death, the great poison of happiness, but the great restraint upon the injustice of mankind, which, while it afflicts and mortifies the individual, guards and protects the society. (Smith [1759] 1976: 12–13)

However, already by the end of the eighteenth century, it seems that very few social commentators were inclined to lend whole-hearted support to such notions, and certainly there appears to have been little political enthusiasm for the suggestion that social justice may be guaranteed above all by the strength of shared feeling for humanity. Indeed, while during his lifetime *The Theory of Moral Sentiments* ([1759] 1976) was widely regarded as his greatest work, after his death in 1790 it appears to have fallen rapidly into disrepute, so that even now he is largely remembered only for writing *An Inquiry into the Nature and Causes of the Wealth of Nations* ([1776] 1979). From the 1750s up to the 1780s it is possible to find many documents that proclaim and celebrate feelings for humanity as the moral basis for social reform and the foundation of civic virtue; but by the turn of the century, such attitudes were more likely to be portrayed as either politically naïve or even as a danger to society.

Initially at least, there appear to be two major explanations for this collective change of heart. In the first place, there is evidence to suggest that social commentators came to be far more alert to the possible ways in which sentimentality may be pursued more as an indulgence of emotion than as part of a genuine concern for humanitarian reform. This is well illustrated in the criticisms Henry Mackenzie directed towards his readers once he understood that his book *The Man of Feeling* ([1771] 2001a) had become popular more as a result of the pleasure his readers derived from revelling in the misery of others, than for the ways it served to inspire them to acts of civic duty. Fourteen years after the publication of the work that established him as a leading proponent of the 'cult of sensibility', Mackenzie is to be found complaining about people who find it all too easy to separate conscience from feeling. He now suspected that his work had done more to turn sentimentality into a vice than to advance it as a moral virtue (Mackenzie [1785] 2001b: 99–103). Indeed, Colin Campbell notes that whereas the word 'sentimental' was used in the middle decades of the eighteenth century to refer to a process of critical thinking about social problems as well as to an experience of humanitarian sensibility, by the end of the century it had begun to lose its positive associations with Enlightenment social reform and was increasingly being used in a purely derogatory sense to signify a disposition to wallow in emotional feeling (Campbell 1987: 138–60, 173–9). On this account, the majority of social commentators were no longer prepared to condone any form of moral philosophy or politics that sought to base its appeal on feelings for humanity, for the potential for sentimentality to degenerate into an entirely self-centred preoccupation had become all too clear.

A second and more disturbing explanation for the subsequent reluctance of theorists to pay serious attention to the virtue of moral sentiment may be related to the understanding that during the French Revolution the language of sentimentalism had been used more as an ideological justification for political atrocity than to promote the ethics of humanitarianism (McCloy 1972). It was widely recognized that the Jacobin government had appealed above all else to the strength of human feeling as a means to gather popular support for their policy of Terror, and as a result, sentimentalism came to be regarded as a 'suspect philosophy' that often served as the pretext for violence and discrimination (Campbell 1987: 174). William Reddy argues that above all it was as a consequence of the shocking discovery that people could be led by their feelings into giving no critical thought to the destructive consequences of their actions that, after the French Revolution, the majority of social commentators were unwilling to identify any positive role for emotions in public life. He maintains that it is particularly as a result of the Terror that social theorists began to represent reason and emotion as opposed forces; henceforth emotion tended to be portrayed as a wholly irrational force with potentially disastrous consequences for self and society, while for the most part, principled self-restraint was viewed as the proper basis for social order (Reddy 2001: 173–256).

The politics of compassion denied

In retrospect, it seems that the critical reaction against sentiment-alism at the end of the eighteenth century was so forceful and comprehensive that even now, social commentators tend to give very little thought to the extent to which the politics of modern societies might take place under the influence and direction of public sentiments of compassion. Over the last 200 years, the majority of social theorists have given no serious consideration to the ways in which the moral foundation of politics, law and civil society might rest upon the strength of 'fellow-feeling'. Indeed, far more sociological attention has been paid to the ways in which, under conditions of modernity, social relationships in the public sphere are increasingly disciplined according to the rules of rational-technical efficiency and commercial exchange. Under these circumstances, it is entirely out of keeping with sociological wisdom to consider public sentiments of compassion as remaining an active force within the political life of modern societies.

For the most part, sociologists have argued that a society dominated by forces of rationalization and capitalist relations of production provides people with few opportunities or, rather, leaves them with no moral inclination to engage in a politics of compassion. It is sociological common sense to emphasize ways in which the emotional warmth of community is drowned within 'the icy water of egotistical calculation' (Marx and Engels [1848] 1967: 82). It is now taken almost as a matter of course that the discharge of professional duties and responsibilities within capitalist market economies requires the majority of people to relate to one another on purely 'objective' grounds and 'without regard for persons' (Weber 1948a: 215). It is generally accepted that in modern societies an intensifying social experience of individualization serves to erode the emotional ties that once bound us to a moral duty of care towards society (Tönnies [1887] 1955).

In this respect, sociologists have generally adhered to a Romantic critique of the social and cultural conditions of modernity that emphasizes the extent to which people lose their capacity to relate to one another by strength of human feeling, the more they are made to live under the tyranny of the market-place and the discipline of bureaucracy (Gouldner 1970; Lepenies 1988; Mazlish 1989). On this account, there is a tendency to represent the Age of Enlightenment more as the harbinger of cold-hearted utilitarianism, than as an intellectual movement that sought to cultivate humanitarian sensibility (Campbell 1987: 180–1). From the early nineteenth century onwards, Enlightenment writers have generally been portrayed as having been so infatuated with the virtues of rationalism, empiricism and materialism that they gave little attention to matters of human feeling (Reddy 2001: 217). Accordingly, ever since, it has been widely assumed that any creed or philosophy that celebrates the power of the emotions as the motive force of thought and action stands radically opposed to the narrow rationalism of the Enlightenment and the ordered 'garden' society it served to inspire (Bauman 1987).

Under the influence of Romanticism, the emotional domain of human experience has been characterized as beyond self-control, opposed to reason, spontaneous, highly idiosyncratic and always liable to disrupt the tightly ordered rules and procedures that govern social life in the public domain (Solomon 1993: 11–12; Lupton 1998: 81–8; Williams 2001: 17–38). For such reasons, emotion has been celebrated by cultural critics of modernity as an 'irrational force of life' whereby individuals might achieve some kind of inner release or personal escape from the 'dehumanizing' and 'alienating' social conditions under which they are made to live out most of their public lives (Jervis 1999). From the dawn of modernity up to the present day, many have sought emotional refuge from a seemingly 'disenchanted' social world through the ecstasy of 'Romantic expressivism' (Taylor 1989). Romanticism has often served as an extremist creed for those privileged enough to be able to devote their time and energies to cultivating some manner of aesthetic or metaphysical flight from reality, while at a more popular level, it may be argued that it has also been used to legitimate the pursuit of sensual pleasure in time spared from the impersonal instrumentality of work in capitalist society. Indeed, in this regard it might well be considered an indispensable component of the hedonistic culture of consumerism to which many people now devote a large portion of their lives (Campbell 1987).

Where the majority of modern social commentators have tended to accept that human emotions are an essentially personal and private concern, little thought has been given to the ways in which they might be collectively organized and promoted as part of projects of social and political reform. Moreover, in so far as there has been a largely unquestioned commitment to the idea that emotional experience is 'irrational' and rooted in 'primitive' animal behaviour, it has seemed entirely out of keeping with the prevailing wisdom to suggest that there are social circumstances in which this might be nurtured as part of an organized attempt to advance the concerns of humanity. Human emotions have generally been represented as being so far removed from reason, and so highly individualized, that it would be absurd to suggest that they may be cultivated so as to make a positive contribution to social life within the public realm.

Such convictions appear to have exerted a strong influence on Hannah Arendt's rejection of any politics that seeks to draw its appeal from the emotive force of compassion. She argues that wherever compassion has served to incite people to engage with political matters, it has almost always degenerated into 'an emotion-laden insensitivity to reality' (Arendt 1963b: 90). In this regard, she argues that we should continue to understand the acts of violence and discrimination perpetrated by the revolutionary Jacobin government as a product of a political system that was so driven by 'the passion of compassion' that it gave no consideration to the value of reasoned debate and lawful process. In Arendt's view, when people are consumed by sentiments of compassion, they are likely to shun public debate in favour of taking direct action to alleviate human suffering, and are easily persuaded to engage in violence in order to achieve their ambition. In this respect, she takes Robespierre to be the archetypal example of how a politics of compassion is liable to corrupt personal integrity. Of him she writes:

> What had perhaps been genuine passions turned into the boundlessness of an emotion that seemed to respond only too well to the boundless suffering of the multitude in their sheer overwhelming numbers. By the same token, he lost the capacity to establish and hold fast to rapports with persons in their singularity; the ocean of suffering around him and the turbulent sea of emotion within him, the latter geared to receive and respond to the former, drowned all specific considerations, the considerations of friendship no less than the considerations of statecraft and principle. (Arendt 1963b: 90)

However, while Arendt's emphasis upon the opposition between reason and emotion supports the modern understanding that feelings are essentially instinctual and 'wild', her discussion also contains a number of insights that go against the sociological view that political life in modern societies is driven largely by the cold, calculating pursuit of economic growth and efficiency. While Marxian and Weberian traditions of sociological analysis have emphasized the extent to which social relationships in the public domain are so disciplined for purposes of rational-technical expediency and commercial gain that matters of human feeling are strictly confined to the private realm, by contrast – at least as far as the politics of compassion is concerned – Arendt is inclined to take the opposing view. For Arendt, the greater danger lies in the extent to which politicians take advantage of public sentiments of compassion in order to make reasoned public debate irrelevant and without consequence. She does not doubt that in modern times compassion remains an extremely potent force of 'human solidarization'; her greater concern is the extent to which our political leaders might exploit this so as to ride rough-shod over any ordered process of 'persuasion, negotiation and compromise' (Arendt 1963b: 86–7).

What should we make of this sharp difference of emphasis? Is this a case of Arendt simply failing to grasp adequately the irresistible force of rationalization and the overwhelming power of the capitalist economy to conform human relationships in the public domain to calculable rules and the pursuit of profit? Alternatively, should we consider the possibility that by concentrating so much attention upon these social characteristics of modernity, sociologists have failed to attend properly to the ways in which compassion remains an active force in the political life of modern societies? Accordingly, should we take this as a further instance of Arendt deliberately working against the dominant wisdom of her time in order to prize open matters for debate that may all too easily be dismissed from the agenda of public concern? If this is the case, then once again we might look back upon her work as containing the seeds of inquiry that only now have begun to germinate and embed themselves in the agenda of sociological research.

The ethics of 'humanity' recovered?

It is only very recently that Western sociologists have been concerned to address the extent to which their tradition has inclined towards an excessively cognitivist bias in its accounts of human agency. While it is possible to trace the development of a distinctive 'sociology of emotions' back to the mid-1970s, it is only during the 1990s that this has been firmly established as a sub-discipline in its own right (Williams 2001: 1–3). In this context, researchers are working hard to reform the sociological stereotype of the 'rational', 'disembodied' social actor by means of a new emphasis upon the extent to which thought and behaviour may be directed by states of bodily feeling. Accordingly, it may be argued that sociology is in the process of developing a far more complex and multidimensional account of social action that concentrates upon the linkages between corporeal experience, cultural outlook and everyday practice; the variety and intensity of our emotionally embodied orientations to the world are thereby perceived to be closely associated with the ways we relate towards self and others (Barbalet 2002).

Within this climate of reform it is possible to identify the development of a renewed interest in the role played by emotions within political campaigns to advance concerns of 'humanity' (Barbalet 2001: 126–48; Berezin 2002; Turner 1993). Efforts are being made to revise the ways in which we account for the cultural history of modernity in order to acknowledge the role played by public sentiments of compassion within the trajectories of political discourse and the formation of social policy. These have also served to inspire cross-disciplinary debate on the interconnections between emotions, ethics and moral practice (Henderson 1987; Nussbaum 1996, 2003; Rorty 1998; Spelman 1997; Woodward 2002). Once again, serious attention is being devoted to the possibilities that exist within our culture for cultivating humanitarian sentiments to effect processes of political and social change.

A number of writers have highlighted the extent to which, from their origins to the present day, human and animal rights campaigners have always sought to advance their concerns with appeals to moral sentiment (Amato 1990, 1994; Sznaider 2001; K. Thomas 1983). Accordingly, rather than adopt the critical view that this provides a surrogate means whereby collective attempts are made to exercise a 'will to power' or defend 'class interests', an emphasis is placed upon the extent to which individuals genuinely and regularly engage in social actions on the basis of a passionate concern to alleviate human suffering. While there is no denying that modern societies are comprised of social systems that lead people to treat one another and the natural world with cruelty and indifference, it is argued that at the same time many display a 'compassionate temperament' that indicates the presence of cultural conditions in which individuals acquire a heightened sensitivity to the experience of pain and a developed imagination for the suffering of others. On these grounds, in opposition to the Romantic strain in critical sociology, it is suggested that modern society may be characterized as 'a *Gesellschaft* of compassionate people' (Sznaider 2001: 16).

Natan Sznaider (1996, 1997a, 1997b, 1998, 2001) highlights the extent to which humanitarian campaigns always tend to be organized on the understanding that narratives of suffering are the most effective means whereby large numbers of people can be mobilized to donate their moral energies and material resources to a political cause. On this analysis, the ethics of humanity that inspired moral philosophy in the eighteenth century has ever since served to promote movements for political and social reform. Although largely ignored as a serious matter for social commentary, it is nevertheless argued that in modern times 'fellow-feeling' has consistently inspired the activities of organizations committed to alleviating the suffering of others. Sznaider notes that throughout the history of Western humanitarianism, campaigners have always relied heavily upon emotive descriptions of bodily pain and personal experiences of injustice, injury and loss as a means to draw public attention to their concerns. In this context, it seems to be taken for granted that, once aroused, public sentiments of compassion have the power to exert a great deal of influence over the official terms of political debate and the direction of social policy. While to date very little sociological attention has been paid to detailing the ways in which this works, it may still be argued that most humanitarian organizations are already well practised in the art of orchestrating 'public opinion' in their favour by 'educating' and/or 'manipulating' sentiment.

Among contemporary moral philosophers, Richard Rorty (1998) and Martha Nussbaum (1996, 2003) would have us recognize this as reason to abandon the attempt to defend human rights on the basis of any purely rational process of argumentation. Both maintain that when it comes to convincing people to take moral responsibility for alleviating the suffering of others, an education in sentiment is far more effective than commands of reason. Indeed, in open recognition of the fact that they are urging a return to the interests of Enlightenment thinkers such as David Hume, Adam Smith and Jean-Jacques Rousseau, who identified 'compassion as a sort of reasoning' (Nussbaum 1996: 28), Nussbaum and Rorty would have us concentrate our attention upon the ways in which people may be 'morally educated' in their imagination for suffering so as to acquire a greater concern for social justice. Nussbaum proposes that it may only be on the basis of a 'compassionate training of the imagination', which involves devoting time and space to reflecting upon literary and artistic representations of what suffering does to people, that it may be possible to develop educational, political and legal systems that uphold principles of civic virtue (ibid., 50–8).

Arguably, it is in the context of legal scholarship that such proposals are now being given most serious attention. In an influential article, Lynne Henderson (1987) contends that judicial proceedings should accord privileged space to narratives of suffering, for this has the potential to enhance decision making with understanding born of 'empathy'. She maintains that 'the avoidance of emotion, affect, and experiential understanding reflects an impoverished view of reason and understanding' that is liable to draw courts towards the 'moral error' of paying no heed to the disabling and tragic choices that many people are forced to make in the social contexts of day-to-day life (Henderson 1987: 1574–93). While Henderson acknowledges the possibility that, on occasion, empathy may cloud moral judgement, she argues that far more harm is done where the 'Rule of Law' is applied as though all aspects of social life were ordered by calculable rules. On this view, it is vital for courts to work at empathizing with personal experiences of suffering, for this 'reminds us of our common humanity and responsibility towards one another' (Henderson 1987: 1653).

By comparing the recorded details of a variety of cases brought to the United States Supreme Court, Henderson begins to trace some of the different ways in which empathy might be brought to bear upon legal rulings. She maintains that in *Brown* v. *Board of Education*, where the court devoted considerable time to listening to stories about the pain and humiliation experienced by children who were victims of racial prejudice, empathy served to broaden legal understanding of the social meaning of being black in a racist white culture. However, this contrasts sharply with the case of *Bowers* v. *Hardwick*, where proceedings allowed no serious consideration to be given to the personal suffering experienced by Michael Hardwick in being victimized for his homosexuality; in this instance it appears that empathy played no part in the court's willingness to uphold the State of Georgia's decision to punish Hardwick for engaging in oral sex with a consenting adult in the privacy of his own home. Such differences lead Henderson to reflect upon the ways in which the time and space allotted for empathy can be severely curtailed or denied by opposing principles, values and prejudices. Here attention is focused upon the possibilities that exist for lawyers and judges to be trained to be more alert to the ways in which empathy occurs, and, further, for them to be persuaded towards the view that this is indispensable for law making.

While being prepared to concede that empathy can occur in different ways and with different degrees of influence upon court proceedings, Henderson is always concerned to underline the positive contribution this makes to legal discourse and understanding. However, Kathleen Woodward (2002) argues that Henderson does not go far enough towards recognizing the potential problems that arise when emotions such as 'compassion', 'sympathy' and 'empathy' are advanced as a moral resource. Woodward seeks to balance the wholly positive association between compassion/empathy and social justice found in the work of writers such as Nussbaum and Henderson, with a greater emphasis upon the complex and contradictory ways in which a new moral economy of emotions might feature within the public sphere of Western societies. In this regard, she is particularly concerned to highlight the ways in which the Republican Party and George W. Bush have appropriated 'the rhetoric of compassion' as an ideological justification for conservative politics. Woodward maintains that, at the moment, a discourse of empathy has 'pivotal power' in American politics, and that appeals to compassion are repeatedly used as a means to defend the Bush Administration's economic and family policy. In this context, she is particularly concerned to draw attention to the extent to which such rhetoric is used not so much in connection with narratives of suffering, but rather to promote the activities of church ministers and business-men involved in programmes to defend conservative family values and reform local economies. From a detailed analysis of key speeches, she maintains:

George W. Bush ... has shrewdly excised the suffering body – one characterized by difference – from his national narrative of the future United States. Foregrounded are not the suffering bodies of African-Americans and the poor, but ministers and businessmen ... If the liberal focus is on the uncertain connection between feeling and action, the calculated response of the conservatives has been to incisively sever the link between feelings of compassion for people and action, eliminating the feeling of compassion altogether. (Woodward 2002: 244)

Woodward takes this as evidence to support her contention that there are two distinct and contradictory ways in which the politics of compassion now appears to take shape. She argues that while, on the one hand, it is possible to identify a return to a politics centred on the task of cultivating 'feelings for humanity', on the other hand, the calculated ways in which compassion is 'performed' by politicians contributes to the creation of cultural conditions where emotional experience loses its intensity so as to be reduced to a mere play on 'sensation'. Where the former accords privileged space to narratives of suffering as a means to protest against social injustice and advance humanitarian concern, the latter is perceived only to pay lip service to 'compassion' where it can be used to promote an ideological agenda. On this account, while writers such as Henderson and Nussbaum seek to contribute to the development of more critically sophisticated forms of moral sentimentality committed to Enlightenment ideals of 'humanity', the 'compassionate conservativism' of the Republican Party seeks to do no more than 'trade on feeling' so as to defend its political commitments to Christian paternalism and the unregulated pursuit of economic gain.

Nevertheless, although Woodward begins to identify some of the contrasting and contradictory ways in which compassion may be either cultivated or performed within the public sphere, it may well be the case that the interrelationship between, on the one hand, an expanded heart for social reform, and on the other, 'the waning of affect', is more complex still. Where she maintains that true narratives of suffering are notably absent within frameworks of political discourse that 'trade on feeling', there is certainly no consensus on this view. For example, Michael Ignatieff (1998) is more alarmed by the ways in which, through the medium of television, large numbers of people can be presented with narratives on human suffering and yet remain unmoved and unmotivated to do anything on behalf of the victims of atrocity, terror and violence. He argues that, ironically, it may be due to the privileged amounts of time and space that news media give to spectacles of human misery that the potential for empathy to exert a positive impact upon contemporary politics is severely curtailed.

Ignatieff maintains that while news media representations of human affliction have contributed to a new 'internationalization of conscience' whereby large numbers of people take for granted that they have a moral responsibility to work at alleviating the suffering of strangers in distant lands, nevertheless, this has also served to create a great deal of moral confusion. He argues that we should be concerned by the extent to which television news works not so much to advance the cause of humanitarianism as to encourage audiences to engage in forms of 'promiscuous voyeurism'. On this view, the sheer volume and persistence of dramatic images of human suffering as a routine part of news media 'infotainment' has the potential to do more to convince people that they are utterly powerless to change the world than to nurture 'a compassionate training of imagination'. Ignatieff suggests that where audiences are presented with a seemingly endless flow of stories of famine, atrocity, war and violence, then this often 'encourages a retreat from the attempt to understand' (Ignatieff 1998: 24). In this context, he contends that our capacity for critical thinking about the most appropriate and effective ways to help people is diminished by the knowledge we acquire of the complexity and magnitude of the disastrous circumstances that destroy human life. The danger here is that while it may be the case that some are moved by empathy to actively support the politics of humanitarianism, the majority will respond with no more than an attitude of 'shallow misanthropy'.

In Ignatieff's view, if news media companies are to make a positive contribution to the development of ethical frameworks for nurturing social commitments to the welfare of others, they should give more time to in-depth reporting on a select number of crises and disasters, rather than crowd news schedules with fleeting footage of as many spectacular images of human suffering as can be crammed into a bulletin on any single day. The assumption here is that news programmes that provide detailed overviews of the networks of human relationships that make both positive and negative contributions to critical situations are also likely to leave audiences with a clearer understanding of the moral actions they might take to combat suffering. On this account, it is not so much the presence or absence of narratives of suffering that serves to nurture compassion as the creative ways in which suffering is framed for public attention.

Indeed, in one of the most sophisticated analyses of the cultural politics of compassion to date, Elizabeth Spelman (1997) argues that the moral complexity of the relationship between narratives of suffering and humanitarian social reform requires us to be particularly attentive to the ways in which symbolic forms of representation are shaped with ideological interests at stake. Citing examples such as Benetton advertisements that use pictures of impoverished children to sell clothes, she is concerned to have us recognize the ways in which both representations of suffering and sentiments of compassion are readily 'appropriated' for political and economic ends that may be far removed from the interests of 'victims'. She maintains that feelings of compassion towards the suffering of strangers are all too easily mixed with values and interests that divert attention away from what suffering does to people and one's responsibility to take actions on their behalf. For instance, she argues that Benetton's advertisements 'are carefully calculated to get viewers and consumers to strongly associate feeling good about their caring response to suffering with the pleasures of purchase and ownership' (Spelman 1997: 10).

As Spelman sees it, if narratives of suffering are to be used effectively to promote a politics of compassion, then the work of Harriot Jacobs, who under the pseudonym of 'Linda Brent' wrote about the experiences of abuse she suffered before escaping slavery, may be taken as an archetypal example of an approach to writing that is reflexively oriented towards the ethical risks this involves. Spelman notes that while working to arouse compassion among her readers for the experiences of suffering endured by slaves in the southern states of North America, Jacobs devotes passages to instructing her readers about the correct ways to think, feel and respond to her narrative. Jacobs seeks to make explicit the possible misreadings and misunderstandings that could be given to her work, so as to make as clear as possible the ways in which she desires to be heard and the kinds of moral attitudes she understands to be most appropriate for her readers to possess in order to respond to the conditions in which black slaves lived.

Accordingly, Spelman suggests that if public sentiments of compassion are to be effectively orchestrated on behalf of humanitarian concerns, then activists need to be particularly alert to the political struggles that shape the social meaning of human suffering, as well as to the methods of communication by which this is expressed and contested in the public sphere. The task of understanding how this works should be founded upon the assumption that the cultural significance of suffering and the moral meaning of how we feel in response to the pain of others are always open to conflicts of interpretation and can be used in opposing and contradictory ways. Moreover, while she is able to cite examples of writers who appear to be sensitive to the moral and political problems of using narratives of suffering as a means to shape public attitudes and behaviours, she advises that by no means are we in a position to surmount these difficulties. Indeed, for the moment at least, it appears that we are still only just discovering the range of ethical dilemmas and political hazards that arise when the concerns of humanity are advanced with appeals to the problem of suffering.

Nevertheless, while the above writers are by no means of one mind in their understanding of the cultural constitution of compassion and its impacts upon the dynamics of political and social reform, I suggest that, at the very least, their works may be taken as evidence of a return to inquiries begun by figures of the Enlightenment into the connections between sentiment and civil society. Once again, it seems that social science is prepared to give serious consideration to the extent to which a society's commitment to defending the rights and promoting the well-being of its citizens is dependent upon the particular quality of people's shared 'feelings for humanity'. However, it is important to add here that, in sharp contrast to a writer such as Adam Smith, who appears to be quite confident that 'the tribute of our fellow-feeling' will prove itself to be 'a great restraint upon the injustice of mankind', today's theorists are far more circumspect when it comes to advancing this as grounds for social organization and moral practice. Contemporary research takes place in a historical and intellectual context that is far more alert to the ethical risks and political hazards associated with social actions driven by the force of moral sensibility. In almost every instance, writers are sensitive to the critical objections that are likely to arise in response to any suggestion that, for the sake of social justice, we should concern ourselves with an education in sentiment. Most contributors to current debates proceed with great caution and, largely speaking, are unwilling to advance any strong claims for the moral worth of 'fellow-feeling'. While prepared to devote their attention to the ways in which moral behaviour may be directed by an imagination for the suffering of others, most emphasize the great difficulty of establishing any clear understanding of the precise ways in which this works.

In this context, it might be argued that it is only as a consequence of theorists now being convinced that reason alone has proved wholly insufficient to persuade and direct people to attend to matters of social justice, that once again they are prepared to recognize sentiment as a significant force in projects of humanitarian reform. More often than not, it appears that it is not so much with enthusiasm for the moral guidance of sentiment as out of despair for reason that such debates are being rehabilitated for a new age. Indeed, when advocating the politics of 'sensibility', authors such as Richard Rorty (1998) refer us not to clear examples of people being morally obliged by strength of feeling to oppose social injustice, but rather to evidence that speaks of the failure of reason to persuade institutionally privileged and powerful people to devote their energies to the care of others. It is out of the conviction that reason has proved itself inadequate to restrain the destructive force of egoism upon the moral organization of society that there is a willingness to return, albeit with trepidation, to debate the possibility that compassion may yet serve to advance principles of humanity.

On these grounds, we may be well placed to develop new insights into Emile Durkheim's conception of the social origins of morality. Indeed, perhaps it is only where there is a heightened concern for the precarious nature of the relationship between rationality and morality that today's sociologists may be persuaded to pay serious attention to Durkheim's reflections upon the ways in which moral behaviour is constituted by social sentiment (Schilling and Mellor 1998). However, where this involves us in questions that Durkheim never fully clarified and which he barely began to answer, I suggest that, while Durkheim may still have much to teach us about the ways in which morality is an emotionally grounded product of society, it is also the case that contemporary debates on the politics of compassion provide us with material for thinking beyond the points at which he leaves his theory. Above all, I would suggest that, as we gather more detailed knowledge of the potential for the experience of suffering to be symbolically represented so as to arouse, manipulate and modify human sentiment, it may be possible to develop a more detailed understanding of the kinds of political intervention that serve to establish and sustain the concerns of humanity. In this context, we may find ourselves in a position to elaborate upon the ways in which 'the cult of the individual' acquires the religious/moral force and legitimation to reform society.

From Durkheim to 'social suffering'

At no point does Durkheim provide us with a sustained analysis of 'moral individualism'. In order to begin to analyse his thoughts on this matter, we must weave webs of significance out of the occasional digressions and suggestive remarks that appear in works devoted to broader topics of concern. However, from these passages it is possible to understand him to have been in the process of developing a sociological account of the politics of compassion that would bring critical attention to bear upon the ways in which the problem of suffering is made to be a part of our social consciousness. Accordingly, we might inquire into the extent to which his work contains some of the focal questions and points of paradox that have led to attention being brought to bear upon the topic of 'social suffering'. Moreover, from current attempts to investigate the potential for narratives of suffering to promote social and political reform, it may be possible to revise our understanding of the forms of politics that are best suited to advance the development of 'organic solidarity'.

In defining 'moral individualism', Durkheim puts particular emphasis upon the extent to which this is founded upon feelings of sympathy for the suffering of humanity. In his essay on 'Individualism and the Intellectuals' ([1898] 1973b) he maintains that the kind of individualism articulated in the 'Declaration of the Rights of Man' is derived from 'sympathy for all that is human, a broader pity for all sufferings, for all human miseries, a more ardent desire to combat them and mitigate them, a greater thirst for justice' ([1898] 1973b: 48–9). He maintains that such sentiments occur as part of a transformation in collective sensibility that is rooted in a widely shared social experience of individualization. As the division of labour increases, and we find ourselves with our own individual social roles and obligations to perform, he argues that it is increasingly the case that we will have very little in common with one another except our shared humanity. Under these circumstances the idea of humanity itself, such as that declared in the works of Enlightenment philosophy, is likely to acquire 'sacred' value in so far as it accords with a common experience of seeking social recognition of one's moral significance and worth as a distinct individual. As far as Durkheim is concerned, above all else, this guarantees that 'the notion that a man suffers without deserving it is intolerable to us', and 'even suffering deserved oppresses and pains us and we try to erase it' (Durkheim 1957: 112). In Durkheimian terms, it is as a manifestation of a 'religious' commitment to 'the cult of man' born out of a transformation in the social experience of moral solidarity that we are liable to be greatly aggrieved by the spectacle of individual suffering.

However, in *The Elementary Forms of the Religious Life* ([1912] 1915), he emphasizes that, in the terms of his analysis, the social development of modern societies has not yet reached the point where it has acquired the religious/moral force to guarantee that the majority of people will be devoted to the advancement of individual human rights. For the moment at least, the 'religion of humanity' is still 'only a very rudimentary cult', for 'the personality of the individual is still only slightly marked', so that 'the cult which expresses it could hardly be expected to be highly developed as yet' (Durkheim [1912] 1915: 424). Accordingly, while Durkheim develops his theory on the understanding that he is witness to the early development of social sentiments and religious/moral forces that have the potential to curb egoistic instinct and combat the pain of anomie, he is also quite clear that by no means should we consider ourselves to have yet reached the point where this can be achieved. With these thoughts he is seeking to scan the horizon of our social development in order to communicate a possible future, but most certainly, we should not consider this to be guaranteed.

Arguably, it is at this point that his work is most vulnerable to criticism; for Durkheim is rather vague when it comes to detailing the forms of social action and political organization that we should now be seeking to promote so as to advance society in this direction. Indeed, Anthony Giddens maintains that one of the greatest problems with Durkheim's theory is that it fails 'to deal in an explicit manner with the relationship between sociological analysis and political intervention in the interests of securing practical social change' (Giddens 1986: 26). While identifying the potential within conditions of modernity to nurture humane forms of society, Durkheim only goes so far as to provide us with the broadest outline of how these might be brought into existence; at no point does he present us with practicable examples of how his sociological insights might be translated into a detailed programme of political reform.

Durkheim affirms that as social processes of individualization intensify, and people become more sentimentally orientated towards 'moral individualism', then we can anticipate that 'the cult of the individual' will increase its influence over the collective conscience of society (Durkheim [1912] 1915: 424–5). However, at the same time he argues that, purely as a product of processes of individualization, such social sentiment is insufficient to guarantee that all of society will be effectively organized so as to advance human rights. Accordingly, in his neglected essays published posthumously as *Professional Ethics and Civic Morals* (1957), Durkheim argues that the state must be the 'prime mover' when it comes to the task of translating principles of humanity into social practice (Durkheim 1957: 64). He maintains that it will only be as a result of this 'organ of social thought' being properly nurtured to work for the good of society as a whole that durable social institutions may be created that allow 'moral individualism' to flourish. To this end, he outlines a vital role for 'intermediary bodies' that continuously maintain close communications and associations between the state and individuals. He maintains that such organizations are indispensable in so far as they guard against the state falling under the dominance of any single section of society, and further, that they serve to caution the state against paying no heed to individual sentiment. It is through the organic bonds between the state, intermediary organizations and individuals that society may be morally reformed so as to achieve organic solidarity.

So long as this ideal conception of the state is not made a present reality or, rather, exists only in embryonic form, Durkheim advises that, as far as our political commitments are concerned, we should be seeking to establish 'secondary organs' that guard against the state being absorbed by sectional interests at the same time as they curb its authoritarian tendencies (Durkheim 1957: 108–9). We are left with no clear directions as to the precise form these should take, or the kinds of actions that may be required in order for them to be brought into existence. Nevertheless, what I consider particularly noteworthy here is his identification of social actions inspired by 'the feeling of human sympathy' as a guide to what might be involved. Durkheim predicts that, as sensibility towards the suffering of individuals intensifies, we may find the future political organization of society to be increasingly determined by the impulse of charity. He contends: '[A]s we go on, charity, in its true meaning becomes ever more significant and so it ceases, as it were, to be optional and to go beyond what it need be, and becomes instead a strict obligation, that may be the spring of new institutions' (Durkheim 1957: 220).

Accordingly, one might argue that the point at which Durkheim leaves his theory invites us to reflect upon the ways in which public sentiments of compassion have subsequently shaped political and humanitarian institutions, as well as the means by which these have been endowed with the moral authority to act upon society for the sake of progressive social change. On these grounds, we may look to the attempts of writers on 'social suffering' to inspire our collective imagination for the suffering of others as an example of how social science might translate some of these sociological insights into political practice. Indeed, where such work seeks to detail the dynamics of the interrelationship between social representations of human suffering, public debate and political action, this may already provide us with the means to think beyond Durkheim with regard to the task of cultivating 'moral individualism'.

Certainly, there is plenty of evidence to suggest that Durkheim was alert to the difficulty of orchestrating moral sensibility so as to advance the development of organic solidarity. For example, with reference to the violence of the French Revolution, he explicitly recognizes that there is always a potential for people to be driven by passionate feelings to engage in acts of 'bloody barbarism' (Durkheim [1912] 1915: 211). Likewise, he is alert to the fact that there are many social occasions on which it appears that large sections of society are unable to engage in thought or feeling for the concerns of others. Indeed, in the closing sections of *The Elementary Forms of the Religious Life*, he emphasizes that social sentiment always leads a precarious existence, and while he contends that symbolic forms of communication may be socially charged with an 'effervescence' that makes individuals passionately devoted to the welfare of others, he is unable to direct us to the precise ways in which this can happen (Durkheim [1912] 1915: 415–47). However, I would argue that, while it is still the case that much obscurity surrounds our understanding of the social constitution of moral sentiment, we are at least in a position to go further than Durkheim towards unravelling the complexity of this phenomenon.

While Durkheim notes that moral individualism is founded upon 'sympathy for all that is human' and 'a broader pity for all sufferings', he never troubles himself with conflicts of interpretation of the social meaning of suffering and the possibility of representing this so as to communicate its moral significance effectively. Contemporary research on 'social suffering' is far more alert than Durkheim ever was to the potential for symbolic forms of communication to be designed for political and ideological ends. Much more critical attention is now devoted to the particular methods and means by which 'the problem of suffering' is brought to public attention. In this context, it is recognized that the social representation of human suffering can take place in many different ways in relation to sectional values and interests. Accordingly, considerable debate now surrounds the potential for experiences of suffering to be 'culturally appropriated' for purposes far removed from, and even contrary to, the interests of 'victims' (Kleinman and Kleinman 1997). This introduces a further layer of complexity to a Durkheimian account of moral individualism; for by no means can we assume that every public discourse on suffering serves to advance concerns of humanity. However, to be alerted to the ways in which social representations of suffering are contrived to effect an ideological 'play on feeling' may leave us in a better position to identify the cultural circumstances under which it becomes possible to involve people in debate over the rights of 'the individual'.

We may also advance our understanding of the social dynamics of 'moral individualism' if we pay more attention to the variety of cultural contexts in which knowledge of suffering is received. While Durkheim's analysis aims to provide the broadest overview of our social development, by contrast, research on 'social suffering' is much more inclined to privilege the details of ethnography as a means of casting light upon our social reality. As a consequence, writers such as Arthur Kleinman, Pierre Bourdieu and Veena Das are far more alert to the potential for variables such as class, gender, age and ethnicity to shape the ways in which individuals relate to suffering, and further, for such factors to bear upon the formation of moral sentiment and the terms of public debate. While Durkheim seeks to expose the moral character of an entire society, in research on 'social suffering', attention is brought to bear upon the multiple ways in which individuals and groups experience 'self' and 'others' across a variety of cultural locations and institutional settings. We are thereby presented with new opportunities to reflect upon the particular ways in which concerns for humanity might be raised in the social context of 'the hospital' (Frank 2001), and to note how this differs from 'the housing estate' (Bourdieu et al. 1999) and 'the courtroom' (Das 1997b). Moreover, according to the social peculiarities of each context, it may be possible to identify the forms of communication and occasions for debate that appear best suited to advance 'sympathy for all that is human'. Indeed, as I have noted elsewhere, this task has already begun to preoccupy the minds of those seeking to reform a politics of sensibility for our time.

In short, whereas Durkheim recognizes that our shared imagination for the suffering of others has a crucial part to play within the social formation of 'moral individualism', contemporary research on 'social suffering' provides us with the opportunity to reflect in more critical detail upon what this involves. While, on the one hand, this leaves us in a position to highlight some of the shortcomings of his programme for the moral reform of society, on the other hand, it presents us with opportunities to revise sociological understanding of the ways in which his insights might be translated into political action. If we are to treat seriously the contention that public sentiments of compassion have a significant influence on the trajectory of our social development, then I suggest that both of these considerations deserve further attention.

Conclusion

It may well be the case that the increasing amount of attention that social science pays to the topic of 'social suffering' is itself a sign of the intensifying force of 'moral individualism' within society. Indeed, it might be argued that perhaps more than in any other field of sociological inquiry, this serves to involve researchers in the most heartfelt concerns of humanity. In this context, perhaps we are presented with the strongest terms by which social science identifies itself with 'sympathy for all that is human' and gives vent to its passion for social justice. Certainly, the majority of writers who seek to use their work as a means to frame public attention to suffering, are highly sensitive to the moral and political significance of their task. Here there is no doubting the potential for social science to become embroiled in the politics of compassion.

In this chapter, I have explored some of the ramifications of the potential for people to be moved by their shared feelings for humanity into taking political action to combat suffering. Whereas, for the most part, sociologists have worked to highlight the ways in which our social relationships are disciplined by the rules of rationalization and unbridled pursuit of economic gain, I have sought to look at the possibilities that exist alongside these conditions for human benevolence to remain an active force within the public domain. This has not been for the purpose of celebrating the extent to which modern societies might be characterized as a 'gesellschaft of compassionate people', but rather to explore the hopes and fears of writers who recognize human thought and behaviour to be not so much subject to the influence of reason as shaped by social sentiment.

I have been principally concerned to investigate debates over the ways in which feelings for humanity might be orchestrated by our shared imagination for the suffering of others. Here there is no doubting the potential for compassion to be heavily implicated within the terms of political debate, concerns of social policy and processes of legal decision. Yet, at the same time, there is certainly no consensus with regard to the precise ways in which this occurs. While alert to the ethical risks and political hazards of designing narratives of suffering so as to nurture moral sentiment, commentators have yet to arrive at a position from which they can offer clear advice on how these are best avoided or minimized. Nevertheless, we might take the view that at least in so far as we are in the process of developing a more sophisticated under-standing of the potential for social representations of suffering to be shaped for ideological purposes and used for corrupt ends, then we might be advancing to a point where it is possible to identify the cultural circumstances and social contexts which allow for the most vital questions of humanity to be raised.

All of this is further reason for sociologists to pay careful attention to the ways in which the problem of suffering is made to comprise social consciousness. Where in other parts of this book I have been mostly interested in exploring the terms whereby we might engage in debate over what the experience of suffering 'is' and what it 'does' to people, here I have begun to investigate how this might be applied in the political domain. In this context, I argue that it is not merely for the purpose of advancing sociological understanding of what it means to be human that we should inquire into the phenomenon of suffering, but also out of concern for the political applications of our sociology. In research on 'social suffering' social science is brought to debate not only its capacity to bring understanding to one of the most pressing of all human concerns, but also its potential to inform public debate in the interests of humanity.

6

MEDIATIZED SUFFERING AND THE INTERNATIONALIZATION OF CONSCIENCE

To what extent might we identify the development of research into 'social suffering' as a sign of the increasing power of the mass media to define the priorities of sociological research and assign the terms whereby we construct knowledge of society? According to John Thompson, one of the most significant ways in which our sense of self and society has been transformed over the last 30 years is in relation to the intermingling of the normal flow of day-to-day life with 'mediatized' forms of experience through which attention is brought to bear upon extreme events of human suffering (Thompson 1995: 226–7). The daily routine of watching television brings us into contact with more violence, war, famine, death and destruction than would have ever been known to previous generations. In this context, critical events that would otherwise be kept at a distance and separate from our practical workaday existence are brought close-up and ever present as a familiar part of our social reality. Arguably, the overall effect is to amplify and accentuate some of the most horrific aspects of human experience, so that these always maintain a significant power of influence over our collective outlook on life. Perhaps it is particularly under these cultural conditions that the ways in which a society accounts for 'the problem of suffering' become a pressing concern for social science.

In the context of sociological attempts to map the cultural dynamics of 'globalization', a number of writers identify media representations of suffering as the dominant means whereby the poor majority of the world are now made known to the minority of us living in the rich enclaves of 'the West' (Bauman 1998: 69–76; Boltanksi 1999; Kleinman and Kleinman 1997; Shaw 1996). As technological advances in communication media are rapidly accelerating and intensifying a collective sense of living in a global society, so this is also working to make known a world of suffering that would otherwise remain obscured from view. Images of starving children, grieving families, violent warfare and terrified refugees have possibly become the most common means by which the populations of developing societies are brought to world attention. On these grounds, one might take the view that any serious attempt to trace the formation of a global consciousness must give careful consideration to the processes of cultural production and exchange that create public knowledge of suffering, and further, the manner in which this informs moral conduct and political opinion. Indeed, one might go so far as to treat this as a matter of utmost urgency if we take seriously the suggestion that, it is with reference to the grief and pain of lived experience that we uncover the common grounds upon which to engage in cross-cultural debate on the terms of human rights.

Initial attempts to develop sociological and cultural analyses of this complex have tended to dwell substantially upon the *negative* influence of the mass media upon the symbolic forms of communication whereby the brute facts of suffering are made known to us, and upon the potential for 'mediatized' forms of experience to erode our capacity to feel for the plight of others. It is generally assumed that the mass media create cultural realities and social experiences that are liable to leave us with a diminished regard for one another's dignity and value as human beings. For the most part, critical attention has focused upon the stereotypical ways in which the news media report human suffering. Cultural commentators consistently complain about the ways in which these fail to provide us with sufficiently detailed information on the social and political dynamics of disaster, famine, war and disease. It is generally assumed that, in order to explain the apparent moral indifference of 'the public' towards the plight of suffering populations, we should concentrate our attention upon the ways in which the news media represent social reality so as to deny opportunities for ethical engagement and political under-standing (Beattie et al. 1999; Philo 1993; Philo et al. 1999).

In this context, critics maintain that news media corporations are not so much interested in providing us with in-depth accounts of the social contexts in which suffering takes place as in visually portraying suffering in sensational terms. It is argued that filmmakers, journalists and editors who are in the business of selling 'news' have made the most gruesome details of personal affliction the common currency of their trade. In the competition to sell stories and maximize their share of the audience, it is claimed that media companies are far more interested in the power of dramatic visual imagery to capture public attention than they are with the attempt to grapple with matters of social complexity. Not only does this have the effect of producing a grossly distorted and ideologically biased account of the social reality of world events, but the sensationalized content of media messages is generally assumed to erode people's capacity for moral outrage in face of the horrors beamed into their living rooms and plastered across the front of their newspapers.

There are a number of different ways in which the mass media are understood to cultivate moral indifference towards suffering. First, it is suggested that where news media corporations treat human suffering as no more than a form of 'infotainment', then publics are socialized to respond to it purely on these terms. It is argued that the news media are in the business of promoting a culture of 'promiscuous voyeurism', which involves audiences in the 'thrill' of being brought face to face with the violent destruction of human life, while at the same time liberating them from any moral responsibility towards the needs of victims (Ignatieff 1998). Here the emphasis is on the extent to which 'the commodification of experiences of atrocity and abuse' and 'the pornographic uses of degradation' encourage publics to relate to media representations of suffering as no more than a form of aesthetic 'pleasure' (Kleinman and Kleinman 1997: 19). It is argued that images designed to create a sense of 'shock and awe' lose their power to provoke moral outrage or to trouble social conscience when audiences learn from an early age that all that is routinely required of them is to sit comfortably at a safe distance and watch.

Second, it is often assumed that the greater the attempt to sensationalize the means by which social problems are brought to public attention, the more likely it is that people will become numbed to the reality of the horrors they are made to witness. However, rather than abandon the thrill of 'disaster pornography' as a means of entertaining their audiences, media organizations are perceived to respond to this state of affairs by intensifying their efforts to bring ever more spectacular and gruesome portrayals of human affliction to public attention. Accordingly, writers such as Susan Moeller maintain that there is a tendency for the mass media to represent the latest catastrophe as more 'extreme', 'calamitous' and 'deadly' than any of its predecessors (Moeller 1999). While in the short term this might prove to be a successful strategy in the competition to sell news, over the long term it is perceived to have the result of further lowering the threshold at which we become bored with the latest round of disaster footage from around the globe. On this account, the 'mediatization' of social life is understood to deprive us of the cultural resources to 'satisfy human needs for an account of our dignity as creatures', and compared to other times and places, leaves us 'less able to treat the human experience of violence and suffering with the respect it deserves' (Ignatieff 1998: 30–1).

Third, where audiences are still thought to retain some capacity to empathize with the pains of others, there are a number of ways in which the mass media are held to have the effect of rendering us unresponsive towards the spectacle of human misery. Some maintain that as people are repeatedly exposed to mediatized experiences of suffering, they are bound to become emotionally wearied and psychically drained to the point where they display signs of 'compassion fatigue' (Kinnick et al. 1996). Others suggest that such terms of analysis do not adequately grasp the reality of human psychology, and maintain that our moral indifference towards the suffering of distant strangers is not so much the result of emotional burnout or sensory overload as a manifestation of 'states of denial' (S. Cohen 2001). Accordingly, it is argued that we are naturally disposed to 'turn a blind eye' to the reality of horrors that place excessive demands upon our moral conscience, and that there are a number of common strategies that people use to 'evade, avoid or shut out unwelcome truths about human suffering' (Cohen and Seu 2002: 1888). On this understanding, we should expect the majority of us to be psychologically inclined to deny the reality of 'distant suffering', and the more the mass media work to present us with the drama of human tragedy, the more practised we become at dissociating ourselves from the moral demands this places upon us.

In this chapter, I do not seek so much to elaborate upon these arguments as to explore the possibility that they may fall short of providing us with a satisfactory account of the influence of the mass media upon the ways in which societies respond to 'distant suffering'. I do not dispute the contention that news media organizations have a commercial interest in sensationalizing their portrayal of human tragedy. And I accept that the content of media messages may be implicated in the development of moral indifference towards the suffering of strangers. However, I am concerned that we do not allow this to colour our overall understanding of the dynamics of the interrelationship between the mass media and the cultural politics of compassion.

Accordingly, in what follows, I present readers with critical questions and points of argument that are designed to highlight the possibility that the moral significance of the mass media lies not so much in their power to exhaust our capacity to feel compassion for others as in their potential to cultivate this capacity to the point where we readily accept that we have a moral duty of care for the needs of strangers in distant lands. I seek to identify an alternative approach to the study of this complex that concentrates more upon the involvement of the mass media in *strengthening* our moral ties to distant others than in their potential for cultivating states of moral indifference. My interest lies in the extent to which we may be witnessing the development of cultural process whereby sections of the population acquire a greater moral imagination for the suffering of others. My purpose is to outline an agenda for research that concentrates more upon the task of tracing how people are moved to acknowledge and respond to 'distant suffering' than on the extent to which they are inclined to deny the moral demands this places upon them.

Recovering historical perspective

At the same time as contemporary cultural critics complain about the ways in which society fails to address the problem of human suffering, they also present us with value positions on what *ought* to be taking place. Those who identify us as displaying signs of 'compassion fatigue' imply that compassion is a natural part of our human condition that under normal circumstances should shape the ways in which we relate to one another. Commentators who express dismay at our capacity to deny the moral demands that the pain of others places upon us are committed to the view that not caring for what suffering does to people is ethically reprehensible. Likewise, where writers perceive mass media portrayals of suffering as displaying no concern for matters of human dignity, they tend to assume that the majority of us share in the understanding that the 'commodification' of experiences of violence, death and destruction is morally objectionable.

I am in full agreement with Keith Tester when he argues that what is most sociologically interesting here is the unquestioned commitment of the majority of writers to the position that we have a moral responsibility to care for the suffering of strangers in distant lands (Tester 2001: 17–22). Historically speaking, for cultural critics to share in the view that media portrayals of suffering *demand* a response of care and compassion from society is quite remarkable. Compared to other times and places, it is highly unusual for such levels of attention to be given to the ways in which the symbolic representation of atrocity and abuse in the public sphere amounts to an assault upon standards of human decency.

In taking this view, I would have us consider the possibility of approaching these debates not so much as evidence of our diminished regard for the suffering of humanity, but as an indication of the existence of cultural conditions in which people acquire a heightened sensibility towards the pains of others. I urge us to take seriously the understanding that the existence of public debate on our failure to address the moral demands that the suffering of others places upon us serves more to display the potential for such matters to feature among our most heartfelt concerns than to chart the processes whereby we distort and ignore the reality of human suffering. Accordingly, rather than accept that such commentary marks the development of cultural conditions under which we 'turn a blind eye' and 'harden our hearts' towards the violation of people's humanity, I contend that it rather reveals our social disposition to be outraged by what suffering does to people. In short, I propose that we interpret this as a sign of the 'naturalization' of moral individualism.

As I noted in the previous chapter, in most historical studies of social sensibility, it is the eighteenth century that stands out as the period of history in which people first began to discover and explore realms of human feeling that have subsequently come to be taken as a 'normal' part of our inner constitution (Reddy 2001). In traditions of sociology, an increasing division of labour, the growth of cities, the extension of market relations, the politics of 'civilization', and the cultural aesthetics of 'sensibility' are all recognized as having contributed to the development of new structures of feeling that comprise the modern sense of self. While there is still no overall agreement as to the precise ways in which embodied states of feeling are constituted as historically contingent products of society, there is nevertheless much recorded evidence to suggest that the quality of our 'inner' life is transformed along with developments at the level of social structure and cultural meaning. On this account, the feelings we have towards self and society are always liable to change.

Within this history, shared feelings for the suffering of humanity are as a distinctively modern social trait (Amato 1990; Arendt 1963b: 70–1; Spierenburg 1984; Sznaider 2001). Within social systems that lead people to treat one another with cruelty and indifference, there also appear to be cultural conditions under which individuals acquire a heightened sensitivity towards the experience of pain and a developed imagination for the suffering of others. Indeed, I have suggested that we touch upon some of the more paradoxical elements in Emile Durkheim's sociology once we are prepared to debate the possibility that the same social processes that give rise to self-centred egoism and the torment of anomie may also involve us in 'a broader pity for all sufferings' and 'sympathy for all that is human' (Durkheim 1973b: 48–9). At the same time as Durkheim understands the conditions of modernity as making us socially disposed to experience a profound sense of inner loneliness and moral confusion, he maintains that we are acquiring a mental outlook which is liable to be greatly aggrieved by the sight of another's suffering. He maintains that it is as a result of a profound transformation in the moral order of society that our sensibility regarding suffering intensifies to a point where 'even suffering deserved oppresses and pains us and we try to erase it' (Durkheim 1957: 112). For Durkheim, such social sensibility guarantees that, as modern people, we are particularly prone to have our passions aroused by issues pertaining to individual human rights.

At the time of writing his sociology, Durkheim could look back over a century of humanitarianism in order to chart the growth of 'moral individualism' in modern societies. A shared imagination for the sufferings of humanity and open expressions of 'fellow-feeling' were central to the advancement of rights for slaves, workers, women and children (McCloy 1972; Sznaider 1996, 1998). While ideological interests and material concerns were always bound to influence the tenor of political debate and practical opportunities for Enlightened social reform, campaigns for prison reform, care for the poor, public health and religious toleration consistently sought to gather public support with appeals to humanitarian sentiment. On this evidence, never before had populations displayed such 'an expanded heart for social reform' (Amato 1990: 103–36). Moreover, writing in the early decades of the twentieth century, Durkheim maintained that this was still only in the early stages of its development (Durkheim [1912] 1915: 424). He argued that the humanitarianism of the nineteenth century marked only the beginning of 'the cult of the individual'. Durkheim anticipated further growth in our shared feelings of human sympathy and that the impulse of charity would grow in influence over the development of society (Durkheim 1957: 199–220).

With the benefit of hindsight, we may well be tempted to dismiss this as an expression of idealism that reflects the innocence of one who never lived to learn of the horror of social systems in which people's humanity is violated to the point of them being rendered utterly superfluous. Perhaps, armed with the knowledge of two World Wars, repeated outbreaks of genocide, and the apocalyptic annihilation of human life in the Third World, he would have seen good reason to reject any suggestion that the concerns of humanity have been advanced over the last century. How is it possible to maintain that moral individualism has flourished when the scale of death and destruction has been so much greater than in any other period of history?

However, while levels of social conflict, political oppression and human misery have exceeded all expectations, at the same time it is possible to argue that never before have such concerted efforts been made to establish and defend people's human rights. Indeed, governments have responded to the atrocities of twentieth-century warfare by developing and elaborating upon the concept of 'human rights' to the point where the idea that individuals have value simply due to their 'humanness' has been enshrined as the most sacrosanct principle of international law. Following the Universal Declaration of Human Rights in 1948, world governments have been in constant debate over how adequately to define and provide for people's rights to existence and self-determination (Felice 1996: 17–34). In most Western societies, the social status of workers, women and children has advanced far beyond anything known in Durkheim's day. Moreover, with the development of campaigns against sex discrimination, racial prejudice, ageism, the abuse of animals, the destruction of the natural environment, and the economic exploitation of the developing world, the language of rights has developed far beyond anything he could have envisaged.

Alongside these developments, it is also possible to chart a considerable expansion of the voluntary sector in Western societies. While some of the voluntary traditions of the nineteenth century have declined and disappeared along with developments in medical technologies and the expansion of state health and welfare services, many new causes have been discovered (Prochaska 1990). In the second half of the twentieth century, the charitable and wider not-for-profit sector of economies has grown in all advanced industrial nations. On average, 2.3 per cent of the work-force in European societies now work for some kind of charity. Over the last 30 years the number of UK registered charities has more than doubled, from 76,000 in 1970 to 187,000 in 2002 (Wolfenden Committee Report 1978; Cabinet Office 2002).

It is estimated that the total annual income of UK charities is now in the region of £30 billion (www.charity-commission.gov.uk). The incomes of the top 500 fund-raising charities are currently increasing by around 7 per cent per annum in real terms. Approximately 45 per cent of this money is derived from government funding, while the rest comes from voluntary sources. Over the last 20 years, the percentage of UK households that gives to charities has remained at around 30 per cent. While there was a decline in household giving during the mid-1990s, the most recent figures show that this has been reversed, in what the Charities Aid Foundation represents as a new 'tide in public spiritness' (Pharoah 2002; NCVO 2001a). Most notably for the purposes of this chapter, humanitarian non-governmental organizations (NGOs) working in areas of disaster/emergency relief and international aid now feature among the largest charities in the UK. Oxfam, the British Red Cross Society, and Save the Children UK all have annual incomes in excess of £100 million (Pharoah 2002; www.charitiesdirect.com). On this evidence, Karen Wright argues that we should understand current trends in charitable giving in the UK as a sign of the development of a new culture of 'cosmopolitan altruism' that reflects the growing influence of the ethics of global humanitarianism on public opinion (Wright 2002).

Indeed, over the last decade the number of international NGOs has increased more than fourfold (The Economist 1999). At a global level, 50 per cent of non-military humanitarian aid is now channelled though the programmes of quasi- and non-govern-mental agencies. Never before in human history have such large-scale co-ordinated international efforts been made to combat poverty, promote peace, fight famine and eradicate epidemic disease. Moreover, the capacity of the mass media to bring social attention to global suffering is widely perceived to be an indispensable component of these developments (Robbins 2002).

From this point of view, to claim that societies are now

displaying signs of 'compassion fatigue' or heightened 'states of denial' is to advance an extremely one-sided view of our social history. At the same time as we are living through the most violent and destructive time for which we have record, it is possible to argue that never before have human societies been so prepared to acknowledge the hurts we inflict upon one another and respond with compassion towards the suffering of strangers in distant lands. Accordingly, I maintain that the reality of our cultural situation is more ambiguous, and possibly more intriguing, than many critics of mass media portrayals of human suffering claim to be the case.

I am not suggesting that we should be congratulating Western societies for their 'generosity' towards the needs of strangers. I do not consider current levels of state welfare expenditure and public giving to be sufficient to meet the demands of our day. I reject the politics of writers, such as Joseph Amato, who argue that 'our hearts are too small and fragile to contain the world's victims' and that we should be looking to establish clear reasons for withholding compassion from strangers who lay claim to our sympathies (Amato 1990: 175–207). I hold to the view that the quality and quantity of aid given to developing societies remains shamefully inadequate, and that the power élites of the G7 donor countries are inclined to treat the populations of the poorest countries of the world as superfluous. I accept that the increasing power and numbers of NGOs is in part a reflection of the extent to which, under regimes of 'neo-liberalism', states are seeking to minimize their involvement in the provision of health, education and welfare (Robbins 2002). I would not hide from the fact that over the last ten years the amount of aid given by OECD countries to less developed societies has declined in real terms by 12 per cent and that on average the richest nations of the world now give only 0.22 per cent of their gross national income (GNI) in aid, and thus fail to meet the UN target figure of 0.7 per cent (German et al. 2002). I contend that the gross inequality between rich and poor nations is morally despicable and should be condemned as a crime against humanity.

However, I am looking to question whether it is appropriate to interpret this as an indication of the extent to which the majority of people are losing or denying an innate capacity to feel for the suffering of others. I would have us acknowledge the historical anomaly of a public debate on how the spectacle of human misery *should* move us to care for the suffering of strangers. Further, I would have us recognize the novelty of social circumstances in which so many people assume that it is right and proper for us to have 'sympathy for all that is human' and to give our money and time to charitable causes. In no way am I suggesting that we should be satisfied with our efforts to combat poverty, social injustice and oppression, but I urge us to consider the popular understanding that we have a moral duty of care for the suffering of strangers as a matter in need of sociological explanation.

When it comes to 'public sentiments of compassion' and their bearing upon the 'internationalization of conscience', I contend that we are dealing with social sensibilities, cultural orientations and institutional arrangements that are distinctively new in our times, and that, for the purposes of sociological understanding, it is important for these to be recognized as such. I suggest that we have scarcely begun to devise the concepts, theories and historical frameworks that are adequate to make proper sense of these developments. Moreover, I hold to the view that this is particularly the case with respect to the influence of 'mediatized' experiences of human suffering upon the formation of our social consciousness.

Media power and moral culture

Most sociological overviews of the history of research into the influences and effects of the mass media upon society emphasize the extent to which many early assumptions about the power of media messages to shape social attitudes and behaviour have been undermined by the discovery of audience 'activity' (Curran et al. 1996; Dickinson et al. 1998). Most commentators now firmly reject the understanding that the content of media messages has an obvious and direct impact upon people's thoughts and feelings, and that it is easy to predict how this is liable to take place. Whereas ethnographic research reveals that individuals interpret and respond to media messages in different ways in relation to the social contexts in which these are received, researchers such as Roger Silverstone maintain that 'a considerable indeterminacy' must always be part of our understanding of the audience (Silverstone 1994: 132–58). Accordingly, we should always anticipate the possibility that the ways in which people make sense of media messages may be far removed from our expectations. Moreover, we should be highly sceptical of any expert claims to understand how publics think and feel that are based exclusively on their interpretations of the 'ideological' content of media messages.

Within the field of media research, it is now commonly assumed that media messages have multiple meanings, and that audiences are actively involved in generating these. On this view, the contents of media messages may only be labelled as 'ideological' when it can be clearly demonstrated that individuals use them in order to establish and sustain unequal power relations in the practical contexts of day-to-day life (Thompson 1995: 213–14). A strong emphasis is placed upon the polysemic nature of media texts and the complexity of communication flows. Here it is widely recognized that the more we learn about the bearing of social context upon the interaction between communication media and their audiences, the more difficult it is to arrive at any comprehensive assessment of the power of mass media to influence our cultural outlooks and social behaviours. While it is accepted that communication media are involved in shaping the social institutions and cultural formations of modern societies, it is also readily acknowledged that we are in a state of theoretical crisis when it comes to the task of describing and analysing how all this takes place.

Where critics comment upon the cultural significance and social implications of mediatized experiences of human suffering, generally speaking, virtually no attempt is made to investigate whether publics share their views. In order to alert us to the moral dangers of the ways in which suffering is framed for social attention, most are inclined to view contemporary news values and practices as a clear indication of what is likely to be taking place in the minds and emotions of members of the audience. Accordingly, where news media are perceived to always work at sensationalizing their accounts of 'violence' and 'atrocity', it is simply assumed that this reflects the extent to which publics have become desensitized to the pain of others (Moeller 1999). Similarly, the extent to which news media are perceived to be more concerned with the business of entertainment than with quality in-depth coverage of social problems is held to indicate general states of misanthropy and moral indifference (Ignatieff 1998).

In light of the findings of audience studies, such forms of analysis are deeply flawed. While they certainly go some way towards exposing dominant news values and the stereotypical frames of reference whereby social problems feature as matters of public debate, they certainly cannot lay claim to any knowledge of how individuals actively receive, interpret and respond to these symbolic forms of communication as routine social behaviour. Writers may well suggest that audiences are wearied and/or emotionally overloaded by the ways in which the mass media portray human suffering, but until this is clearly established with the evidence of ethnographic research, then it remains no more than a matter for speculation. To date, researchers have shown very little interest in the social situations in which audiences create meanings out of the messages they receive about the suffering of humanity. Moreover, on the rare occasions when researchers have investigated the empirical reality of the involvement of the mass media in people's 'compassion fatigue' or 'states of denial', the terms of their inquiries have been set within narrow limits, and the samples of populations involved are by no means adequate as resources for generalization.

In possibly the most detailed study of the phenomenon of 'compassion fatigue' to date, Katherine Kinnick and colleagues (1996) conducted a telephone survey with 316 residents of Atlanta on their attitudes towards media portrayals of violent crime, AIDS, homelessness and child abuse. They were particularly interested to note the extent to which respondents reported themselves to experience a state of 'emotional burnout' as a consequence of coming into repeated contact with these issues via the mass media. The study concluded that 'mass-mediated compassion fatigue' does exist, but that it is 'issue-dependent' and more likely to be reported as part of the experience of white, male college graduates. Their results indicated that 40.1 per cent of respondents admitted to feeling 'burnt out' on the issue of violent crime, 35 per cent on AIDS, 33.1 per cent on homelessness and 14.7 per cent on child abuse. Kinnick and colleagues interpret these findings both as an indication of the extent to which people are more emotionally sensitive to issues of 'personal salience' and also as a reflection of the tendency of the news media to concentrate their attention upon the most terrible aspects of crime.

There are no other studies that bear direct comparison with this work. However, in a British context, Stanley Cohen and Bruna Seu (2002) have sought empirical evidence to support the argument that, in response to media reports on the gross violation of people's human rights, individuals are more likely to engage in 'states of denial' than to experience 'compassion fatigue'. In their study, fifteen participants, most of whom were university students, were divided into three focus groups and asked to discuss their responses to leaflets from Amnesty International campaigns that draw attention to atrocities committed in Afghanistan and massacres of population in Bosnia. Cohen and Seu then documented the different rationalizations used by individuals to avoid confronting the reality of human suffering and to distance themselves from the moral demands that the information from Amnesty places upon them. They take this as evidence to support the hypothesis that, although 'bystander alibis' are always shaped by distinctive cultural points of view, nevertheless, it is 'human nature' for us to work at distancing ourselves from the suffering of strangers in foreign lands, and thereby any need to take moral responsibility

I do not doubt that these studies serve to establish that some people consider themselves to be emotionally wearied by their interactions with news media reports of human suffering, and that there are various strategies we might adopt in order to dissociate ourselves from ties of moral responsibility towards the victims of atrocity and abuse. But I would question whether it is appropriate to let this colour our *overall* understanding of the interactions between the mass media and the dynamics of social conscience. There are a number of levels at which I am dissatisfied with the conclusions drawn from these studies.

First, these researchers do not distinguish between the many different ways in which human suffering is represented by the mass media. In common with much of the literature on society's moral indifference towards the suffering of others, attention is focused exclusively upon the ways we appear to respond to items of 'news' and the instant 'shock' of being confronted with the terrible facts of human affliction. Little or no thought is given to some of the alternative formats by which human suffering is framed for public attention.

To date, as far as I am aware, there are no empirical studies of the ways in which audiences actively interpret and respond to the pains of others when these are represented as part of 'documentary' or 'docudrama'. Michael Ignatieff (1998) speculates that such forms of reporting are better suited to inspire publics to act to support the work of humanitarian organizations; but so far this has not been taken up as a matter for empirical investigation. Moreover, as Keith Tester points out, social scientists have paid very little attention to the ways in which audiences are involved in and respond to 'telethon' events such as the BBC's *Children in Need* appeals and Comic Relief's *Red Nose Day* (Tester 2001: 104–31). There is evidence to suggest that people are more responsive to humanitarian appeals that demonstrate that 'something can be done' to alleviate human misery (Devereux 1996; Dyck and

Coldevin 1992; Sargeant 1999). Thus it may be the case that where representations of human suffering are contextualized within the framework of positive messages on how time and resources can be used to make a difference to people's lives, then we shall find audiences more willing to meet the moral demands that this places upon them. Indeed, Comic Relief claims that over 70 per cent of the British population have been moved to take part in *Red Nose Day* (www.comicrelief.com/comicrelief/story.shtml).

Secondly, such studies display no concern for the extent to which the social contexts in which their respondents interact with the content of media messages serve to shape the ways in which they interpret and respond to the suffering of others. An audience response to media portrayals of human suffering in the context of a university seminar room may be quite different from that which takes place among families at home, friends at a pub, gatherings at a church, or children in a school assembly. Before concluding that 'compassion fatigue' is a socially pervasive phenomenon, or that it is 'natural' for human beings to practice 'states of denial', we should be careful to consider the extent to which individuals express these attitudes/behaviours as a response to particular social settings and institutional arrangements.

Thirdly, when it comes to the task of interpreting their data, these researchers make no attempt to relate their findings to research on patterns of voluntary giving. From data collected by the Charities Aid Foundation (CAF), the National Council of Voluntary Organizations (NCVO) and the Family Expenditure Survey (FES), considerable amounts of information are now available on both the level of voluntary giving in the UK and the social characteristics of individuals who are most likely to support charitable causes. Class, age and gender all appear to have a considerable bearing upon the amount of money people give to charity. In the UK the most affluent 20 per cent of the population donate only 0.7 per cent of household expenditure to charity, while the poorest 10 per cent give 3 per cent (Banks and Tanner 1997; L. Edwards 2002). The percentage of people who give regularly to charity, as well as the average size of their donation, generally increases with age (Walker and Pharoah 2002). More-over, it appears that, while the average wage of British men is 25 per cent higher than that of British women (Walby and Olsen 2002), this does not lead them to be any more generous towards the needs of strangers. Indeed, the NCVO claims that in the year 2000, British women gave over £400 million more to charity than men did (NCVO 2001b). In addition, it is now established that in the UK, donations to charity are influenced most directly by factors such as the amount of growth in the national economy, changes in taxation policy, the time of year in which appeals are made, and the level of people's participation in the National Lottery (Passey and Hems 1997; Walker and Pharoah 2002; Wright 2002).

I contend that we should take such information as an indication of the extent to which the interrelationship between mass media and moral conscience is liable to be shaped by the dynamics of national economies, the political culture of nation-states and the social characteristics of sections of the audience. The ways in which people feel and respond to the suffering of others is by no means purely a consequence of the quality of their relationships with the mass media; there are many other social factors involved. Indeed, the mass media may contribute only a small part to the overall formation of our social sensibilities. We need to work more at recognizing how an individual's structural location, material circumstances and cultural outlook are liable to moderate the ways in which they respond to mediatized spectacles of human misery.

Finally, and perhaps most importantly, in focusing their attention upon the extent to which people may be 'losing' or 'denying' a capacity to care about the suffering of strangers, these studies display little concern for the occasions on which individuals may be so moved by the spectacle of misery that they become motivated to involve themselves in the politics of compassion. Hardly no thought is given to the *particularity* of the social occasions and cultural circumstances under which some of us are prepared to commit ourselves to taking moral responsibility for the suffering of strangers in distant lands. To my mind it is more interesting to inquire into the historical novelty of social conditions where not only is it popularly accepted that we should be morally outraged by what suffering does to people, but also that this should be taken up as a pressing matter of political concern.

An agenda for research

I want to suggest an agenda for research that begins from the understanding that the idea that we have a moral obligation to care about the suffering of others, by virtue of the fact that we share in a common humanity, is a peculiarly modern social trait. This requires us to work at identifying the cultural formations and social processes that appear to involve people in heightened experiences of pain and a greater imagination for the suffering of others. I consider it vital for us to start from the recognition that the ethics of humanitarianism has a distinct history, and that in this regard we are dealing with moral sensibilities, political outlooks and cultural orientations that are still in the *process* of being developed as a potential part of our social character.

There are passages in Adam Smith's *The Theory of Moral Sentiments* ([1759] 1976) where he reflects upon the strength of feeling that we might hold towards the suffering of people in distant parts of the globe. He writes:

> Let us suppose that the great empire of China, with all its myriad of inhabitants was suddenly swallowed up by an earthquake, and let us consider how a man of humanity in Europe, who had no sort of connexion [sic] with that part of the world, would be affected upon receiving intelligence of this dreadful calamity. He would, I imagine, first of all, express very strongly his sorrow for the misfortune of that unhappy people, he would make many melancholy reflections upon the precariousness of human life, and the vanity of all the labours of man, which could thus be annihilated in a moment ... [But] when all this fine philosophy was over, when all these humane sentiments had been once fairly expressed, he would pursue his business or his pleasure, take his repose or his diversion, with the same ease and tranquillity, as if no such accident had happened. The most frivolous disaster which could befall himself would occasion a more real disturbance ... [P]rovided he never saw them, he will snore with the most profound security over the ruin of a hundred millions of his brethren and the destruction of that immense multitude seems plainly an object less interesting to him, than this paltry misfortune of his own. (Smith [1759] 1976: 136–7)

There are two levels at which I am interested in this passage. In the first place, I suggest, it is useful for the extent to which it points to some of the novelty of our present age. While in most of his work Smith is inclined to put great faith in the power of moral sentiment to unify us with concern for the suffering of humanity, in this passage he warns us against trusting this too far. He holds to the view that, all too quickly, our thoughts and feelings regarding the suffering of strangers on the other side of the world are liable to be overtaken by more immediate concerns of everyday life. Smith readily accepts that there are limits to our moral imagination, and for the most part does not trouble himself over the extent to which we should preoccupy ourselves with the quality of our social attachments to humanity on a global scale. Accordingly, this gives us cause to reflect upon the peculiarity of social circumstances where the terms of public debate assume that 'distant suffering' is an ever-present part of our cultural reality. Moreover, it may appear stranger still that we have reached the point where critical attention is focused upon the extent to which individuals have to work at denying the moral demands placed upon them by the knowledge they acquire of disaster and atrocity in faraway lands.

Secondly, I would have us dwell upon this passage for the extent to which Smith identifies the 'visibility' of suffering as vital for the development of our moral imagination. He readily accepts that so long as the victims of disaster remain beyond our field of vision, then whatever concerns we may express for their misfortune are likely to be short-lived and without moral consequence. Smith assumes that so long as we never have to set our eyes upon the suffering of these people, then it will be all too easy for us to ignore or forget their plight. He does not envisage the possibility of there being cultural circumstances in which 'distant suffering' is made readily 'visible' to us as a routine part of our social life. His analysis does not include social circumstances in which we are regularly positioned by the mass media as moral spectators of worlds of violence and atrocity. Accordingly, Smith touches on a factor in our cultural develop-ment that involves us in quite different forms of social reality than were available to him to experience. He draws us to the point where we might take the 'visibility' of suffering as a matter for sociological investigation.

It is only since the mid-1980s that scholars have begun to attend to the ways in which the mass media make 'visible' the suffering of humanity, and how this might serve to either advance or obstruct the politics of humanitarianism. It is only since the mid-1990s that social scientists have begun to debate the possible effects of this upon the quality and character of our moral sensibilities. There are aspects of these debates that restate some of the concerns of cultural critics at the end of eighteenth century. Once again, we have cultural commentators expressing anxieties over the ways in which human feelings can be managed and manipulated for selfish and unscrupulous ends. Whereas writers such as Henry Mackenzie were criticized for creating a genre of literature which readers used to pleasure themselves in knowledge of the misery of others, similarly, modern news media are deplored for the ways in which they work to provide people with the thrill of being involved in scenes of death and destruction. Contemporary critics who claim that we are witness to the 'commercialization' of human suffering and the development of a culture of 'promiscuous voyeurism' echo the worries of those who first argued that 'sensibility' could all too easily degenerate into self-indulgence. Moreover, those who object to the ways in which media industries work to 'commodify' human suffering repeat long-standing concerns about the ways in which capitalism reduces matters of personal worth to purely economic considerations.

While I acknowledge that all these issues are cause for great concern, my suspicion is that these also serve to divert attention away from cultural developments that may have more radical consequences for the ways in which we assess the character of our times. I am far more intrigued by the extent to which it is possible to identify the terms of these debates as an indication of ways in which people's social consciousness and moral feelings are in the process of changing. To my mind, it is not so much with questions about the ways in which people are made morally indifferent towards 'distant suffering', but rather with a concern to understand why a growing minority are in no doubt that they have a moral duty to combat the suffering of humanity on a global scale, that we come closer to addressing the peculiarity of our cultural situation.

Certainly we should be asking ourselves what kinds of 'visibility' human suffering acquires through the mass media; but we should be more interested in understanding how this strengthens ties of moral responsibility towards distant others than in dwelling upon the ways in which this is met with moral indifference. If we have arrived at a position such that it is possible to consider Adam Smith as having *underestimated* the powers of our moral imagination, then we should be far more concerned to understand why the reality of 'distant suffering' might now weigh so heavily upon our minds. To my mind, what is most sociologically interesting here is the involvement of the mass media in the creation of social sensibilities (or forms of collective conscience) whereby people readily accept that they are under a moral obligation to donate their time and resources to alleviating the miseries of strangers in foreign lands.

It is possible that we are witnesses to the development of a new sense of 'common humanity'. It could be, as John Thompson describes, that the mass media are nourishing a new kind of 'moral-practical reflection which has broken free from the anthropocentric and spatial-temporal limitations of the traditional conception of ethics' (Thompson 1995: 265). If this is the case, then we should be seeking better understanding of the cultural occasions and social contexts in which individuals appear to display a heightened level of 'global consciousness'. We should be working to identify the social characteristics of the types of people who appear most able and willing to take on these new responsibilities. We should be looking to analyse the ways in which a shared imagination for 'distant suffering' serves as a guide to moral action and as an impulse for political decision.

This should involve us in a programme of research that is concerned not so much to chart the cynical manipulation and commercial exploitation of images of suffering as to identify the positive ways in which this might be framed so as to educate compassion (Nussbaum 2003). We should be looking to identify the ways in which media messages are received within different social settings and cultural arrangements so as to be attentive to the bearing of class, gender, age and ethnicity upon the ways in which individuals actively interpret their moral responsibilities towards others. Moreover, we should be concerned not so much to dwell in broad terms upon the failure of NGOs to gather public support for humanitarianism as to understand the micro-dynamics of the occasions where campaigns succeed in setting the terms of political debate that command people's moral attentions (Rotberg and Weiss 1996).

Conclusion

At best, we can hope to achieve only highly tentative accounts of the role of the mass media in the historical transformation of our experience of self and society. Our capacity to understand the interactions between technologies of the mass media, cultural values and social behaviour is limited by the difficulty of keeping pace with the various speeds at which the dimensions of this complex change. Under these conditions we can only ever hope to achieve highly partial, provisional and uneven accounts of the significance this holds for people's political concerns and moral relationships. The ways in which we interpret the novelty of our cultural situation will always be open to debate.

In this chapter, I have explored the possibility of seeing contemporary debates on 'compassion fatigue' and 'states of denial' not so much as an indication of the failure of society to attend to the reality of 'distant suffering', but rather as a sign of the extent to which this might animate the terms of our moral imagination. I have sought to highlight the historical peculiarity of cultural circumstances in which we accept without question that the spectacle of human misery *should* move us to pity, and that on this basis, we *ought* to take moral responsibility for the needs of strangers in faraway lands. I have urged readers to reflect upon the extent to which this does more to reveal the *strength* of people's moral feelings for humanity than to expose their capacity for moral indifference.

To my mind, the most sociologically interesting questions arise when we consider the possibility that we are witness to the development of cultural conditions in which people are acquiring new sensitivities towards pain and a greater imagination for the suffering of others. On this understanding, the moral significance of the mass media may lie not so much in their power to exhaust our capacity to feel compassion as in their potential to cultivate it to the point where it becomes central to our politics. I do not consider myself to be in a position to understand the full consequences of these developments. Moreover, I am not seeking to present them as grounds for optimism when it comes to assessing the possible futures that are available to us. One of my few certainties is that 'the truth' about our historical situation is liable to prove itself more complex and uncertain than that found in the work of sociology. Here I am concerned only to draw us to the point of identifying new possibilities for questioning the social character of our times and the extent to which this might be brought under the direction of a cultural politics of compassion.

TOWARDS A CRITICAL SOCIOLOGY OF SUFFERING

Sociology is founded on the understanding that we are living through one of the most critical junctures in human history. While recognizing the unparalleled opportunities within conditions of modernity for people to develop their human potential, sociologists have always been particularly alert to the glaring discrepancy between the ideals of 'progress' and the bitter realities of our social world. It is the character of sociology to expose the human costs of modernization and to interrogate the rationality of its achievements and ambition. In so doing, sociology amounts to more than a peculiarly modern attempt at self-understanding; it also presents itself as a means to engage in debate over the morality of our times.

However, as I write, the majority of sociologists seem more reluctant than at any other time in their history to speak with confidence on 'the truth' about our social situation. Moreover, most appear to want to dissociate themselves from any strong points of view on the values by which we should live. Over the last decade, an unprecedented number of publications have taken as their starting point 'the fact' that sociology is in a chronic state of epistemological uncertainty and moral confusion (Horowitz 1993; Lemert 1995; Levine 1995; Mouzelis 1995; Schilling and Mellor 2001; Seidman 1994; Turner and Rojek 2001). It has become commonplace to declare sociology to be in a state of 'crisis'.

In part this reflects a more widespread disenchantment with the 'progressive' potential of modern civilization. The crisis of sociology is fuelled by the knowledge of industrial genocide, the oppressive force of totalitarianism, escalating military conflict, the threat of global environmental catastrophe and the apocalyptic annihilation of human life in the so-called Third World. Such catastrophes may be judged sufficient in themselves to chasten severely any sociological attempt to legislate on behalf of 'the good society' (Bauman 1987, 1989, 1993). These brute facts stand to caution any move to present modern rationality and science as the obvious answer to our problems. Indeed, over the last century it has become all too clear that, while conditions of modernity provide for the health, material prosperity and cultural enlightenment of large sections of population, they are also the means by which unprecedented extremes of violence, cruelty and oppression have destroyed the lives of hundreds of millions of people.

Our sociological malaise is further sustained by the understanding that there are no longer any serious alternatives to capitalism. The crisis of sociology is wedded to the crisis of socialism. In the aftermath of the collapse of Soviet communism and the intensifying force of global capitalism, the majority of social commentators seem convinced that it is now impossible for individual nation-states to adopt any alternative path to modernization. The traditional politics of the radical Left appear to be both intellectually moribund and practically irrelevant. While new 'anti-capitalist' and 'anti-globalization' social movements may revitalize the critique of political economy, for the most part, they are not recognized as exemplars of radically new ways of living in the world; their passion for protest is not matched by any certainty over how we might build a truly humane society. We may yet be presented with opportunities to introduce some measures of social reform to curb the most wild and destructive tendencies of the global market system, but no longer does it seem possible to imagine a world without capitalism (Hutton and Giddens 2000). Without the imminent possibility of some form of Marxist or socialist solution to the dilemmas of milieu and social structure, sociology seems to many to be bereft of hope and political purpose.

Under these conditions, some go so far as to claim that the tenor of debate within Western sociology is now largely divorced from fundamental questions of economics, politics and ethics. Sociology appears to have become a repository for expressions of personal discontent, with little or no effort being made to reflect critically upon how it may be intellectually oriented towards the concerns of common humanity. On this understanding, the aesthetics of self-identity, personal risk and individual consumer life-style seem more important to our discipline than elementary principles of social justice and the quest for moral solidarity (Turner and Rojek 2001). Most may readily acknowledge that the new demands and complexities of life in 'late modern' or 'postmodern' global society require that we abandon excessively bourgeois, ethnocentric and male-centred frameworks of analysis; but in attacking the anachronisms of our 'classical' heritage, all too often it appears that sociology is left ever more fragmented and disorientated by its latent tendency towards parochialism and ideologies of difference.

Nevertheless, should there only be talk of 'crisis'? While it may be tempting to conclude that such critical commentary amounts to the death throes of sociology, it is also possible to associate much of this with a shared desire to create new languages that speak more meaningfully to the pressing issues of our times. Might we yet venture to understand such collective mourning for sociology's lost promise as a necessary part of a work of critical reconstruction? Where now there may be much talk of the dearth of sociological ambition, can we not relate to this as a measure of critical impulse that must be welcomed if we are to revitalize a shared imagination for a better world?

I would like to suggest that a critical sociology of suffering has the potential to make some important contributions to our intellectual and political reformation. I maintain that in learning to 'think with suffering' sociologists may have opportunities not only to establish new creative relationships with their history, but also to uncover grounds on which to build a global sociology that speaks to the concerns of our shared humanity. In this final chapter, I offer a summary account of the main problems and points of argument that have inspired the writing of this book. I also outline some of the possible directions in which this might lead sociological inquiry, as well as the political significance they could hold.

For dialogue and debate

From the outset, I have presented this book as part of 'a work in progress'. It has been written with the purpose of initiating further dialogue and debate within social science, and sociology in particular, over the social constitution of human suffering and the forms of culture through which this is experienced and made known to others. While individual chapters have raised arguments in the context of debates that may not be readily identified in terms of a 'sociology of suffering', in these various theoretical and methodological excursions, I have been working to clear the ground for such research to be recognized as a legitimate and necessary field of study.

A great deal of this has involved a critical dialogue with contemporary writing on 'social suffering'. Indeed, at one level my book may be approached as an attempt to introduce a wider audience to forms of literature that, while placing 'the problem of suffering' on the agenda of social science, challenge us to radically rethink the ways we conceptualize human experience and the methods by which we engage in the empirical study of society. In this literature we are called upon to be particularly attentive to the cultural practices and social processes by which people embody conditions of modernity as subjective forms of 'moral-emotional' experience. Moreover, it is argued that we should devote ourselves to the development of styles of writing and methods of research that go as far as possible to convey the existential realities of the dehumanizing social circumstances in which large numbers of people are made to live.

Arthur Kleinman (1999) is perhaps the most forthright when it comes to identifying what such a project implies for the conduct of social science. In the first place, he argues that we should be particularly concerned to raise the sociological value of ethnography. He aims to persuade us not only to make more effort to bring the brute facts of suffering in human *experience* to the fore of sociological thinking and debate, but also to recognize the potential for the *practice* of ethnography to involve us in questions of personal integrity and moral purpose. Kleinman maintains that the critical power of ethnography derives not only from its capacity to draw social attention to the standpoint of individuals living in conditions of extreme adversity, but also from the existential anxieties that ethnographers are liable to experience in their work. He writes:

> What is special about ethnography, then, is the practice it realizes
> ... The ethnographer's angle of exposure places her so uncomfor-
> tably between distinctive moral worlds and local and global ethical
> discourse and, what is more, creates such a destabilizing tension
> between them that she is forced to become, even at times it seems
> from published accounts against her will, self-reflexively critical of

her own positioning as well as attentive to the new and unexpected possibilities that can (and so often do in real life) emerge. (Kleinman 1999: 414–15)

Kleinman presents us with a vision for social science where the *act* of researching experiences of human suffering, as much as the writing up of this work, is identified as part of our critical praxis. At the same time as ethnographers of 'social suffering' challenge us to engage with sociological thinking in a more human frame, their work is identified as a moral engagement that, by force of *feeling*, has a potential to initiate far-reaching debates within social science over the political values that shape its intellectual orientations and practice.

Secondly, he urges us to work at prying open 'a space' for ethnographies of human suffering in forums of policy decision and political debate. Adopting a Weberian emphasis upon the extent to which the language of policy and political/legal procedure is liable to be dominated by purely economic and technical-rational considerations, Kleinman argues that as a matter of ethical responsibility, social scientists should aim to communicate the brute facts of lived experience in the most sentimentally charged terms available to them. At the same time as he celebrates the potential for the practice of ethnography to engage social scientists in debate over the humanitarian value of their research, he also associates the published results of this work with a capacity to bring moral sentiment to bear upon proceedings within the public domain. Accordingly, Kleinman invests hope in the capacity for a 'self-reflexive sensibility' to initiate a wider process of critical inquiry into the social consequences of our scholarship as well as the human significance of societies' political practices and policy decisions.

While exploring some of the ways in which works of social suffering are designed to perform these tasks, I have also developed some sociological lines of inquiry that provide an analytical setting for debating the cultural and political value of this manner of research and writing. In this context, I have sought to focus critical attention on the extent to which the concerns of writers such Arthur Kleinman are advanced not so much as a consequence of the achievement of a fine-grained ethnographic account of suffering in lived experience, but rather as a result of the ways in which this research is perceived to remain *inadequate* to the tasks it sets itself. While attending to the ways in which embodied experiences of affliction may be moderated at the level of cultural meaning, I would also have us recognize the political and moral consequences of continually *failing* to arrive at a satisfactory account of what suffering *does* to people.

It is as a result of the *pain of failing* to come to terms with 'the problem of suffering' that social scientists such as Pierre Bourdieu, Vieda Skultans and Veena Das debate the moral meaning and political value of their work. While *struggling* to devise frameworks of representation and analysis that make clear the socio-cultural dynamics of suffering in human experience, these researchers have become preoccupied with fundamental questions of origins, significance and purpose; it is the acute sense of *lacking* a sufficient account of the most important aspect of what happens to people 'in' suffering that maintains their (com)passion and interest. It is the epistemological frustrations and moral anguish experienced in the effort to bring 'meaning' to the brute facts of human suffering that serves as the motive force of their critical inquiry and concern for public debate. I have argued that it is the open confession of a failure of understanding that provides 'a space' in which attention is brought to human suffering; what may be most important to recognize is the extent to which writing on social suffering succeeds in its aims and objectives where it leaves people with a lasting sense of *dissatisfaction* with its efforts to provide an authentic account of the pains of human experience.

In my readings of Karl Marx, Emile Durkheim and Max Weber, I have outlined a theoretical groundwork for sociological explorations of the ways in which suffering acquires the sense and appearance of being 'utterly useless' and 'for no purpose'. I have outlined the possibilities within the works of these major theorists for further thinking about the social constitution of this traumatic 'sense of senselessness'. Moreover, I have sought to draw attention to the various ways in which these writers account for the force and dynamics of this within processes of social and cultural change. I have argued that these 'classical' founders of our discipline still have a great deal to teach us about the social conditions whereby 'the problem of suffering' is made to comprise embodied experience and cultural consciousness; much remains here to inspire our questioning of the sociological and political value of writing on 'social suffering'.

However, perhaps above all, it is by engaging in debate with Hannah Arendt's methods of writing on the horrors of totalitarianism that we uncover the analytical terrain that is best suited for developing our understanding of the political ramifications of this work. One of Arendt's most important contributions to social science may be a style of writing that is fashioned for the purpose of communicating the perplexities of the process of thinking more than the points on which this comes to rest. I have suggested that her work represents a pioneering example of the ways in which writing on 'the problem of suffering' may be designed to focus social attention on a world where 'senselessness is daily produced anew' (Arendt 1973: 457). Arendt works to establish and maintain a burden of analytical frustration in face of the horrors of Auschwitz, for she understands that it is on these terms that her writing acquires the potential to draw readers into critical thinking about the social conditions that enable such events to take place. While writing on social suffering may not directly associate itself with this project, nevertheless, I suggest that in giving vent to the burden of making experiences of suffering productive for thought and action, it finds itself in the position of working to this purpose. Moreover, where the comparisons and contrasts between these bodies of literature provide us with opportunities to reflect critically upon the force of moral sentiment within our political thinking, I suspect that we have scarcely begun to grasp the analytical value of Arendt's writing as well as the new directions in which works of 'social suffering' might lead the terms of sociological inquiry.

In chapters where I investigate our cultural capacity for compassion I have made efforts to highlight just one of the pressing matters for debate with which works of 'social suffering' might inspire a critical sociology for our times. I have argued that one of the possible 'effects' of such writing may be to bring more sociological interest to the understanding that conditions of modernity involve us in both a heightened sensitivity towards pain and a developed imagination for the suffering of others. Where the ultimate aim of writing on social suffering may be to 'educate' a politics of compassion, this in itself may stand as testimony to the intensifying force of 'moral individualism' within our society; the sociological appeal of this manner of writing may also reflect the development of social processes in which 'sympathy for all that is human' is more likely than ever before to become an active force in the public domain. However, it is most important to add that by no means does this necessarily serve to promote the development of compassionate forms of society; for such 'feelings of humanity' coexist with the intensifying force of capitalist market relations and rationalization upon our lives. Moreover, it is all too clear that our cultural capacity for compassion may be cynically manipulated for a wide range of pernicious purposes. We are part of a culture in which an ideological 'play' on compassion may serve as the means to lend legitimacy to bloody acts of barbarism and where the suffering of humanity may be 'commodified' and reduced to no more than a sentimentalized form of consumer entertainment. All too often our passion for compassion appears morally misguided and blind to its negative social consequences.

Nevertheless, I have argued that there remain some grounds for hope here. There is empirical evidence to illustrate the ways in which public sentiments of compassion might still be orchestrated so as to advance a politics of humanitarianism. It is now almost 20 years since Live Aid, the greatest example we have to date of the possibilities that exist within our culture for societies to be united by a shared imagination for the suffering of the others, and on this basis, organized to save human life. Moreover, we may take the ongoing and increasing levels of public support that are given to charities such as Oxfam, Save the Children, Comic Relief and the Red Cross as evidence of the power of common feelings for humanity to sustain global institutions in this work. By no means would I present this as good reason to be optimistic for the future of human societies, but I would certainly argue that this amounts to a significant departure in our cultural and political history that calls for more sociological understanding. Moreover, I would cautiously suggest that a critical sociology of suffering might yet prove itself to be of value within efforts to increase the power and appeal of this movement.

The sociological task at hand

As far as Alvin Gouldner (1975) is concerned, for sociology to become a liberating force in society, it must be politically engaged with the task of communicating the social character of human suffering. Indeed, for Gouldner, combating 'needless suffering' is the essential purpose of all 'humane sociology'; further, it is on this basis that our discipline may recover the passion and conviction to speak meaningfully to the crisis of our times. A critical sociology of suffering is a necessary part of the attempt to engage sociology in the struggle to tell the truth about our world so as to imagine how it can be made to change (Levine 1995: 198).

In this book I have endeavoured to treat such arguments with the utmost seriousness. Moreover, following Gouldner, I have suggested that this endeavour calls for a sociology of sociology.

The sociological study of human suffering requires us to question, and if necessary oppose, disciplinary boundaries that drive us into narrow fields of technical expertise. Wherever possible, we should be thinking about the diverse realities of human experience; for 'the problem of suffering' is such that it touches upon every aspect of our personhood. In addition, it seems that in attending to the existential reality of this phenomenon, it is practically impossible to avoid questioning the essential meaning and value of our work (Skultans 1998). The negative impact of suffering on our lives is such that it demands debate over what we are fundamentally for. In this respect, we should expect all research and writing in this area to involve a critical engagement with the morality and politics of our times. Finally, in so far as it is in terms of an attempt to understand 'the difficulty of understanding' that we touch upon some of the most vital aspects of what suffering does to people, then it may well be the case that this field of study amounts to one of the most critical settings in which sociology is made to confront the *failures* of its scholarship, methods and thinking. Yet, as I have argued, we might still relate to such failings as a necessary part of 'thinking with suffering'.

There are many more questions to be considered, and as part of our response to these we may well find ourselves in the position of having to make substantial revisions to our terms of theoretical inquiry, methodological practice and approaches to writing. I have merely attempted to clear some space for this work to take place. For now, I suggest we pay critical attention to the following.

First, there is still much more work to be done in order to establish problems of 'human suffering' within sociological terms of analysis and conceptual debate. From the outset of my discussion I have worked with the understanding that a focus upon 'the problem of suffering' provides us with opportunities to revise the ways we relate to our classical heritage. While it has become fashionable in some quarters to suggest that the frameworks of inquiry devised by Marx, Durkheim and Weber are no longer relevant to understanding a social world undergoing intensifying processes of individualization and globalization (Beck 2000 and Urry 1999), I have taken an opposing view. Although I acknowledge that there is much novelty in the societies, cultures and technologies of global capitalism that requires us to engage in programmes of research that are beyond the imagination of our classical forebears, I maintain nevertheless that their writings are still relevant in assessing the negative human consequences of the world in which we live. I am inclined to argue that sociological thinking within the classical tradition still holds great value for raising fundamental questions of humanity. Our 'founding fathers' all shared a basic concern to expose the existential meaning of conditions of modernity; further, they were all alert to the potential for society and culture to be experienced by individuals as idioms of pain and suffering. While such concerns are to the fore in developments within new sociologies of the body and emotions, I maintain that there is still much work to be done to locate these within analytical frameworks that engage with the historical and social formation of conditions of modernity. I suggest that this should be a central concern of a critical sociology of suffering. I hold that we have scarcely begun to explore the sociological significance of our embodied cultural consciousness of society and how this might be dynamically related to our moral sentiments and political orientations. It is on this ground that sociologists have opportunities to develop new productive relationships with their past, so as to engage anew with the project of 'humanizing' the ways in which we relate to one another.

Second, while I have discussed some of the possible ways in which 'the problem of suffering' is made to comprise social consciousness, and how this in turn might become a force of cultural innovation and social change, nevertheless, I have only gone so far as to present readers with some founding terms of inquiry and ongoing points of interest. It is far beyond the scope of this book to chart the variety of ways in which this takes place in the contexts of day-to-day life. In edited collections of studies of 'social suffering' this work has begun, but it is still no more than a beginning (Bourdieu et al. 1999; Kleinman et al. 1997; Das et al. 2000, 2001). One of my aims in writing this book has been to broaden and elaborate upon a means of theorizing the findings of ethnographies of social suffering, and further, to draw out some of the implications of this manner of research and writing for the task of theorizing society. This is a work that aims to involve sociological theory with empirical research and empirical research with sociological theory. To develop a critical sociology of suffering, we must be more attentive to the many different ways in which people encounter and give voice to their suffering. There is a great amount of work to be done to uncover the determining influence of particular institutional settings, cultural formations and patterns of relationships upon the ways individuals are made to suffer. Moreover, we have scarcely begun to chart the *specific* ways in which personal encounters with 'the problem of suffering' exert pressures for change upon shared cultural meanings and common social practices. In short, there is a need for research that aims to discover how the negative force of suffering is brought to bear upon people's lives, and what they do under the compulsion to escape this experience and/or make it productive for thought and action.

Third, at the end of this study I am left in no doubt that a sociological study of human suffering must involve programmes of research into the cultural frames of reference whereby attempts are made to bring public attention to this experience. In almost every instance, studies of 'social suffering' are devised on the under-standing that societies are failing to attend properly to what suffering *does* to people. In this context, we are called to reflect critically upon the cultural discourses that are used to communicate the social meanings of personal affliction, so as to take note of the ways in which these may be designed (sometimes quite deliberately) to 'silence' the genuine voices of people in extremes of hardship and pain. In this regard, the 'commodifying' and 'mediatizing' of human experience may well be recognized as a pressing matter for concern, for so much of the politics of suffering (and compassion) is perceived to take place in relation to the symbolic forms of communication by which 'famine', 'war', 'violence', 'poverty' and 'atrocity' are brought to our attention as 'news'. However, in addition, we should also be concerned to reflect upon the ways in which the cultural discourse of sociology fails to expose the 'reality' of suffering in lived experience. While seeking to expose the symbolic acts of violence against people's experience that take place within the wider public sphere, we should not be so naïve as to deny that this also takes place wherever the effect of our sociological writing is to remove human vitality from our accounts of social life (Bourdieu 1999).

Finally, in developing our moral understanding of the processes whereby the problem of suffering is brought to social attention, we should be particularly attentive to the variety of ways in which individuals are liable to respond to the suffering of others. In this work, our sociological task should be to explain the bearing of social context upon the ways in which individuals interpret and respond to symbolic forms of culture that 'make known' the misery of our world. We should be concerned to recognize the bearing of class, gender, occupation, ethnicity and nationality upon the ways in which people respond with 'acts of compassion' or 'states of denial' to their cultural apprehension of what suffering does to people. In this context, we might even trace the social and political effects that a sociological study of suffering has upon society.

Under what circumstances might such research acquire the power to direct the terms of social policy and revise political decision? What kinds of people are moved by this work to take up the concerns of 'common humanity'?

By no means am I suggesting that a critical sociology of suffering would be sufficient to meet 'the demands of our day'. I am not so naïve as to claim that this would amount to an adequate 'solution' to the crisis of sociology. However, I am prepared to argue that such work may be a necessary part of the creative task of revitalizing 'the promise' of our discipline. Those who engage in this work should recognize from the start that there is no morally comfortable or intellectually satisfying approach to research and writing on what suffering does to people. Indeed, by working to bring social attention to seemingly unendurable realities and addressing the 'human meaning' of critical events and situations that somehow remain 'unassumable' in consciousness, I suspect that we will always be dogged by the *pain of failure*. Our task begins with the courage to suffer this for the sake of building humane forms of society.

REFERENCES

Abercrombie, N., Hill, S. and Turner, B. S. (1984) *The Penguin Dictionary of Sociology.* Harmondsworth: Penguin.

Adelson, N. (2001) Reimagining aboriginality: an indigenous people's response to social suffering. In V. Das, A. Kleinman, M. Ramphele, M. Lock and P. Reynolds, (eds), *Remaking a World: Violence, Social Suffering and Recovery,* Berkeley: University of California Press, 76–101.

Alexander, J. C. (1988) Introduction: Durkheimian sociology and cultural studies. In J. C. Alexander (ed.), *Durkheimian Sociology: Cultural Studies,* Cambridge: Cambridge University Press, 1–21.

Althusser, L. (1969) *For Marx.* London: Allen Lane.

Amato, J. A. (1990) *Victims and Values: A History and a Theory of Suffering.* New York: Greenwood Press.

Amato, J. A. (1994) Politics of suffering, *International Social Science Review,* 69 (1–2), 23–30.

Amnesty International (1973) *Report on Torture.* London: Gerald Duckworth.

Amnesty International (1984) *Torture in the Eighties.* London: Amnesty International Publication.

Amnesty International (1996) *International Conference on Torture: Final Report.* London: Amnesty International Publications.

Amnesty International (2000) *Take a Step to Stamp Out Torture.* London: Amnesty International Publications.

Amnesty International (2002) *Amnesty International Report 2002.* London: Amnesty International Publications.

Arendt, H. (1958) *The Human Condition.* Chicago: University of Chicago Press.

Arendt, H. (1963a) *Eichmann in Jerusalem: A Report on the Banality of Evil.* Harmondsworth: Penguin.

Arendt, H. (1963b) *On Revolution.* Harmondsworth: Penguin.

Arendt, H. (1968) *Men in Dark Times.* Harmondsworth: Pelican.

Arendt, H. (1973) *The Origins of Totalitarianism.* New York: Harcourt Brace Janovich.

Arendt, H. (1978) *The Life of the Mind: Thinking.* London: Secker and Warburg.

Arendt, H. (1994a) Nightmare and flight. In *Essays in Understanding 1930–1954,* New York: Harcourt Brace & Co.

Arendt, H. (1994b) Understanding and politics (the difficulties of understanding). In *Essays in Understanding 1930–1954,* New York: Harcourt Brace & Co., 307–27.

Arendt, H. and Jaspers, K. (1992) *Correspondence 1926–1969.* New York: Harcourt Brace Janovich.

Aschheim, S. (1997) Nazism, culture and the origins of totalitarianism: Hannah Arendt and the discourse of evil, *New German Critique,* 70 (Winter), 117–39.

Banks, J. and Tanner, S. (1997) *The State of Donation: Household Gifts to Charity, 1974–96.* London: The Institute for Fiscal Studies.

Barbalet, J. M. (2001) *Emotion, Social Theory and Social Structure: A Macrosociological Approach.* Cambridge: Cambridge University Press.

Barbalet, J. M. (ed.), (2002) *Emotions and Sociology.* Oxford: Blackwell Publishing/The Sociological Review.

Bates, M. S. (1987) Ethnicity and pain: a biocultural model, *Social Science and Medicine,* 24 (1), 47–50.

Bauman, Z. (1987) *Legislators and Interpreters.* Cambridge: Polity.

Bauman, Z. (1989) *Modernity and the Holocaust.* Cambridge: Polity.

Bauman, Z. (1991) *Modernity and Ambivalence.* Cambridge: Polity.

Bauman, Z. (1993) *Postmodern Ethics.* Oxford: Blackwell Publishers.

Bauman, Z. (1998) *Globalization: The Human Consequences.* Cambridge: Polity.

Beattie, L., Miller, D., Miller, E. and Philo, G. (1999) The media and Africa: images of disaster and rebellion. In G. Philo (ed.), *Message Received: Glasgow Media Group Research 1993–1998,* Harlow: Longman, 229–67.

Beck, U. (2000) Risk society revisited: theory, politics and research programmes. In B. Adam, U. Beck and J. Van Loon, *The Risk Society and Beyond: Critical Issues for Social Theory.* London: Sage.

Beecher, H. K. (1956) Relationship of significance of wound to pain experienced, *Journal of the American Medical Association,* 161 (17), 1609–12.

Bellah, R. N. (1999) Max Weber and world-denying love: a look at the historical sociology of religion, *Journal of the American Academy of Religion,* 67 (2), 277–304.

Bendelow, G. A. and Williams, S. J. (1995a) Pain and the mind–body dualism: a sociological approach, *Body and Society,* 1 (2), 83–103.

Bendelow, G. A. and Williams, S. J. (1995b) Transcending the dualisms: towards a sociology of pain, *Sociology of Health & Illness,* 17 (2), 139–65.

Bendelow, G. A. and Williams, S. J. (1998) *Emotions and Social Life: Social Theory and Contemporary Issues.* London: Routledge.

Bennett, O. (2001) *Cultural Pessimism: Narratives of Decline in the Postmodern World.* Edinburgh: Edinburgh University Press.

Berezin, M. (2002) Secure states: towards a political sociology of emotions. In J. M. Barbalet (ed.), *Emotions and Sociology,* Oxford: Blackwell Publishing/The Sociological Review, 33–52.

Berger, P. L. (1969) *The Sacred Canopy: Elements of a Sociological Theory of Religion.* New York: Anchor Books.

Berger, R. J. (1993) The 'Banality of evil' reframed: the social construction of the 'final solution' to the 'Jewish problem'. *The Sociological Quarterly,* 34 (4), 597–618.

Bernstein, R. J. (1996) Did Hannah Arendt change her mind? From radical evil to the banality of evil. In L. May and J. Kohn, (eds), *Hannah Arendt: Twenty Years Later,* Cambridge, Mass.: MIT Press, 127–47.

Bernstein, R. J. (2002) *Radical Evil: A Philosophical Interrogation.* Cambridge: Polity.

Besterman, T. (1962) Voltaire and the Lisbon earthquake or, The death of optimism. In Theodore Besterman (ed.), *Voltaire: Essays,* Oxford: Oxford University Press, 24–41.

Bloch, M. (1961) *Feudal Society.* London: Routledge & Kegan Paul.

Boltanski, L. (1999) *Distant Suffering: Morality, Media and Politics.* Cambridge: Cambridge University Press.

Bourdieu, P. (1999) The space of points of view. In P. Bourdieu et al., *The Weight of the World: Social Suffering in Contemporary Society,* Cambridge: Polity, 3–5.

Bourdieu, P. et al. (1999) *The Weight of the World: Social Suffering in Contemporary Society.* Cambridge: Polity.

Bowker, J. W. (1970) *Problems of Suffering in Religions of the World.* Cambridge: Cambridge University Press.

Bowker, J. W. (1997) Religions, society, and suffering. In A. Kleinman, V. Das and M. Lock, (eds), *Social Suffering,* Berkeley: University of California Press, 359–81.

Burger, T. (1993) Weber's sociology and Weber's personality, *Theory and Society,* 22 (6), 813–36.

Cabinet Office (2002) *Private Action, Public Benefit: A Review of Charities and the Wider Not-For-Profit Sector: Strategy Unit Report.* London: Cabinet Office.

Campbell, C. (1987) *The Romantic Ethics and the Spirit of Modern Consumerism.* Oxford: Blackwell Publishing.

Canovan, M. (1974) *The Political Thought of Hannah Arendt.* London: J. M. Dent & Sons.

Cassell, E. J. (1982) The nature of suffering and the goals of medicine, *New England Journal of Medicine,* 306 (11), 639–45.

Chuengsatiansup, K. (2001) Marginality, suffering and community: the politics of collective experience and empowerment in Thailand. In

V. Das, A. Kleinman, M. Ramphele, M. Lock and P. Reynolds, (eds), *Remaking a World: Violence, Social Suffering and Recovery*, Berkeley: University of California Press, 31–75.

Cohen, R. I. (1993) Breaking the code: Hannah Arendt's Eichmann in Jerusalem and the public polemic – myth, memory, and historical imagination, *Michael*, 13, 29–85.

Cohen, S. (1996) Witnessing the truth, *Index on Censorship*, 1, 36–45.

Cohen, S. (2001) *States of Denial: Knowing about Atrocities and Suffering*. Cambridge: Polity.

Cohen, S. and Seu, B. (2002) Knowing enough not to feel too much: emotional thinking about human rights appeals. In M. P. Bradley and P. Petro, (eds), *Truth Claims: Representation and Human Rights*, New Brunswick, NJ: Rutgers University Press, pp. 187–201.

Collins, R. (1988) The Durkheimian tradition in conflict sociology. In J. C. Alexander (ed.), *Durkheimian Sociology: Cultural Studies*. Cambridge: Cambridge University Press, 107–28.

Conway, D. (1987) *A Farewell of Marx: An Outline and Appraisal of his Theories*. Harmondsworth: Penguin.

Cowling, M. (1989) The case for two Marxes restated. In M. Cowling and L. Wilde, (eds), *Approaches to Marx*, Milton Keynes: Open University Press.

Curran, J., Morley, D. and Walkerdine, V. (eds), (1996) *Cultural Studies and Communications*. London: Arnold.

Daniel, E. V. (2000) Mood, moment and mind. In V. Das, A. Kleinman, M. Ramphele and P. Reynolds, (eds), *Violence and Subjectivity*, Berkeley: University of California Press, 333–66.

Das, V. (1994) Moral orientations to suffering: legitimation, power and healing. In L. C. Chen, A. Kleinman and N. C. Ware, (eds), *Health and Social Change in International Perspective*, Boston: Harvard School of Public Health, 139–67.

Das, V. (1995) *Critical Events: An Anthropological Perspective on Contemporary India*. Delhi: Oxford University Press.

Das, V. (1997a) Language and body: transactions in the construction of pain. In A. Kleinman, V. Das and M. Lock, (eds), *Social Suffering*, Berkeley: University of California Press, 67–92.

Das V. (1997b) Sufferings, theodicies, disciplinary practices, appropriations, *International Journal of Social Science*, 49, 563–72.

Das, V. (2000) The act of witnessing: violence, poisonous knowledge, and subjectivity. In V. Das, A. Kleinman, M. Ramphele and P. Reynolds, (eds), *Violence and Subjectivity*, Berkeley: University of California Press, 205–25.

Das, V. and Kleinman, A. (2001) Introduction. In V. Das, A. Kleinman, M. Ramphele, M. Lock and P. Reynolds, (eds), *Remaking a World: Violence, Social Suffering and Recovery*, Berkeley: University of California Press, 1–30.

Das, V., Kleinman, A., Ramphele, M. and Reynolds, P. (eds), (2000)

Violence and Subjectivity. Berkeley: University of California Press.

Das, V., Kleinman, A., Ramphele, M., Lock, M. and Reynolds, P., (eds), (2001) *Remaking a World: Violence, Social Suffering and Recovery*. Berkeley: University of California Press.

Deaux, G. (1969) *The Black Death, 1347*. London: Hamilton.

DelVecchio Good, M.-J., Brodwin, P. E., Good, B. J. and Kleinman, A., (eds), (1992) *Pain as Human Experience: An Anthropological Perspective*. Berkeley: University of California Press.

Denby, D. (1994) *Sentimental Narrative and the Social Order in France, 1760–1820*. Cambridge: Cambridge University Press.

Descartes, René ([1664] 1972) *The Treatise of Man*. Cambridge, Mass.: Harvard University Press.

Devereux, E. (1996) Good causes, God's poor and telethon television, *Media, Culture and Society*, 18: 47–68.

Dickinson, R., Harindranath, R. and Linné, O. (eds), (1998) *Approaches to Audiences: A Reader*. London: Arnold.

Dostoyevsky, F. ([1864] 1972) *Notes from Underground/The Double*, London: Penguin.

Dow, T. E., Jnr (1978) An analysis of Weber's work on charisma, *British Journal of Sociology*, 29 (1), 83–93.

Durkheim, E. ([1912] 1915) *The Elementary Forms of the Religious Life*. London: Allen & Unwin.

Durkheim, E. (1952) *Suicide: A Study in Sociology*. London: Routledge & Kegan Paul.

Durkheim, E. (1957) *Professional Ethics and Civic Morals*. London: Routledge & Kegan Paul.

Durkheim, E. (1964) *The Division of Labour in Society*. New York: The Free Press.

Durkheim, E. (1973a) The dualism of human nature and its social conditions. In R. N. Bellah (ed.), *Emile Durkheim on Morality and Society*, Chicago: University of Chicago Press, 149–63.

Durkheim, E. ([1898] 1973b) Individualism and the intellectuals. In R. N. Bellah (ed.), *Emile Durkheim on Morality and Society*, Chicago: University of Chicago Press, 43–57.

Dyck, E. J. and Coldevin, G. (1992) Using positive vs. negative photographs for Third-World fund raising, *Journalism Quarterly*, 69 (3), 572–9.

Dynes, R. (2000) The dialogue between Voltaire and Rousseau on the Lisbon Earthquake: the emergence of a social science view, *International Journal of Mass Emergencies and Disasters*, 18 (1), 97–115.

Edwards, L. (2002) *A Bit Rich? What the Wealthy Think about Giving*. London: IPPR.

Edwards, R. B. (1979) *Pleasures and Pains: A Theory of Qualitative Hedonism*, Ithaca, NY: Cornell University Press.

Edwards, R. B. (1984) Pain and the ethics of pain management. *Social Science and Medicine*, 18 (6), 515–23.

Elias, N. (1994) *The Civilizing Process*. Oxford: Blackwell Publishing.

Elliott, A. M., Smith, B. H., Penny, K. I., Smith, W. C. and Chambers, W. A. (1999) The epidemiology of chronic pain in the community, *The Lancet*, 354, 1248–52.

Elster, J. (1985) *Making Sense of Marx*. Cambridge: Cambridge University Press.

Engels, F. ([1844] 1973) *The Condition of the Working-Class in England: From Personal Observation and Authentic Sources*. London: Lawrence & Wishart.

Fairley, P. (1978) *The Conquest of Pain*. London: Michael Joseph.

Farmer, P. (1997) On suffering and structural violence: a view from below. In A. Kleinman, V. Das and M. Lock, (eds), *Social Suffering*. Berkeley: University of California Press, 261–84.

Farmer, P. (1999) *Infections and Inequalities: The Modern Plagues*. Berkeley: University of California Press.

Felice, W. F. (1996) *Taking Suffering Seriously: The Importance of Collective Human Rights*. Albany, NY: State University of New York Press.

Fine, R. (2000) Crimes against humanity: Hannah Arendt and the Nuremberg debates, *European Journal of Social Theory*, 3 (3), 293–311.

Fine, R. (2001) Hannah Arendt: politics and understanding after the Holocaust. In R. Fine and C. Turner, (eds), *Social Theory after the Holocaust*, Liverpool: Liverpool University Press, 19–45.

Fine, R. and Turner, C. (2000) *Social Theory after the Holocaust*. Liverpool: Liverpool University Press.

Finn, W. F. (1986) Patients' wants and needs: the physicians' responses. In R. DeBellis, C. S. Torres, V. Barrett, E. Marcus, M.-E. Siegel and A. H. Kutscher, (eds), *Suffering: Psychological and Social Aspects in Loss, Grief, and Care*, New York: The Haworth Press.

Foucault, M. (1965) *Madness and Civilisation*. New York: Random House.

Foucault, M. (1977) *Discipline and Punish*. New York: Pantheon.

Frank, A. W. (1992) The pedagogy of suffering: moral dimensions of psychological therapy and research with the ill, *Theory & Psychology*, 2 (4), 467–85.

Frank, A. W. (1995) *The Wounded Storyteller: Body, Illness and Ethics*. Chicago: University of Chicago Press.

Frank, A. W. (1996) Reconciliatory alchemy: bodies, narratives and power, *Body and Society*, 2 (3), 53–71.

Frank, A. W. (2001) Can we research suffering?, *Qualitative Health Research*, 11 (3), 353–62.

Freud, S. ([1929] 1985) Civilization and its discontents. In *Civilization, Society and Religion: Group Psychology, Civilization and its Discontents and Other Works*, trans. J. Strachey, London: Penguin Books Ltd, 251–340.

Fromm, E. (1942) *The Fear of Freedom*. London: Routledge.

Gay, P. (1966) *The Enlightenment, An Interpretation, vol. 1: The Rise of Modern Paganism*. New York: W. W. Norton.

Gay, P. (1969) *The Enlightenment, An Interpretation, vol. 2: The Science of Freedom*. New York: W. W. Norton.

Geras, N. (1983) *Marx and Human Nature: The Refutation of a Legend.* London: Verso.

German, T., Randel, J. and Ewing, D. (eds), (2002) *The Reality of Aid: An Independent Review of Poverty Reduction and International Development Assistance.* Manila: IBON Foundation.

Giddens, A. (1986) Introduction. In A. Giddens (ed.), *Durkheim on Politics and the State*, Stanford, Calif.: Stanford University Press, 1–31.

Giddens, A. (1994) Living in a post-traditional society. In U. Beck, A. Giddens and S. Lash, *Reflexive Modernization: Politics, Tradition and Aesthetics in the Modern Social Order*, Cambridge: Polity, 56–109.

Giddens, A. (1995a) Durkheim and the question of moral individualism. In *Politics, Sociology and Social Theory*, Cambridge: Polity, 116–35.

Giddens, A. (1995b) Durkheim's political sociology. In *Politics, Sociology and Social Theory*, Cambridge: Polity, 116–35.

Glover, J. (1999) *Humanity: A Moral History of the Twentieth Century.* London: Pimlico.

Goldman, H. (1993) Contemporary sociology and the interpretation of Weber, *Theory and Society*, 22 (6), 853–60.

Gottfried, R. S. (1983) *The Black Death: Natural and Human Disaster in Medieval Europe.* London: Macmillan.

Gouldner, A. (1962) Introduction. In E. Durkheim, *Socialism*, New York: Collier Books, 7–31.

Gouldner, A. (1970) *The Coming Crisis of Western Sociology.* London: Heinemann.

Gouldner, A. (1975) The sociologist as partisan: sociology and the Welfare State. In *For Sociology: Renewal and Critique in Sociology Today*, Harmondsworth: Pelican Books, 27–68.

Graubard, S. R. (1996) Preface to the issue 'Social Suffering', *Daedalus*, 125 (1), v–x.

Greden, J. F. (2001) The burden of recurrent depression: causes, consequences, and future prospects. *Journal of Clinical Psychiatry*, 62 (22), 5–9.

Gureje, O., Von, K., Michael, G., Simon, E. and Gater, R. (1998) Persistent pain and well-being: a WHO study in primary care, *JAMA*, 280, 233–8.

Gurr, T. R. (2000) *Peoples versus States: Minorities at Risk in the New Century.* Washington: United States Institute of Peace.

Gurr, T. R., Marshall, M. G. and Khosla, D. (2000) *Peace and Conflict 2001: A Global Survey of Armed Conflicts, Self-Determination Movements and Democracy.* University of Maryland: Centre for International Development and Conflict Management.

Harff, B. and Gurr, T. R. (1996) Victims of the state: genocides, politicides and group repression from 1945 to 1995. In A. J. Jongman (ed.), *Contemporary Genocides: Causes, Cases, Consequences*, Leiden: PIOOM, 33–58.

Harris (Louis) & Associates (1999) *National Pain Survey 1999.* Rochester, NY: Louis Harris & Associates.

Hegel, G. W. F. ([1820] 1996) *Philosophy of Right*, New York: Prometheus Books.

Henderson, L. (1987) Legality and empathy, *Michigan Law Review*, 85 (6), 1574–1653.

Hennis, W. (1983) Max Weber's central question, *Economy and Society*, 12 (2), 135–79.

Hennis, W. (1988) *Max Weber: Essays in Reconstruction*. London: Allen & Unwin.

Hewitt, K. (1983) The idea of calamity in a technocratic age. In K. Hewitt (ed.), *Interpretations of Calamity*, Boston: Allen & Unwin, 3–31.

Hick, J. (1966) *Evil and the God of Love*. London: Macmillan.

Hobsbawm, E. (1994) *An Age of Extremes: The Short History of the Twentieth Century 1914–1991*. London: Penguin.

Hochschild, A. R. (1983) *The Managed Heart: Commercialization of Human Feeling*. Berkeley: University of California Press.

Hochschild, A. R. (1989) *The Second Shift*. New York: Avon Books.

Horkheimer, M. and Adorno, T. W. (1972) *Dialectic of Enlightenment*. New York: Continuum.

Horn, S. and Munafò, M. (1997) *Pain: Theory, Research and Intervention*. Buckingham: Open University Press.

Horowitz, I. L. (1993) *The Decomposition of Sociology*. New York: Oxford University Press.

Hutton, W. and Giddens, A. (2000) *On the Edge: Living with Global Capitalism*. London: Jonathan Cape.

Hydén, L. (1997) Illness and narrative, *Sociology of Health and Illness*, 19 (1), 48–69.

Ignatieff, M. (1998) *The Warrior's Honour: Ethnic War and the Modern Conscience*. London: Vintage.

Illich, I. (1976) *Limits to Medicine. Medical Nemesis: The Expropriation of Health*. London: Penguin.

Ingram, J. C. (1993) The politics of human suffering. *National Interest*, 33, 39–67.

Jervis, J. (1999) *Transgressing the Modern: Explorations in the Western Experience of Otherness*. Oxford: Blackwell.

Johnson, A. G. (1995) *The Blackwell Dictionary of Sociology: A User's Guide to Sociological Language*. Oxford: Blackwell.

Jordan, Z. A. (1971) Introductory essay: Karl Marx as a philosopher and sociologist. In Z. A. Jordan (ed.), *Karl Marx: Economy, Class and Social Revolution*, London: Nelson, 9–67.

Käsler, D. (1988) *Max Weber: An Introduction to his Life and Work*. Cambridge: Polity.

Kendrick, T. D. (1956) *The Lisbon Earthquake*. London: Methuen.

Kim, J. Y., Millen, J. V., Irwin, A. and Gersham, J. (2000) *Dying for Growth: Global Inequality and the Health of the Poor*. Monroe, Me.: Common Courage Press.

Kinnick, K. N., Krugman, D. M. and Cameron, G. T. (1996) Compassion fatigue: communication and burnout toward social problems, *Journalism and Mass Communications Quarterly*, 73 (3), 687–707.

Kitto, H. D. F. (1957) *The Greeks*. Harmondsworth: Penguin.

Kleinman, A. (1986) *Social Origins of Distress and Disease: Depression, Neurasthenia and Pain in Modern China*. New Haven: Yale University Press.

Kleinman, A. (1988) *The Illness Narratives: Suffering, Healing and the Human Condition*. New York: Basic Books.

Kleinman, A. (1992) Pain and resistance: the delegitimation and relegitimation of local worlds. In M. DelVecchio Good, P. E. Brodwin, B. J. Good and A. Kleinman, (eds), *Pain as Human Experience: An Anthropological Perspective*, Berkeley: University of California Press, 169–97.

Kleinman, A. (1995) Pitch, picture, power: the globalization of local suffering and the transformation of social experience. *Ethnos*, 60 (3–4),181–91.

Kleinman, A. (1996) Bourdieu's impact on the anthropology of suffering. *International Journal of Contemporary Sociology*, 33 (2), 203–10.

Kleinman, A. (1999) Experience and its moral modes: culture, human conditions and disorder. In G. B. Peterson (ed.), *The Tanner Lectures on Human Values*, Salt Lake City: University of Utah Press, 355–420.

Kleinman, A. (2000) The violences of everyday life: the multiple forms and dynamics of social violence. In V. Das, A. Kleinman, M. Ramphele and P. Reynolds, (eds), *Violence and Subjectivity*, Berkeley: University of California Press, 226–41.

Kleinman, A. and Kleinman, J. (1991) Suffering and its professional transformation: toward an ethnography of interpersonal experience, *Culture, Medicine and Psychiatry*, 15 (3), 275–301.

Kleinman, A. and Kleinman, J. (1997) The appeal of experience; the dismay of images: cultural appropriations of suffering in our times. In A. Kleinman, V. Das and M. Lock, (eds), *Social Suffering*, Berkeley: University of California Press, 1–23.

Kleinman, A., Brodwin, P. E., Good, B. J. and DelVecchio Good, M. (1992) Pain as human experience: an introduction. In M. DelVecchio Good, P. E. Brodwin, B. J. Good and A. Kleinman, (eds), *Pain as Human Experience: An Anthropological Perspective*, Berkeley: University of California Press, 1–27.

Kleinman, A., Das, V. and Lock, M. (eds), (1997) *Social Suffering*. Berkeley: University of California Press.

Koestler, A. and Myers, A. (2002) *Understanding Chronic Pain*. Jackson, Miss.: University Press of Mississippi.

Kotarba, J. (1983) *Chronic Pain: Its Social Dimensions*. Beverly Hills: Sage Publications.

Kroker, A. and Cook, D. (1988) *The Postmodern Scene: Excremental Culture and Hyper-Aesthetics*. London: Macmillan.

Kumar, K. (1995) Apocalypse, millennium and utopia today. In M. Bull (ed.), *Apocalypse Theory and the Ends of the World*, Oxford: Blackwell, 200–24.

Kung, H. (1977) *On Being a Christian*. London: William Collins.

Langer, L. (1997) The alarmed vision: social suffering and holocaust atrocity. In A. Kleinman, V. Das and M. Lock, (eds), *Social Suffering*, Berkeley: University of California Press, 47–66.

Lawrence, P. (2000) Violence, suffering, Amman: the work of oracles in Sri Lanka's eastern war zone. In V. Das, A. Kleinman, M. Ramphele and P. Reynolds, (eds), *Violence and Subjectivity*, Berkeley: University of California Press, 171–204.

Leadbeater, C. (2002) *Up the Down Escalator: Why the Global Pessimists are Wrong*. New York: Viking Press.

Leder, D. (1990) *The Absent Body*. Chicago: University of Chicago Press.

Leibniz, G. W. ([1710] 1969) *Essais de Théodicée*. Paris: Garnier-Flammarion.

Lemert, C. (1995) *Sociology after the Crisis*. Oxford: Westview.

Lepenies, W. (1988) *Between Literature and Science: The Rise of Sociology*. Cambridge: Cambridge University Press.

Levi, P. (1987) *If This Is a Man; and, The Truce*. London: Abacus Books.

Levi, P. (1989) *The Drowned and the Saved*. London: Abacus.

Levinas, E. (1988) Useless suffering. In R. Bernasconi and D. Wood, (eds), *The Provocation of Levinas: Rethinking the Other*, London: Routledge, 156–67.

Levine, D. N. (1995) *Visions of the Sociological Tradition*. Chicago: University of Chicago Press.

Love, J. (1993) Developmentalism in Max Weber's sociology of religion: a critique of F. H. Tenbruck. *Archives Européennes de Sociologie*, 34 (2), 339–63.

Löwith, K. (1993) *Max Weber and Karl Marx*. London: Routledge.

Lukes, S. (1973) *Emile Durkheim: His Life and Work*. Harmondsworth: Penguin.

Lupton, D. (1998) *The Emotional Self*. London: Sage Publications.

Mackenzie, H. ([1771] 2001a) *The Man of Feeling*. Oxford: Oxford University Press.

Mackenzie, H. ([1785] 2001b) Henry Mackenzie, the lounger, no. 20 (Saturday, 18 June 1785). In *The Man of Feeling*, Oxford: Oxford University Press, pp. 99–103.

Mann, M. (1999) The dark side of democracy: the modern tradition of ethnic and political cleansing, *New Left Review*, 235, 18–45.

Margoles, M. S. and Weiner, R. (eds), (1999) *Chronic Pain: Assessment, Diagnosis, and Management*. Boca Raton, Fla.: CRC Press.

Marx, K. ([1844] 1959) *Economic and Philosophic Manuscripts of 1844*. Moscow: Progress Publishers.

Marx, K. (1959a) Critique of the Hegelian dialectic and philosophy as a whole. In *Economic and Philosophic Manuscripts of 1844*, Moscow: Progress Publishers, 133–57.

Marx, K. (1959b) Private, property and communism. In *Economic and Philosophic Manuscripts of 1844*, Moscow: Progress Publishers, 93–108.

Marx, K. (1973) *Grundrisse: Foundations of the Critique of Political Economy.* Harmondsworth: Penguin.

Marx, K. ([1867] 1976) *Capital: A Critique of Political Economy, vol. 1.* Harmondsworth: Penguin.

Marx, K. (1977) Towards a critique of Hegel's philosophy of right: introduction. In D. McLellan (ed.), *Karl Marx: Selected Writings*, Oxford: Oxford University Press, 63–74.

Marx, K. and Engels, F. ([1848] 1967) *The Communist Manifesto.* Harmondsworth: Penguin Books.

May, R. (1969) *Love and Will.* New York: W. W. Norton & Co.

Mazlish, B. (1989) *A New Science: The Breakdown of Connections and the Birth of Sociology.* Oxford: Oxford University Press.

McCloy, S. (1972) *The Humanitarian Movement in Eighteenth-Century France.* New York: Haskell House Publishers Ltd.

McLellan, D. (1971) *The Thought of Karl Marx: An Introduction.* London: Macmillan.

McLellan, D. (1973) *Marx's Grundrisse.* St Albans: Paladin.

McLellan, D. (1977) *Engels.* Glasgow: Fontana/Collins.

Meek, R. (1962) Marx's 'Doctrine of increasing misery'. In *Economics and Ideology and Other Essays: Studies in the Development of Economic Thought*, London: Chapman and Hall, 113–28.

Mehta, D. (2000) Circumcision, body, masculinity: the ritual wound and collective violence. In V. Das, A. Kleinman, M. Ramphele and P. Reynolds, (eds), *Violence and Subjectivity*, Berkeley: University of California Press, 79–101.

Melzack, R. and Wall, P. (1965) Pain mechanisms: a new theory, *Science*, 150, 971–9.

Melzack, R. and Wall, P. (1988) *The Challenge of Pain.* Harmondsworth: Penguin.

Merrifield, A. (1999) Notes on suffering and freedom: a Marxian and Dostoevskian encounter, *Rethinking Marxism*, 11 (1), 72–86.

Merton, R. K. (1957) *Social Theory and Social Structure.* New York: The Free Press.

Meštrović, S. G. (1989) The theme of civilization and its discontents in Durkheim's division of labour: philosophical assumptions and practical consequences, *Journal for the Theory of Social Behaviour*, 19 (4), 443–56.

Meštrović, S. G. (1991) *The Coming Fin de Siècle: An Application of Durkeim's Sociology to Modernity and Postmodernity*, London: Routledge.

Meštrović, S. G. (1993) *The Barbarian Temperament: Towards a Postmodern Critical Theory.* London: Routledge.

Meštrović, S. G. (1997) *Postemotional Society.* London: Sage Publications.

Meštrović, S. G. and Brown, H. (1985) Durkheim's concept of anomie as dérèglement. *Social Problems*, 33, 81–99.

Mészáros, I. (1970) *Marx's Theory of Alienation.* London: Merlin Press.

Moeller, S. (1999) *Compassion Fatigue*. London: Routledge.

Mommsen, W. J. (1987) Personal conduct and societal change. In S. Lash and S. Whimster, (eds), *Max Weber, Rationality and Modernity*, London: Allen & Unwin, 35–51.

Morgan, D. G. and Wilkinson, I. (2001) The problem of suffering and the sociological task of theodicy, *European Journal of Social Theory*, 4 (2), 199–214.

Morris, D. (1991) *The Culture of Pain*. Berkeley: University of California Press.

Morris, D. (1997) About suffering: genre, voice, and moral community. In A. Kleinman, V. Das and M. Lock, (eds), *Social Suffering*, Berkeley: University of California Press, 25–46.

Morris, D. (1998) *Illness and Culture in the Postmodern Age*. Berkeley: University of California Press.

Mouzelis, N. (1995) *Sociological Theory: What Went Wrong? Diagnosis and Remedies*. London: Routledge.

National Council of Voluntary Organizations (NCVO) (2001a) Charitable giving – the tide has turned: the fall and rise of charitable giving 1995–2000, *Research Quarterly*, 13 (June).

National Council of Voluntary Organizations (NCVO) (2001b) *Women Give Over £400 Million More to Charity than Men in a Single Year*. London: NCVO.

Nemo, P. (1998) *Job and the Excess of Evil*. Pittsburgh: Duquesne University Press.

Nussbaum, M. C. (1996) Compassion: the basic social emotion, *Social Philosophy and Policy*, 13 (1), 27–58.

Nussbaum, M. C. (2003) Compassion and terror, *Daedalus* (Winter 2003), 10–26.

Office for National Statistics (ONS) (2002) *Psychiatric Morbidity among Adults Living in Private Households, 2000*. London: HMSO.

Ortony, A., Clore, G. L. and Collins, A. (1990) *The Cognitive Structure of Emotions*. Cambridge: Cambridge University Press.

Parsons, T. (1966) Introduction. In M. Weber, *The Sociology of Religion*, London: Methuen.

Passey, A. and Hems, L. (1997) *Charitable Giving in Great Britain 1996*. London: NCVO, pp. xix–lxvii.

Pearce, F. (1989) *The Radical Durkheim*. London: Unwin Hyman.

Perkins, J. (1995) *The Suffering Self: Pain and Narrative Representation in the Early Christian Era*. London: Routledge.

Pharoah, C. (2002) *Dimensions 2002: Annual Update of CAF's Top 500 Fundraising Charities*. London: Charities Aid Foundation (CAF).

Pharoah, C. and Tanner, S. (1997) Trends in charitable giving, *Fiscal Studies*, 18 (4), 427–43.

Philo, G. (1993) From Buerk to Band Aid: the media and the 1984 Ethiopian famine. In J. Eldridge (ed.), *Getting the Message: News, Truth and Power*, London: Routledge, 104–25.

Philo, G., Hilsum, L., Beattie, L. and Holliman, R. (1999) The media and the Rwanda crisis: effects on audiences and public policy. In G. Philo (ed.), *Message Received: Glasgow Media Group Research 1993–1998*, Harlow: Longman, 213–28.

Pickering, W. S. F. (1984) *Durkheim's Sociology of Religion: Themes and Theories*. London: Routledge & Kegan Paul.

Pickering, W. S. F. and Miller, W. W. (eds) (1993) *Individualism and Human Rights in the Durkheimian Tradition*. Oxford: British Centre for Durkheimian Studies.

Podhoretz, N. (1964) *Doings and Undoings: The Fifties and After in American Writing*. New York: Farrar, Straus & Giroux, Inc.

Prochaska, F. (1990) *The Voluntary Impulse: Philanthropy in Modern Britain*. London: Faber & Faber.

Ramp, W. (1998) Effervescence, differentiation and representation in *The Elementary Forms*. In N. J. Allen, W. S. F. Pickering and W. Watts Miller, (eds), *On Durkheim's Elementary Forms of the Religious Life*, London: Routledge, 136–48.

Ramphele, M. (1997) Political widowhood in South Africa: the embodiment of ambiguity. In A. Kleinman, V. Das and M. Lock, (eds), *Social Suffering*, Berkeley: University of California Press, 99–118.

Reddy, W. M. (2001) *The Navigation of Feeling: A Framework for the History of Emotions*. Cambridge: Cambridge University Press.

Rey, R. (1993) *The History of Pain*. Cambridge, Mass.: Harvard University Press.

Ricoeur, P. (1995) Evil, a challenge to philosophy and theology. In *Figuring the Sacred: Religion, Narrative and Imagination*, Minneapolis: Fortress Press, 249–61.

Robbins, R. (2002) *Global Problems and the Culture of Capitalism*. New York: Allyn & Bacon.

Robinson, D. N. (1978) Pain and suffering: psychobiological principles. In Warren, T. Reich, (ed.), *Encyclopedia of Bioethics*. New York: The Free Press, 1177–81.

Romano, T. (1999) Fibromyalgia. In M. S. Margoles and R. Weiner, (eds), *Chronic Pain: Assessment, Diagnosis, and Management*, Boca Raton, Fla.: CRC Press.

Rorty, R. (1998) Human rights, rationality and sentimentality. In *Truth and Progress: Philosophical Papers, vol. 3*, Cambridge: Cambridge University Press, 167–85.

Rose, G. (1996) *Mourning Becomes the Law: Philosophy and Representation*. Cambridge: Cambridge University Press.

Rose, H. (1994) *Love, Power and Knowledge: Towards a Feminist Transformation of the Sciences*. Cambridge: Polity.

Rotberg, R. and Weiss, T. G. (eds), (1996) *From Massacres to Genocide: The Media Public Policy and Humanitarian Crises*. Washington: The Brookings Institution.

Rotenstreich, N. (1984–5) Can evil be banal?, *The Philosophical Forum*, 16 (1), 50–62.

Rotfeld, A. D. (2002) Introduction: global security after 11 September 2001. In *Stockholm International Peace Research Institute (SIPRI) Yearbook 2002: Armaments, Disarmaments and International Security*, Oxford: Oxford University Press, 1–18.

Rummel, R. J. (1994) *Death by Government*. New Brunswick, NJ: Transaction Publishers.

Rummel, R. J. (1996) The Holocaust in comparative and historical perspective. In A. J. Jongman (ed.), *Contemporary Genocides: Causes, Cases, Consequences*, Leiden: PIOOM, 17–31.

Sadri, A. (1992) *Max Weber's Sociology of Intellectuals*. Oxford: Oxford University Press.

Salomon, A. (1935) Max Weber's sociology, *Social Research*, 2 (1), 60–73.

Sargeant, A. (1999) Charitable giving: toward a model of donor behaviour, *Journal of Marketing Management*, 15, 215–38.

Sayer, D. (1991) *Capitalism and Modernity: An Excursus on Marx and Weber*. London: Routledge.

Scaff, L. A. (1989) *Fleeing the Iron Cage: Culture, Politics and Modernity in the Thought of Max Weber*. Berkeley: University of California Press.

Scaff, L. A. (1993) Weber after Weberian sociology, *Theory and Society*, 22, 845–51.

Scaff, L. A. (2000) Weber on the cultural situation of the modern age. In S. Turner (ed.), *The Cambridge Companion to Weber*, Cambridge: Cambridge University Press, 99–116.

Scarry, E. (1985) *The Body in Pain: The Making and Unmaking of the World*. Oxford: Oxford University Press.

Scheff, T. J. (1988) Shame and conformity: the defence–emotion system. *American Sociological Review*, 53, 395–406.

Scheff, T. J. (1994) *Bloody Revenge: Emotions, Nationalism and War*. Boulder, Colo.: Westview Press.

Scheff, T. J. and Retzinger, S. M. (1991) *Emotions and Violence: Shame and Rage in Destructive Conflict*. Lexington, Mass.: D.C. Heath.

Scheper-Hughes, N. (1992) *Death without Weeping: The Violence of Everyday Life in Brazil*. Berkeley: University of California Press.

Scheper-Hughes, N. (1997) Peace time crimes. *Social Identities*, 3, 471–97.

Scheper-Hughes, N. (1998) Undoing: social suffering and the politics of remorse in the new South Africa, *Social Justice*, 25 (4), 114–42.

Schilling, C. and Mellor, P. A. (1998) Durkheim, morality and modernity: collective effervescence, homo duplex and the sources of moral action, *British Journal of Sociology*, 49 (2), 193–209.

Schilling and Mellor (2001) *The Sociological Ambition: Elementary Forms of Social and Moral Life*, London: Sage Publications.

Schluchter, W. (1981) *The Rise of Western Rationalism: Max Weber's Developmental History*. Berkeley: University of California Press.

Schluchter, W. (1996) *Paradoxes of Modernity: Culture and Conduct in the Theory of Max Weber*. Stanford, Calif.: Stanford University Press.

Schopenhauer, A. (1970) On the suffering of the world. In *Essays and Aphorisms*, Harmondsworth: Penguin, 41–50.

Seidman, S. (1994) *Contested Knowledge: Social Theory in the Postmodern Era*. Oxford: Blackwell.

Seybolt, T. B. (2002) Major armed conflicts. In *Stockholm International Peace Research Institute (SIPRI) Yearbook 2002: Armaments, Disarmaments and International Security*, Oxford: Oxford University Press.

Shaffer, J. A. (1978) Pain and suffering: philosophical perspectives. In Reich, Warren T. (ed.), *Encyclopedia of Bioethics*, New York: The Free Press, 1181–4.

Shaw, M. (1996) *Civil Society and Media in Global Crises: Representing Distant Violence*. London: Pinter.

Sica, A. (1988) *Weber, Irrationality and Social Order*. Berkeley: University of California Press.

Sica, A. (2000) Rationalization and culture. In S. Turner (ed.), *The Cambridge Companion to Weber*, Cambridge: Cambridge University Press, 42–58.

Silver, A. (1989) Friendship and trust as moral ideals: an historical approach, *European Journal of Sociology*, 30, 274–97.

Silver, A. (1990) Friendship in commercial society: eighteenth-century social theory and modern sociology, *American Journal of Sociology*, 95 (6), 1474–1504.

Silverstone, R. (1994) *Television and Everyday Life*. London: Routledge.

Simmel, G. (1971) The transcendent character of life. In D. N. Levine (ed.), *On Individuality and Social Forms*, Chicago: University of Chicago Press, 353–74.

Simmel, G. (1997) The concept and tragedy of culture. In D. Frisby and M. Featherstone, (eds), *Simmel on Culture*, London: Sage Publications, 55–74.

Skultans, V. (1998) *The Testimony of Lives: Narrative and Memory in Post-Soviet Latvia*. London: Routledge.

Slack, P. (1985) *The Impact of Plague in Tudor and Stuart England*. London: Routledge.

Smail, D. (1993) *The Origins of Unhappiness: A New Understanding of Personal Distress*. London: Constable.

Smith, A. ([1759] 1976) *The Theory of Moral Sentiments*. Oxford: Clarendon Press.

Smith, A. ([1776] 1979) *An Inquiry into the Nature and Causes of the Wealth of Nations*. Oxford: Clarendon Press.

Smith, B. H. (2001) Chronic pain: a challenge for primary care, *The British Journal of General Practice*, 51 (468), 524–6.

Solomon, R. C. (1993) *The Passions: Emotions and the Meaning of Life*. Indianapolis: Hackett Publishing.

Sontag, F. (1981) Anthropodicy and the return of God. In Stephen T. Davis (ed.), *Encountering Evil*, Edinburgh: T & T Clark, 137–51.

Spelman, E. V. (1997) *Fruits of Sorrow: Framing Our Attention to Suffering*. Boston: Beacon Press.

Spierenburg, P. (1984) *The Spectacle of Suffering*. Cambridge: Cambridge University Press.

Stedman Jones, S. (2001) *Durkheim Reconsidered*. Cambridge: Polity.

Steiner, G. (1967) *Language and Silence*. London Faber & Faber.

Syrkin, M. (1963) Hannah Arendt: the clothes of the empress, *Dissent*, 10, 344–52.

Sznaider, N. (1996) Pain and cruelty in socio-historical perspective, *International Journal of Politics, Culture and Society*, 10 (2), 331–53.

Sznaider, N. (1997a) Compassion and control: children in civil society, *Childhood*, 4, 223–40.

Sznaider, N. (1997b) Democracy and child welfare, *International Journal of Politics, Culture and Society*, 11, 325–50.

Sznaider, N. (1998) The sociology of compassion: a study in the sociology of morals, *Cultural Values*, 2 (1), 117–39.

Sznaider, N. (2001) *The Compassionate Temperament: Care and Cruelty in Modern Society*. Lanham, Md.: Rowman & Littlefield.

Sztompka, P. (2000) Cultural trauma: the other face of social change, *European Journal of Social Theory*, 3 (4), 449–66.

Taylor, C. (1989) *Sources of the Self: The Making of the Modern Identity*. Cambridge, Mass.: Harvard University Press.

Taylor, C. (1992) *Multiculturalism and 'The Politics of Recognition': An Essay*. Princeton: Princeton University Press.

Tenbruck, F. (1989) The problem of the thematic unity in the works of Max Weber. In K. Tribe (ed.), *Reading Weber*, London: Routledge, 42–84.

Tester, K. (1994) *Media, Culture and Morality*. London: Routledge.

Tester, K. (1999) The moral consequentiality of television, *European Journal of Social Theory*, 2 (4), 469–83.

Tester, K. (2001) *Compassion, Morality and the Media*. Buckingham: Open University Press.

The Economist (1999) After Seattle: a global disaster, 11 December, 21–4.

Thomas, K. (1983) *Man and the Natural World: A History of Modern Sensibility*. New York: Pantheon.

Thomas, V. N. (1997) Psychological and social factors influencing pain: individual differences in the experience of pain. In V. N. Thomas (ed.), *Pain: Its Nature and Management*, London: Ballière Tindall.

Thompson, J. B. (1995) *The Media and Modernity: A Social Theory of the Media*. Cambridge: Polity.

Todeschini, M. (2001) The bomb's womb? Women and the atomic bomb. In V. Das, A. Kleinman M. Ramphele, M. Lock and P. Reynolds, (eds), *Remaking a World: Violence, Social Suffering and Recovery*, Berkeley: University of California Press, 102–56.

Tönnies, F. ([1887] 1955) *Community and Association*. London: Routledge & Kegan Paul.

Tribe, K. (1989) Introduction. In K. Tribe (ed.), *Reading Weber*, London: Routledge, 1–14.

Turner, B. S. (1992) *Max Weber: From History to Modernity.* London: Routledge.

Turner, B. S. (1993) Outline of a theory of human rights, *Sociology*, 27 (3), 489–512.

Turner, B. S. (1996) Introduction: Marx and Nietzsche. In *For Weber: Essays on the Sociology of Fate*, London: Sage, pp. ix–xl.

Turner, B. S. (1999) *Classical Sociology.* London: Sage.

Turner, B. S. (2002) Cosmopolitan virtue, globalization and patriotism, *Theory, Culture & Society*, 19 (1–2), 45–63.

Turner, B. S. and Rojek, C. (2001) *Society and Culture: Principles of Scarcity and Solidarity.* London: Sage.

United Nations (UNDP) (2000) *Human Development Report 2000: Human Rights and Human Development.* New York: UNDP.

United Nations Population Fund (UNFPA) (2001) *The State of World Population 2001. Footprints and Milestones: Populations and Environmental Change.* New York: UNFPA.

Urry, J. (1999) *Sociology beyond Societies: Mobilities for the Twenty-First Century.* London: Routledge.

Voltaire ([1759] 1947) *Candide or Optimism.* Harmondsworth: Penguin.

Walby, S. and Olsen, W. (2002) *The Impact of Women's Position in the Labour Market on Pay and Implications for UK Productivity.* London: Department for Trade and Industry Women and Equality Unit.

Walker, C. and Pharoah, C. (2002) *A Lot of Give: Trends In Charitable Giving for the 21st Century.* London: Hodder & Stoughton/Charities Aid Foundation (CAF).

Wall, P. (1999) *Pain: The Science of Suffering.* London: Wiedenfeld & Nicolson.

Weber, M. (1920–1) *Gesammelte Aufsatze zur Religionssoziologie*, 3 vols, Tubingen: J. C. B. Mohr.

Weber, M. ([1921] 1968) conomy and Society, Totowa, NJ: Bedminster Press.

Weber, M. (1948a) Bureaucracy. In H. H. Gerth and C. W. Mills, (eds), *From Max Weber: Essays in Sociology*, London: Routledge, 196–244.

Weber, M. (1948b) Politics as a vocation. In H. H. Gerth and C. W. Mills, (eds), *From Max Weber: Essays in Sociology*, London: Routledge, 77–128.

Weber, M. (1948c) Religious rejections of the world and their directions. In H. H. Gerth and C. W. Mills, (eds), *From Max Weber: Essays in Sociology*, London: Routledge, 323–59.

Weber, M. (1948d), The social psychology of the world religions. In H. H. Gerth and C. W. Mills, (eds), *From Max Weber: Essays in Sociology*, London: Routledge, 267–301.

Weber, M. (1966) Theodicy, salvation and rebirth. In *The Sociology of Religion*, London: Methuen, 138–50.

Weil, S. (1950) The love of God and affliction. In *Waiting on God*, Glasgow: William Collins, 76–93.

Weiss, J. (1987) On the irreversibility of western rationalization and Max Weber's alleged fatalism. In S. Whimster and S. Lash, (eds), *Max Weber, Rationality and Modernity*. London: Allen & Unwin, 154–63.

Whimster, S. and Lash, S. (1987) Introduction. In S. Whimster and S. Lash, (eds), *Max Weber, Rationality and Modernity*, London: Allen & Unwin, 1–34.

Whitfield, S. J. (1980) *Into the Dark: Hannah Arendt and Totalitarianism*. Philadelphia: Temple University Press.

WHO (1999) *The World Health Report 1999: Making a Difference*. Geneva: World Health Organization.

Wilkinson, I. (2001a) *Anxiety in a Risk Society*. London: Routledge.

Wilkinson, I. (2001b) Thinking with suffering, *Cultural Values*, 5 (4), 421–444.

Wilks-Heeg, S. (1998) The Communist Manifesto and working-class parties in Western Europe. In M. Cowling (ed.), *The Communist Manifesto: New Interpretations*, Edinburgh: Edinburgh University Press, 119–31.

Williams, S. J. (2001) *Emotion and Social Theory*. London: Sage Publications.

Williams, S. J. and Bendelow, G. A. (1998) *The Lived Body: Sociological Themes, Embodied Issues*. London: Routledge.

Wolfenden Committee Report (1978) *The Future of Voluntary Organisations*. London: Croom Helm.

Woodward, K. (2002) Calculating compassion, *Indiana Law Journal*, 77 (2), 223–46.

World Bank (2000) *Entering the 21st Century: World Development Report 1999/2000*. New York: Oxford University Press.

World Health Organization (WHO) (2001) *The World Health Report 2001, Mental Health: New Understanding, New Hope*. Geneva: World Health Organization.

Wright, K. (2002) Generosity vs. altruism: philanthropy and charity in the United States and United Kingdom, *Voluntas*, 12 (4), 399–416.

Zborowski, M. (1952) Cultural components in response to pain, *Journal of Social Issues*, 8, 16–30.

Ziegler, P. (1969) *The Black Death*. London: Collins.

Zola, I. (1966) Culture and symptoms: an analysis of patients presenting complaints, *American Sociological Review*, 31, 615–30.

INDEX